MEDIUM ÆVUM MONOGRAPHS
NEW SERIES VII

LE VOYATGE D'OULTREMER EN JHERUSALEM

DE NOMPAR, SEIGNEUR DE CAUMONT

Edited by

PETER S. NOBLE

The Society for the Study of
Medieval Languages and Literature, Oxford

THE SOCIETY FOR THE STUDY OF
MEDIEVAL LANGUAGES AND LITERATURE

http://mediumaevum.modhist.ox.ac.uk

© Peter S. Noble, 1975

First published for the Society for the Study of Mediæval
Languages and Literature by Basil Blackwell, Oxford, 1975

This digital reprint first issued 2015

ISBN-13: 978-0-907570-70-7(pb)

Contents

	Page No.
Introduction	4
Abbreviations	5
Bibliography	7
Le Voyatge d'Oultremer en Jherusalem	10
Notes	83
Glossary	109
Index of Proper Names	117
Index of Place Names	121
The Author, his Family and his Work	131
Family Tree	139
Syntax and Morphology	
a) Nouns and the Declension	140
b) Articles	143
c) Adjectives, Adverbs and Participles	147
d) Pronouns:	
Personal	150
Disjunctive	152
Possessive Pronouns and Adjectives	154
Demonstrative Pronouns and Adjectives	156
Relative Pronouns and Adjectives	157
Interrogative Pronouns and Adjectives	158
Indefinite Pronouns and Adjectives	159
e) Verbs:	160
Number	161
Mood	161
Conditionals	162
Infinitives	163
Imperative	164
Tenses	164
Passive	166

		Page No.
	Pronominal Verbs	167
	Past Participles	168
f)	Negatives	169
g)	Invariable Words	171
	Subordinating Conjunctions	172
	Adverbs	175
	Prepositions	182
h)	Numbers	187
i)	Word Order	187
j)	Conclusion	190
Orthography		191
Influence of Provençal and the Dialects		198
Map of Caumont Possessions		203

Introduction

This book is based on a thesis presented to the University of London. In it I have tried to reproduce the main conclusions of my work on the life and writing of Nompar de Caumont. These reveal the grammatical usages of a prominent southern noble of the early fifteenth century, which illustrate the tendency of the provinces to lag linguistically behind the main metropolitan centres of France. The diverse influences at work in the south west of France are also shown, as is their effect on the life of this not wholly typical nobleman.

The text is to be found in a manuscript in the British Museum, Egerton 890 which also contains a text of a poem by the same author.[1] The manuscript has been written by one scribe, and although the hand cannot be dated exactly, it is certainly contemporary or almost so with the life of the author.[2] Folio 3 has been repaired with a paper patch, resulting in the loss of some words. Folio 13 is torn so that the lower half is missing and has been replaced by a blank paper patch. Folio 22 is out of position as it should follow 18, and similarly folio 29 should follow 32. The scribe has indicated both misplacings. In some places the manuscript has been corrected by a later hand, which has decorated forty-six initials.

I must thank my supervisor, Professor D.J.A. Ross, for all his help and encouragement and Dr. L. Polak for her advice on pilgrimages. Professor T.J. Brown, Dr. W.M. Hackett, Dr. P. Clifford, Dr. C. Thacker, Dr. M. Blanc have all helped me most kindly with different aspects. Professor L. Butler, Dr. A. Ruddock and Dr. P. Earle have helped me with the history. In France the Duc de la Force give me every assistance, as did Monsieur J. Burias and his staff in the Archives at Agen, Mademoiselle D. Viez at Pau and the staff at the Bibliothèque Municipale at Périgueux. To them and to the staffs of the Bibliothèque Nationale and the British Museum I offer my sincere thanks. The responsibility for any errors remains mine.

I must also thank the University of Reading and the Central Research Council of the University of London for grants which enabled me to undertake this research, while it is thanks to the generosity of the University of Reading and Birkbeck College that this publication is possible. Above all I must thank my family for all their help in every way. Mrs. M. Edwards typed this book with great patience, and I am extremely grateful to her and to all connected with its production.

---

1. See p. 134.
2. Professor T.J. Brown kindly dated it for me.

Abbreviations

Anglade:	J. Anglade, <u>Grammaire de l'ancien Provençal</u>
Aspland:	C. Aspland, <u>A Contribution to the Syntactical Study of -ant Forms in Twelfth Century French Verse</u>
Beaulieux:	C. Beaulieux, <u>Histoire de l'Orthographe Française</u>
Belabre:	Baron de Belabre, <u>Rhodes of the Knights</u>
Bloch and von Wartburg:	O. Bloch and W. von Wartburg, <u>Dictionnaire Etymologique de la Langue Française</u>
Brunot:	F. Brunot, <u>Histoire de la Langue Française des Origines à 1900</u>
Brunot and Bruneau:	F. Brunot and C. Bruneau, <u>Grammaire Historique de la Langue Française</u>
Butler:	Thurston and Attwater, <u>Butler's Lives of the Saints</u>
C.M.F.A.:	Classiques Français du Moyen Age
C.M.H.:	Cambridge Medieval History
Demus:	O. Demus, <u>The Mosaics of Norman Sicily</u>
Dubois:	L'abbé Dubois, <u>Cahiers</u>
Fonds Périgord:	Fonds Périgord, Bibliothèque Nationale.
Fouché:	P. Fouché, <u>Le Verbe Français, Etude Morphologique</u>
Gardner and Greene:	R. Gardner and M. Greene, <u>A Brief Description of Middle French Syntax</u>
Godefroy:	F. Godefroy, <u>Dictionnaire de l'Ancien Français</u>
Goerlich:	E. Goerlich, <u>Die Südwestlichen Dialecte der Langue d'Oil</u>
Grandgent:	C. Grandgent, <u>Provençal Philology and Morphology</u>
Lévy:	E. Lévy, <u>Provenzalisches Supplement Wörterbuch</u>
Morawski:	J. Morawski, <u>Proverbes Français, antérieurs au XVe siècle</u>
Norwich:	J. Norwich, <u>The Kingdom in the Sun</u>
Nyrop:	K. Nyrop, <u>Grammaire Historique de la Langue Française</u>
Polak:	L. Polak, <u>Le Pelerinage de Jehan de Tournay</u>
Pope:	M.K. Pope, <u>From Latin to Modern French</u>
Schwan-Behrens:	Schwan-Behrens, <u>Grammaire de l'Ancien Français</u>
Tobler-Lommatzsch:	Tobler-Lommatzsch, <u>Altfranzösisches Wörterbuch</u>

Wagner: R.-L. Wagner, *Les Phrases Hypothétiques commençant par Si dans la Langue Française des Origines à la fin du xvie siècle*

Walther: H. Walther, *Carmina Medii Aevi Posterioris Latina*

Bibliography [1]

Archives

Archives Départementales de Lot et Garonne, Agen.
Archives Départementales des Pyrénées Atlantiques, Pau.
Chroniques de Saint Denis, Bibliothèque Nationale.
Fonds Périgord, Bibliothèque Nationale.

Books and Articles cited

J. Andrieu, L'Histoire de l'Agenais, Paris 1893.
J. Anglade, Grammaire de l'ancien Provençal, Paris 1921.
Anselme, le père: Histoire Généalogique et Chronologique de la Maison Royale de France, Paris 1730
L'Art de vérifier les Dates, Paris 1818.
C. Aspland, A Contribution to the Syntactical Study of -ant Forms in Twelfth Century French Verse, Unpublished Ph.D. thesis, London 1967.
K. Baedeker, South Italy and Sicily, London 1930.
C. Beaulieux, Histoire de l'Orthographe Française, Paris 1927.
Baron de Belabre, Rhodes of the Knights, Oxford 1908.
M. Blanc, Time and Tense in Old French Narrative, Archivum Linguisticum, Vol.16, 96-124.
O. Bloch and W. von Wartburg, Dictionnaire Etymologique de la Langue Française, Paris 1950.
C. de Boer, Ovide Moralisé, Amsterdam 1915.
J. Boudon de Saint Amans, Histoire de Lot et Garonne, Agen 1836.
C. Briquet, Les Filigranes, Paris 1907.
F. Brunot, Histoire de la Langue Française des Origines à 1900, Paris 1905.
F. Brunot and C. Bruneau, Grammaire Historique de la Langue Française, Paris 1933.
Cambridge Medieval History, Cambridge 1936 and revised 1966.
Catholic Encyclopedia, New York 1911.
H.J. Chaytor, History of Aragon and Catalonia, London 1933.
L. Constans and E. Faral, Le Roman de Troie en Prose, Paris 1922, Classiques Français du Moyen Age, 29.
A. Dauzat, Dictionnaire Etymologique des Noms de Famille et Prénoms de France, Paris 1951.
O. Demus, The Mosaics of Norman Sicily, London 1949.
Dubois l'abbé, Cahiers, unpublished, Archives Départementales de Lot et Garonne.
A. Ewert, The French Language, London 1956. (First published 1933.)
P. Fouché, Le Verbe Français. Etude Morphologique, Paris 1967.
L. Foulet, Petite Syntaxe de l'Ancien Français, Paris 1930.

---

1. I have listed only the works which are actually cited in the thesis. They are arranged alphabetically by author. Where there is no author, as with some dictionaries or encyclopedias, they are listed according to the initial letter of the title, excluding the articles.

J. Galy, Le Livre Caumont où sont contenus les dits et enseignemens du Seigneur de Caumont composés pour ses enfans l'an 1416, Paris 1845.
R. Gardner and M. Greene, A Brief Description of Middle French Syntax, University of North Carolina, Studies in Romance Languages and Literature, 29, Chapel Hill, 1958.
F. Godefroy, Dictionnaire de l'Ancien Français, Paris 1881-1902.
----- Lexique de l'Ancien Français, Paris 1901.
E. Goerlich, Die Südwestlichen Dialecte der Langue d'Oil, Heilbronn 1882.
C. Grandgent, Provençal Philology and Morphology, New York 1905.
C. Hassler, Fratris F. Fabri evagatorium in Terra Sanctae Arabiae et Egypti peregrinationem, Stuttgart 1843.
W. Heyd, Histoire du Commerce du Levant, tr. Raynaud, Leipzig 1885-6.
Isidore of Seville, Etymologiae, Paris 1509.
Duc de la Force, Dix Siècles d'Histoire de France, Paris 1960.
L. Lalanne, Dictionnaire Historique de la France, Paris 1879.
J. Lelewel, Géographie du Moyen Age, Brussels 1852.
Marquis Lelièvre de la Grange, Voyaige d'oultremer en Jherusalem, Paris 1858. (Reviewed by M. de Xirey, Bibliothèque de l'Ecole des Chartes, 1858, p.381.)
E. Lévy, Provenzalisches Supplement Wörterbuch, Leipzig 1880-1924.
R. Lodge, The Close of the Middle Ages, London 1915.
M. Maloux, Larousse Dictionnaire des Proverbes, Sentences et Maximes, Paris 1960.
W.H. Mathews, Mazes and Labyrinths, London 1922.
J.P. Migne, Patrologiae Cursus Completus, Paris 1854.
J. Morawski, Proverbes Français, antérieurs au xve siècle, Paris 1925, Classiques Français du Moyen Age, 47.
M. Newett, Canon Pietro Casola's Pilgrimage to Jerusalem in the Year 1494, Manchester 1907.
J.J. Norwich, The Kingdom in the Sun, London 1970.
K. Nyrop, Grammaire Historique de la Langue Française, Copenhagen 1902-1932.
R. Pernoud, Un guide du Pèlerin de Terre Sainte au xve siècle, Cahiers d'Histoire et de Bibliographie, 1, Nantes 1940.
L. Polak, Le Pelerinage de Jehan de Tournay, unpublished Ph.D. thesis, London 1958.
M.K. Pope, From Latin to Modern French, Manchester, rev. 1952.
F.J. Raby, A History of Christian Latin Poetry, Oxford 1953.
R. Roehricht, Bibliotheca Geographica Palestinae, Berlin 1890.
S. Runciman, History of the Crusades, Cambridge 1951.
Schwan-Behrens, Grammaire de l'Ancien Français, Leipzig 1923.
J. Stefanini, La Voix Pronominale en Ancien et en Moyen Français, Publications des Annales de la Faculté des Lettres, Aix en Provence, Nouvelle Série, 31, 1962.
S. Thompson, A Motif Index of Folk Literature, Bloomington, Indiana 1955.
Studer and Evans, Anglo-Norman Lapidaries, Paris 1924.

J.P. Trevelyan, A Short History of the Italian People, rev. D. Mack Smith, London 1956.
Tobler-Lommatzsch, Altfranzösiches Wörterbuch, Berlin 1925-.
Thurston and Attwater, Butler's Lives of the Saints, London 1956.
R-L. Wagner, Les Phrases Hypothétiques commençant par "Si" dans la Langue Française des Origines à la fin du xvie siècle, Paris 1939.
H. Walther, Carmina Medii Aevi Posterioris Latina, Göttingen 1963.
B. Woledge, The Plural of the Indefinite Article in Old French, Modern Language Review, 1956, vol.1, 17-30.
T de Wyzewa, tr. La Légende Dorée, Paris 1935.

Le Voyatge d'Oultremer en Jherusalem

[2R] FERM CAUMONT¹

C'est le livre que je, le seigneur de Caumont et de Chastel Nuef ay fayt ou voyatge d'oultre mer en Jherusalem et du fleuve Jourdeyn ou sont compris les royaumes,*(i) principés, comtés, et autres païs et terres et les nomps dez lieux et nombre dez lieues d'aler et de venir tant par terre que par mer et combien de tamps je demouray le complir despuys mon department jusques a mon retour.

Et premierement sont lez ordenances que je lessay en ma terre a mon pueple avant mon departement.

10 Item l'ordenance dez gentils hommes et autres qui alerent avec moy ou dit voyatge.
Item le voyatge de Jherusalem.
[2V] Item les serements que font les chevaliers ou saint Sepulcre.
Item le desert de Jerico.
Item le chemin ou fleuve Jourdeyn.
Item les peregrinacions, indulgences et pardonances de payne et coulpe de le sainte terre Jherusalem.
Item le devize que je prins a pourter ou dit voyatge.
Le retour de Jherusalem.
20 Les joyes que je pourtay d'icelluy païs d'outremer.
Item ung autre voyatge que je fis a mon seigneur saint Jacques et a Nostre Dame de Finibus terre.²
Item ung autre romans que je fis d'enseignemens.³

[3R] FERM CAUMONT

Ce sont les ordenances que je, Caumont, ay leissees en ma terre quant je en parti pour fere le saint passatge d'outremer en Jherusalem.

Je, le seigneur de Caumont, de Chastel Nauf*(ii) et de Berbeguieres⁴ notiffique et faiz assavoir a toute le université de ma terre, a toux en general que come jadis mon tres redoubté seigneur, mon seigneur mon
30 pere,⁵ cuy Dieux absolle par sa sainte pitié et misericorde, le temps qu'il vivoit, eusse entreprins de fere le saint voyatge d'outremer au saint Sepulcre en Jherusalem ou Jhesu Crist nostre redemptor voulsist prendre mort et passion pour nous pouvres pecheurs et pecheresses rachater dez paines d'enfer ou nous fussions esté perdus, se son precieux [3V] corps ne fust. Et pour ce que Nostre Seigneur Dieux l'a tiré a sa cort a la glorie du royalme celestial de paradis, il n'a peu*(iii) acomplir sa

---

*(i)   Ms. reading: ... les royaumes, principés, comtés, illez et autres païs ... illez is added in a different hand.
*(ii)   After Chastel Nauf there is an erasure of de Chastel Cullier.
*(iii) peu ... The manuscript has been repaired, half obliterating the word. The damage caused by the repair means that several words are lost. The other possible reading is puet.

volonté et desir a y aler ainsi que son entente estoit. Je, comme son
vray filz et universal heretier tant a contemplacion de sa bonne devocion
que par ycelle que je mesmes y ay par moy en remission de mes griefs
pechiés que encontre Dieu mon createur j'ay acommiz et faiz me suis de
bon et vray cuer exposé de fere et enteriner le dit saint voyatge et
passatge d'outremer visiter le saint Sepulcre Nostre Seigneur ou l'aide
duquel et de ...*(i) seigneur saint George est mon entencion et ...*(ii)
parfere et mettre a bonne fin vraye. Pour quoy ...*(iii) affectuosament
je prie a vous mes chiers foyals et ...*(iv) a mes bonnes gens de ma
10   ditte terre, tant gentils religieux pestres et gens de sainte eglize et
autres de quelque estat ou condicion que soyés qu'il vous pleise prier
Jhesu Crist, nostre sauveur, avec bonne et parfeite devocion qui luy
vigne a plesir par sa sainte benigne humilité me donner povoir, grace et
auctorité ainsi que mon corps forment desire. Et a la benoite Vierges
Marie, sa precieuse mere plaine de toute misericorde et de humilité
vueilliés auxi prier qu'elle soit ma advocade envers son precieux cher
[4R] filz que par le merite de sa sainte passion me donne aler et venir
sauvement et seurement, sain et haytiez ratourner entre vous mes bons
amiz et freres et me donne fere les euvres*(v) que soient a honneur de
20   mon corps et sauvacion de mon arme. Et a cause que j'ay en voulor a
vous declarer ung poy de mon cuer pour ce que escripture est chouse
ferme et clere et a toudiz mais manifeste et certayne, a celle fin que
vous puissés mieux veoir et entendre une partie de mon entente quant
je n'y seray, je vous lesse par escript certaines ordenances cy desoubz
escriptes, feites et par articles ourdentés, les quelles, vous prie, vueillés
avoir en memoire et pour l'amour de moy mettre paine a les complir,
chascun endroit soy, sellon leur fourme et teneur par la maniere que de
mot a mot s'en suivent.

Premieremant que, comme vous soyés tous dis estés envers mon dit [4V]
30   tres redoubté seigneur de pere et envers moy et toux nostres predecesseurs,[1]
ausi qu'il n'est memoire du contraire, bons, vrays et foyals liges, je
contfisant de vostre bonne prodomie et loyauté vous recomande bien
affectuosament et de cuer et molt bien chierement vous prie que vous
ayés par recomandés ma tres chiere et ma tres bien amee m'amye et
m'amour vraye et mes petis enfans.[2] Aussi que je vous lesse par bien
entiegrement recomandés et par mesmes toux mes lieux, plasses, chasteaus

---

*(i)   There is a gap in the manuscript. The usual formula is ... de
         mon seigneur saint George.
*(ii)   . A gap in the manuscript. Possible reading is volonté.
*(iii)   A gap in the manuscript. Tres?
*(iv)   A gap in the manuscript. Probable reading is liges.
*(v)   Ms. reading: ... et me donner fere les euvres ...

et fortalesses et toute ma terre par entier[1] come ceux esquelx j'ay tres
parfeite comfiance et fere que le doy par rayson.   Car tousjours m'avés
mostré bon seignal de vraye amour et a present en mon abscence quant
je n'i seray vous prie icelle bonne vraye amour, que me pourtés, vueilliez
moustrer tellement que a mon retour je vous en aye a mercier et de vous tel
report puisse oïr que par jamais je et mes successeurs vous en soyons tenus
d'ayssi en avant.   Et vous en aye a rendre tel bon gueredon, ainssi que
je y ay bonne voulenté et esperance de le fere, s'il plast a Dieu.

Item mes bons vray amix, comme vous [5R] savez le monde est aujourduy
10   plein de tribulacions et aucune foix quant l'en pensse estre en paix et
bonne tranquillité, aucuns debas et discensions sourdent par le païs tant
par enviez, par malvaix repors que autrement en pluseurs diversses voyes
et manieres voulentaires.   Si que se nul accident vous avenoit en aucune
maniere ou aucune noveleté vous estoit fette maintenent quant je seray hors
de païs longtain de ma terre que sans vous esmovoir chaudement ne aster
vous vueillés premierement avoir bonne deliberacion et advis et vous
governer bien saigemant par avant que nul soubde esmovemant soit par vous
commis ne artempté mes par bon et amoderé conseil vous regissiez serlont
Dieu, raison et bonne iustice*, en maniere que par nulle guise decens
20   puissés estre par houstinité, affin que nul mal ne vous en puisse advenir
couvertement, ne l'en puisse dire que en vous ne soit tout bon gouvern-
mant.

Item a vous freres religieux, reteurs, [5V] vicaires et toute autre maniere
de pestres qui estes et demorés en ma terre, je vous prie umblement et de
cuer que de bon voloir vous plaise dire chascun de vous deux foiz chascune sempmence le <u>Confitemini domino quoniam bonus</u> par tel que Nostre
Seigneur Dieux Jhesu Crist me vueille garder et deffendre en mer et en
terre de tout perilh et temptacion du maligne esperit.   Et chescun dimenche
auxi que vous chanterés messe et farés le saint sacrifice a Nostre Seigneur
30   que expressemment de moy fassiez commemoracion en vostre memento et
bonnes prieres que ferés a Dieu.   Et en les prieres que ycelluy jour sont
acostumees a feire en l'eglize vous me vueillés denuncier au bon pueble
qu'ilz m'aient en remembrance envers Nostre Seigneur qu'il me ottroye
par son plaisir que je puisse retourner liez et joyeux entre eux.

Item a vous gentilz femmez et autres quelxconques de ma ditte terre a
toutes en general et a chascune par soy vous prie si affectuosament comme
je puis, [6R] que de vostre bonne volenté et especiale amour que j'ay

---

*   Ms. reading: ... iustice.   En maniere que par nulle guise decens
puissés estre par houstinité ...   This would result in a sentence
without a main clause.

bonne comfiance que me pourtés que vueilliez dire par moy jusques a
mon retour toux lez samediz de l'an a comensser le jour de mon departement sept foix le Ave Marie en honneur et en remenbransse des sept
joyes que le Vierges Marie precieuse heut de son benoit chier filz, ou
si le samedi n'avés loisir ou ne le poves feire que les dittes le dimenche
avec bonne et vraye devocion par affin que par icelles bonnes prieres a
la pucelle Nostre Dame qui ne pourta que ung enfant plaise me achater
grace avec luy que je puisse sain et sauf fere mon voyatge a mon honneur
et sauvacion.

10 Item si le cas avenoit que estant en icest saint voyatge Nostre Seignor
faisoit son commandemant de moy attendu que tous somes venuz en cest
monde de nient et nez de noz meres pour morir et trespasser de cest
siecle plein de labour et de tristece en [6V] l'autre qui perdurablement
sens fin durera, je vous prie moult cheremant que en ycelluy cas vous
pleise avoir ma pouvre arme chaytive par recomandee et ne le mettre
pas en obly ains vueillés prier toux et toutes devotemant icelluy seigneur
qui nous fist et fourma assa semblance et nous desfera quant luy plaira
que par sa sainte misericorde et pitié aie compassion et merci de mon
arme ainssi que de bon cuer de vraie et entiere devocion me transporte
20 visiter le saint lieu ou il prist mort et passion pour nous le jour du
venredi ahouré et le saint Sepulcre ou les bons prodomes Josep
d'Arimacias et Nicodemus mistrent son precieux corps quant l'eurent
demandé a Pilat,[1] le faulx malveis tirant, que par sa sainte resureccion
qu'il ressuscita de mort a vie le jour de pasques luy plaise resusciter mon
corps et mon arme en la compaignie dez sains angels de paradis ou est la
joie perdurable sains fin m'egeussant lesquelles prieres et autres bonnes
oraisons vous dont grace et pouvoir que puissés fere choses que soient au
profitz de vostres corps et sauvacion de vos armes.

Item mes bon et parfais amix s'il estoyt [7R] ainssi comme dit est que
30 Nostre Seigneur fist son comandemant de moy, j'ay establi, ordenné
et institui et a present en celluy cas fais, ordenne et instituisse emprés
moy mon vray et universal heretier Noper de Caumont,[2] mon premier
filz de toute ma terre et de toux mes biens et de tout quant que j'ay
entierement, ainssi comme estre doit par droite ligne et parfoite raison
sellon Dieu et le monde, et vous prie bien affectuosament tant par
vostre devoir fere que par vostre honneur observer et garder et suis
certain que vous ne farés pas du contraire que le dit Noper mon filz et
vray heretier vueillés recevoir par seigneur et luy estre bons vrays et
foyals ligez et obeïsans, comme estre devés et toux dis avés acoustumé
40 estre a mon dit tres redouté seigneur mon pere et a moy et a nostres
predecesseurs. Et que par mesmes il vous fasse ce que feire vous devra,
cousi que tout bon seigneur doit fere a ces vassaux, et je que vueil que
ainssi soit. Et par consequent si Dieux faizoit son comandemant de luy
que fusse alés de vie a trespassement que ainsi le farés de mes autres
enfans ainsi come de gre en gre seront descenduz que par semblable

maniere et par semblant cas les vueillez recevoir par seigneur ou par
dames[1] sains nulle contradiccion et continuer envers eux en toute bonne
loyauté, laquelle [7V] avez tosdiz acoustumé et farés par le plaisir de
Dieu jusques a la fin.

Item se aucuns vous repourtoient de moy aucunes paroles que ou voyatge
je fusse trespassé de cest siecle en l'autre que Nostre Seigneur eusse
fait de moy son plaisir que soubdaynement ne les vueillés pas croire.
Car si par aventure pour vous fere despleisance au cuer aucuns messongiers
et jongleurs[2] vous repourtoient que se seroit ainssi pour vous mettre en
10 miencolie et tristece et n'en seroit riens en aucune maniere ni quelsque
repourteurs que soient, ne vueillez croire nul d'eulx si non que se
fussent souffisans gens et dignes de foy et parfeitement bien enfourmés
de la verité et peussent prover et moustrer bonnement que ainssi fusse et
encores que entieremant ung an soit passé ainçoys que vous en croyés
rien ne d'un ne d'autre.

[8R] Item sachiés que je lesse tout amplemant m'amye, mes petis enfans
et toute ma terre par entier ou guouvernemant de monseigneur le conte
de Foiz,[3] qui m'a norri, comme en celluy ou j'ay plus de espoir de parfeite comfiance.

20 Item plus mes bons amix j'ay deputé et ordenné mon beau oncle Arnaut
de Caumont et mon ben amé escuier Galhardet de Tozeux[4] pour avoir le
regiment et estre residentemant guouverneurs de ma tres chere et ma tres
bien amee m'amye, de mes enfans et de vous autres et auxi de toute ma
terre de Guascoigne, d'Agenois, de Pierregour et de Bazadés come
ceulx esquells je me confize grandemant de leurs sens, loyauté, bonne
discrecion et diligence pour vous regir et gouverner paisiblement et
pasciffiquemant, en vous priant que a ce qu'il vous diront, demonstraront,
conseilleront et aministraront, lez vueillés aryre et estre vrays,
obeïssans et les secourre et aidier se mestier en ont, comme [8V] a nostre
30 propre persone et vous demounstrés de partide ou eulx encontre toutz
autres, qui mal ni despleisir leur vouldroient fere, si par gardant mon
devoir et touchant mon bien et mon honneur et de m'amye, de mes
enfans, de vous et de toute ma terre leur querrient discensions en quelque
maniere. Et par semblant cas ceulx que j'ay commis et leissé pour la
garde de mes lieux, plasses, chasteaux et fortelesses leur vueillez estre
obeïssans et favorables en toute necessité et feire pour eulx ce qu'ilz
vous comanderont et verrés estre faisable touchant le sauvacion et fortiffi-
cacion d'icelles par affin que en deffaute de reparacion et bonne diligence ne se ayent a perdre.

40 Item vous prie a vous toux en general que vueillés avoir l'un envers
l'autre bonne pais, amour, acort et vraie tranquillité sans avoir nulle
noise, discencion ne debat emsemble, ain vueillez estre bons et foyals
amix comme freres, ainssi que estre devez. [9R] Car par discencions

et debatz toux les maulx du monde (ne) viennent, mes si vous avez nulle
demande a calanger l'un sur l'autre en quelques maniere que ce soit que
par devant mes officiers a ce deputés les feites venir et mettre en ma
cort laquelle vous sera ouverte a vous fere droit et raison et toute
loyale justice. Toutes foix si aucun grant debat ou querelle sourdoit
de l'un a l'autre et vous semblasse que mes officiers ne fussent assés
suffisans pour icelluy debat declarer, vous prie, les vueillez remettre
et cesser de celluy pleyt et debat jusques a ma venue et retour. Et par
la grace de Nostre Seigneur oyez que j'aie les parties, je les metray a
10   bonne paix et acourt.

Item sachiés que j'ay grant joie de ce que je cognois que vous toux
prenés en gre que je acomplisse cest saint voyatge que j'ay en propos de
fere et, a par que plaisir y prenés, a la grande amour que [9V] mostré
m'avez, de ce que de tres bon voloir m'avez aidé et secouru largement
du vostre en maniere que je m'en tiens par bien content et vous en
mercie de tout mon cuer. Et plaise a Dieu le pere omnipotent que me
donne tant vivre en bonne prosperité que je vous en puisse rendre bon
queredon, ainssi que j'ay bonne affeccion et vouloir de la fere. En
vous priant de bon cuer que se je vous ay feit chouse que vous desplaise
20   qu'il vous plaise le me pardoner. Et si vous en avés feit a moy ne dit
que ne me doye tourner a desplaisir par afin que Jhesu Crist nostre
redemptor me pardonne mes pechiéz et deffallimens, ainsi qu'il pardonna
ceulx qui le mirent en croix, je vous pardonne de bon cuer et de bonne
foy.

Pour quoy mes bons, vrays amix et amiez pour acomplir ma devocion huy
que est le xx jour du mois de fevrier l'an de l'incarnacion de Nostre
[10R] Seigneur mil ccccxviii je prins orendroit mon chemin s'il plest
a Dieu le tout poissant et a la Vierges precieuse, sa chere mere, et
au bon chevalier, monseigneur saint Gorge, auxquelz plaise me ottroier
30   que sauvement et seurement je y puisse aller et retourner paisiblement
a honneur de moy et sauvacion de mon arme et en remission de mes
pechiés que Jhesu Crist par sa benigne grace vueille remettre et par-
donner, quant vendra a mes derreniers jours, ainssi qu'il pardona la
Marie Magdalene. Et ycelle sainte parolle me vueille denuncier que
fist au bon lairon en l'abre de la vraie croix, quant il li pria; "Sire,
souveigne te de moy quant en ton regne seras' et Nostre Seigneur luy
respondi; 'Huy seras avec moy en paradis';[1] toux et toutes le vueillez
prier que par la merite de sa sainte passion au pas de la fin, celle sainte
parolle et pardurable don a moy et a vous luy plaise ottroier que puissons
40   venir au saint lieu dez bons esleuz a la sua dextre. Et quant je seray
part dela, je le prieray pour vous tous et toutes que dez bien faiz que je
diray ne feray vous en done* bonne part et de tout mal vous vueille

---

*   done. The e of done is added in a different hand.

garentir. En vous priant que tout jour vous vueille souvenir de ma tres
chere et ma tres bien amee m'amye et mes petis enfans ignocens que
sont tous vostres et seront tant comme [10V] vievront. Et a Dieu soiês
vous recomandês tous et toutes. Ore me baisiez et le saint esperit soit
aveques vous et garde moy et de mon arme. Et en tesmoing de ce les
ordennances sus dittes j'ay signê de ma propre main pour plus de fermetê
avoir.

FERM CAUMONT

[11R] Ce sont les apointtemens et ordenances fettes, acordees et
10 passees entre moy, le seigneur de Caumont, de Chastel Neuf* et de
Berbeguieres d'une part et mes escuiers, Bertran Chastel, Gonsalvo de
Bonelles[1] et autres de ma compaignie d'autre part sur le partiment de
nostre voyatge pour aler au saint Sepulcre d'oultremer en Jherusalem
par le maniere que de mot a mot s'ensuivent.

Premieremant que les diz mes escuiers et autres m'ont jurê et promis,
promettent et jurent sur les sains evangelis Nostre Seigneur qu'ilz me
serviront bien et loyaument sain et malade en toutes et quantes voies
et manieres qu'ilz porront a leur loial povoir sans nul travail de leur
corps espargnier.

20 Item qu'ilz ne me lesseront jamais ne se partiront [11V] de ma compaignie
en quelque part ou je vueille aler par quelconque cause ou occasion
que ce soit jusques a tant que je soie retournês en ma terre se non que
ce fusse par cas de mort que Dieux eusse fait son comandemant de moy
et autrement non en aucune maniere.

Item si aucun debat, discenssion ou noise sordoit de l'un a l'autre come
aucune foiz avient par le chemin, qu'ilz seront tenus lendemain par tout
le jour demander pardon l'un a l'autre et de leissier toute error et
iniquitê.

Item je leur ay promis, promet et jure et leur faire bonne compaignie
30 et ne lez leissier nullemant se non que ce fusse par cas de mort ou
aucune [12R] grande enfermetê leur sorvenoit a l'alant en laquelle je en
eusse aperdie mon voyatge. Et si en celluy cas les me convenoit lessier que me seroit bien grief, je seray tenus de les leissier de quoy ilz se
puissent fere gouverner et retourner part dessa en ma terre. Et si le cas
estoit que au retour en nous en venent l'accident sus dit avenoit que
aucun d'eulx fusse malade que Dieux deffende de ne lez leissier point
jusques a la mort.

---

*   de Chastel Neuf. After this the words de Chastel Culier
have been erased.

Lesquelles chouses sus dittes et chacune d'icelles furent fettes, promises
et jurees le xxvii jour du mois de feuvrier l'an mil ccccxviii que nous
partimes de Caumont pour acomplir le dit voyatge, a ce presens et
tesmoingz Galhardet de Tozeuz, Nandonet [12V] Gaubert, Guassion
de le Causee, Archambaud de le Mote, Jehan de Lauriole, Jehan de
Taris et Clement de Salungnac, escuiers de ma terre.[1]

FERM CAUMONT

[13R] LE PROLOGUE

DU VOYATGE ... *(i)

10 [13V] Noper, seigneur de Caumont, de Chasteau Nuef, de Chasteau
Cullier[2] et de Berbeguieres. Chouse notoire, manifeste et vraie
que Nostre Seigneur Dieu, Jhesu Crist fist et crea le siel, le terre, les
quatre helemens, tout le firmament et tout quant est et nous forma assa
semblance, et pour ce que chascun scet que par le peché de nostre
premier pere Adam, pour le desobiassence qu'il fist de mangier du fruit
de vie[3] que li avoit eté defendu, nous estions dampnez en enfer ...
par le grant amour qu'il pourtoit ... ama mieulx mourir et prendre ...
que ce nous fussions esté ... *(ii) [14R] de son precieux sanc lequel par
sa debonayreté espandi pour nous en l'albre de le vraie croix, ou il
20 souffri si cruelle mort et amere, comme vous savez et avez oÿ dire, de
le quelle nous devroit bien souvenir, et devrions considerer lez griefs
travaillz duites, males lengors et engoysses que par nostre sauvacion il
ha voulu souffrir pour nous. Si que de corps, d'arme et de foy devrions
estre tous jours en luy et fere ces comandemans. Car sans doubte il
m'est bien advis que se ung seigneur terren m'avoit sauvé le vie et
gardé*(iii) de mourir, que jamais ne ly fauldroie, ains auroit toux dis
comandemant sur moy et tout ainxi seroit il bien raison que a Nostre
Seigneur, qui de le perpetuele mort nous ha gardé, nul jour ne eure ne
ly devons faillir ne pourrions assés fere pour luy, mes toux tamps devons
30 prier que nous dont le sue grace et amour et toux jours que en avons
besoing. Car nous n'avons bien ne honneur ne avoir ne povons si de
luy ne vient, et pour ce devons estre obeïssans acomplir sa voulenté et
plaisir, se voulons vievre en sa glorie perdurablement. Car chascun
puet bien savoir que cest monde n'est pas nostre domicille ne demeure,
ains est mort et paine miserable, pleine de trevail et de tristece. Et

*(i)   The lower half of the page has been torn away. There are
        traces of other words, probably d'oultremer en Jherusalem.
*(ii)   Again half the page has been torn away, leaving these dis-
        jointed phrases.
*(iii) gardé. The ms. reading is garder, which makes no sense.
        This mistake is consistent with the theory that the author dic-
        tated his account.

donques devons nous estre diligens avoir la vie de duree non pas tant
se attendre ez chouses [14V] mondaines ne avoir tant le cuer aux deliz
de cest siecle que ayons aperdie le joie sans fin et au derrier l'aurons
nous tout a lessier et ne savons l'eure ne quant, car nulh ne puet faillir
a le mort. Et cellon ce que chescun aura fait part dessa sera gueredon-
nés part dela, n'en doubtés point, et si nous y somes huy par aventure
n'y serons pas demein. Car le sainte escripture dit ainssi; Nullus tam
fortis cui pareant vincula mortis.[1] C'est a dire; qu'il n'y a nul si fort
que le mort en aie point de mercy. Et par esperience le povez veoir
10   que tantost l'en sera sain et en bon point, bel, jeune et fort, et encontinent devendra malade et tantost cherra ou lit de le mort.[2] Si me
semble qu'il n'y a que de mettre paine et trevail fere en maniere que
puissions entrer ou regne celestiel, quant departirons de cest siecle
miserable que n'est que rozee. Et certainemant je ne doubte point que
se nous voulons que n'y entrons bien, si nous gardons de mal fere, car
sachiez que nulh n'y puet entrer s'il n'est souparé du mal purement et
acompaignié du bien. Et qui ne ce tient a bien fere est chouse de sa
dapnacion et pourront avoir grant duel au jour du jutgemant ceulx a qui
Nostre Seigneur dira de sa propre bouche; Ite maledicti in ignem
20   eternum;[3] Alez malediz ou feu eternal. Et je ay souvant panssé en ces
[15R] chouses et suy moult trist, doulant et marri, quant me souvient de
le mort que fera le departiment du corps et de l'arme, et ne say quel
chemin aura a tenir, mes bon se Dieu plest. Et s'il nous souvenoit du
perill que avons a passer, quant avons voulenté de mal fere ne fallirons
pas si souvant ne si largemant, mes poy nous en membre et appar que
l'en ne cesse de fere guerres, prendre lieux, bouter feux, forsser femmez,
destruire le pueple qui tant a Nostre Seigneur ha cousté et tuer les
hommes, pilher les serviteurs de Dieu et lez eglizes, qui sont temple
Nostre Seigneur, et pluseurs autres violences que je ne nomme pas. Et
30   j'ay ouy dire ha aucunes gens que au tamps passé les rois, lez princes et
les grans seigneurs et barons fesoient bastir lez mostiers, lez eglizes et
a present est au revers qu'ilz les desfont et abatent et font destruire, et
ce n'est que l'enemi qui lez a lassiez et conjoins a soy que n'ont le cuer
que en fere mal et bastir guerres et discenssions par lez païs l'un contre
l'autre et a leurs prouchains voisins contre droit et raison, dont ilz en ont
grant pechié de ce que font et font fere et moustrent bien qu'il ne leur
chaut de l'emour de Dieu ne dez bonnes gens ne prouchains voisins, ne
n'ent en memoire le parolle que l'escripture dit; Tam regibus quam
principibus mors nulli miseretur.[4] Sachiez de certain que le mort
40   n'a merci des rois, dez princes ni de null autre si grant seigneur [15V]
soit, que toux ne lez preigne. Et ceulx qui vuellent guerres, devroient
fere comme le loup sellont que ce lit es fables * que une foiz s'en monta

---

    *   lit. The ms. reading is; ... sellont que ce liti es fables ... This
        is presumably a scribal slip.

sur une haulte montaigne avec toux ces petis lombas qu'il avoit bien
chieremant norris pour leur demostrer le païs a l'entour et leur dit;
"Or regardés mes filz, je vous ay norris tant comme j'ay peu et maintenant je suy si vieux que je ne puis cheminer, mes vous estes assés grans
et fors pour vous donner conseil dores en avant. Toutes fois je vous
vueil aviser d'une chouse de le quelle vous vueillés bien garder. C'est
assavoir que ou païs ou vous vouldrés fere vostre prise ne fettes point
vostre maison ne habitacion. Si vous vueillez vivre sans doubte et ce
ne fettes ce, vous ne porriez avoir si longe duree comme j'ay. En cas
10   si je eusse fait le contraire, je n'eusse pas tant vescu ne vous si bien
norris.   Pour ce a mon propoux ceulx qui ont leur meson et habitacion
en ung païs et ont entente y demourer, se deyvent garder fere mal au
gens du païs entour eulx par especiel a leurs prouchains voisins. Car
ilz porient bien savoir qu'ilz ne seront pas asseur ne ni auront duree.*
Car nuyt et jour s'auront a garder, et j'ay ouy dire souvant que qui ha
mal voisin si ha maul matin." ¹   Pour ce [16R] vouldroie je plus avoir
cent livres de rente et estre amez du pueple et dez voysins a l'entour
que ne feroie mille que me voulsissent mal ne fusse en leur desgrace.
Car qui est amez du pueple est amez de Dieu.   Or regardons que ma
20   proufiteroit il le rente que jour et nuyt me fausist estre armés? Je ne
tendroie pas que ce fusse rente, ains se pourroit bien appeller le mort.
Pour ce n'est si belle chouse que quant Dieu donne le grace et l'amour
du pueple et de son voisin, ausi est il le segont comandemant Nostre
Seigneur qui dit; <u>Dilige proximum tuum sicut te ipsum.</u> ²   C'est a dire
que amez ton prosine comme toy mesmez et qui fera le comandement de
Dieu sera sauvez et bien se doit aviser donques que l'en ne face mal ex-
pressemant a son voisin et aviser se ce sera bien (bien) fait ou mal. Car
quant l'en le fait après s'en repant, et alors n'est pas tamps, et vous di
que trop asceste n'est pas sagesse, mes nous n'y avisons pas ains avons le
30   cuer et le voulenté plus au mal fere que au bien continuer et a paines
sera que qui mal fet que mal ne ly viegne. ³   Car l'en dit voulentiers
que ou monde n'a si belle chouses comme barat car il tourne de la don
vient, et c'est bien raison.   Et vous di que qui veult tenir tel voie
n'entrera ja en paradis. Et pour ce que n'avons le cuer en bien, Nostre
Seigneur nous envoye tempestes, [16V] mortalités et pluseurs tribulacions
et meschances pour lez malx et orribles pechiéz et tirennie que aujourduy
acometons tant que je en suis bien mereville que ne prenons a cuer ce
que l'escripture dit; <u>Fac bene dum vivis post mortem vivere si vis.</u> ⁴
Fay du bien en dementies que vivras si veulx vivre quant mort seras.
40   C'est a dire; Si veulx avoir paradis. Mes nous n'y avons pas l'imagin-
assion mes que audions fere huellz de siere ⁵ a Nostre Seigneur, si comme
se il ne veoit goute.   Mes en bonne foiz nous ne povons riens fere,

---

*   Ms. reading; Car ilz porient bien savoir qu'ilz ne seront pas asseur
ne ni duree.   Clearly a verb is missing, probably auront.

pansser ne cogiter qu'il ne le sache tout et coqnoiscions a les fin qu'il
n'avoit riens davant lez yeulx.   Pour ce nous devrions amender nostres
vies et fere du bien puis que tamps avons.   Car l'en dit voulentiers;
que qui temps ha et tamps demeure, tamps li faut,[1] et ainxi l'escripture
dit; Non modo leteris quia forsan cras morieris.[2]   Ne te alegres pas
tant maintenant non obstant que soies sain et en bon point, car par
aventure demain morras.   Pour ce faissions le bien et lassions le mal.
Car le bon angel que Dieux nous ha baillié a le part droite nous con-
seille tout pour le bien, et l'ennemi qui est a le part senestre le mal
pour nous decevoir.   Pour ce prenons le meilleur et soions umbles et
courtois et ne fassions pas comme [17R] Lucifer qui estoit le plus res-
plendens angel de paradis et pour son grant ergull Jhesu Crist le fist
descendre al abisme d'enfer ou il est le plus orrible deable qui soit et
yci avons bon exemple que ne soions*point ourgueleux ne fassions contre
le mandemant Nostre Seigneur.   Car le chouse que plus li desplet,
c'est ourgulh qui est le plus orrible pechié de touts les sept pechiéz
mortelz et par lequel viegnent plus de mals, et qui en pechié mortel
muert, il est dampnez; pleise a Dieu que nous en puissions garder, mes
ung tigneux vouldroit que tous fussent comme luy, aussi est l'ennemi
que vouldroit que tous fussent dampnez comme il est.   Pour ce devons
aler le droit chemin et estre en Nostre Seigneur et non pas fere comme
pluseurs font en cest monde que leissent leurs propres seigneurs pour se
mettre avec leur hennemix pour or ou par argent, comme pluseurs font
que lessent Dieu pour le deable, que son parens de la turpe que change
lez yeulx pour le coue;[3] ainxi font cels changeurs de mestres que ven-
dent leur honneur, que est le plus belle chouse que home puisse avoir
et qui plus vaut, et le changent pour or et par argent que ne vaut neant,
mes tels audent toux embrassier et qui trop embrasse, poy estraint;[4] pour
ce devons fere bien et estre en Dieu et le prier qu'il ayt pitié et [17V]
merci de nous.   Car Dieux demeure tout jour que ayons en nous repen-
tance et retournons a luy.   Car il ha dit dessa bouche; Nolo mortem
peccatoris sed ut convertatur et vivat.[5] Je ne veulx pas, dit Nostre
Seigneur, la mort du pecheur mes que se converte et vive, et qui ne se
convertira envers luy sera dapnez en enfer a la mort perdurable.   Pour
ce devons juner et fere du bien et aumosnes as pouvres tant comme
povons ne avons loisir, et fassions ce que Nostre Seigneur dit; Da tua
dum tua sunt quia post mortem tua non sunt, quia dare non poteris, quando
sepultus eris.[6]   Que veult tant dire; donne le tien en dementres qu'il
est tien et as loisir.   Car après le mort ne sera pas tien, car donner ne
le pourras pas quant en terre seras.   C'est assavoir quant seras mort.
Et en ycelle maniere pourras acquerir l'amour Nostre Seigneur qui est
le(s) plus precieuze chouse que soit et serons bons marchans et ferons

*   soions.   The ms. reading is sions which is probably a scribal slip.

21

        beau gaing acquerre tel noble heretatge que toux jours durera, mes plu-
        seurs ne le font pas ains acquerent le puis d'enfer en pluseurs de manieres,
        mes l'en se devroit estudier a ayder a bastir eglizes, comforter les des-
        consollês, visiter les melades en leurs liz et pensser d'eulx premieremant
        que de nous, et c'est le mandemant Nostre Seigneur qu'il dit propremant
        de sa bouche; [18R] <u>Cum sis in mensa primo de paupere pensa</u>.[1] Quant
        tu seras a ta table a ton disner ou a ton sopper avant toutes choses penssa
        premier dez pouvres de Dieu; et qui fait ce qu'il comende il s'en va tout
        droit en paradis. Et ainxi est moult bonne et honnorable chose et de
10   grant prouffit qui enprant aler visiter le saint lieu ou le precieux corps
        Nostre Seigneur fut mis amprês qu'il fut crucifiê en croix pour nous.
        Car c'est le sauvemant de toux ceulx qui de bonne devocion y vont et
        ce doit fere qui puet, mes toux ceulx qui povent ne le font pas que bien
        sont clers ceulx que j'oy dire qui y vont, toutes foiz je croy bien qui en
        y a pluseurs qui le lessent affere pour ce qu'il est si loingtain et de grant
        despensse qu'ilz ni pourroient contribuir, et ceulx je tiens que ont plus
        souffisant raison que ceulx qui ont bien de quoy et demeurent pour
        prendre l'aise de leur corps que par aventure leur vausist mieulx ne
        prendre pas tant de sojour ne repoux, car ung poy de travail est bon
20   afere qui aprês retourne a tout bien*(i) et grant prouffit. Car qui du
        bien veult avoir mettre le faut les mains, et ainxi dit le fransois que a
        paines vient null bien sans paine,[2] et pour ce null ne doit estre necligent
        a travailler pour atquerir honneur et [18V] sauvacion. Et sachiez que
        necligence est une de plus pires taches que l'en puisse avoir sur soy fors
        que tracion. Car l'ostel*(ii) del homme necligent jamais sa fin ne sera
        de null bien, ains par necligence vient en cheitivece et pouvresse. Et
        pour ce lez gens qui son diligens et prudens en leurs besoignes et negoces;
        tels sont sages et ne puent avoir se bien non; ores pourra l'en dire que
        celluy qui ha ordonnê cessi, ne le scet mye rettenir pour soy mes ce je
30   leur ottroie que je n'ay pas si grant discrecion en moy. Toutes foiz je
        vouldroie bien par le plaisir Dieu que je eusse le grace que je le sceusse
        dire et ordonner en celle maniere que ceulx qui en auront besoing le
        sceussent a prendre et estancher pour eulx, car ce seroit a moy plaiser et
        a eulx prouffit. Mes pour declarer mon entencion que n'est pas grans
        j'ay prins ceste matiere a conclure pour moy que ne say quant ay a
        demorer en cest monde fors tant comme au plaisir Dieu sera. Et ay con-
        siderê ces chouses sus dittes bien que le tamps fait son devoir et va en
        decheant et nous que de heure en heure allons tout jour a le mort, si que
        je ne voy que nous ayons point de tarde de fere du bien qui bon vouloir
40   y a; et en veritê je vouldroie que, ainxi comme je y ay bonne*(iii) [22R]

        *(i)   Ms. reading is: ... qui aprês retourner a tout bien. There are
                   other examples of this mistake on p.11, l.19 and p.17, l.26.
        *(ii)   The ms. reading does not make sense, as it stands. There must
                   be an omission, perhaps of a preposition. Car en l'ostel ...
        *(iii)   je y ay bonne ...   These are the last words of the folio 18 in
                   the manuscript. There is a folio misplaced at this point, because
                   the folio which should follow is folio 22. The scribe has made a
                   mark to indicate this.

affeccion que null me tombast, non pourtant que, se Dieux plest, je ne
mueray point mon propoux que je ne fasse mon devoir tant come je pour-
ray. Et pour lez grans tribulacions, discencions et enviez que je voy
en cest païs semener lez uns envers lez autres, et ycelles plus prestes de
croistre que de laissier, que me desplet, pour ycelles eschiver et fouir a
leurs temptacions voulentaires et a toute maulvaise vie deshordennee et
que je ne vueil pas ainxi exploier mon tamps attendre tant en lez chouses
mondeines que je ne pansse en les chouses espirituelles a contemplacion
de le sainte passion que Nostre Seigneur souffri pour tant l'omaing linatge

10   et par avoir pardonance et remission de mos pechiêz que encontre mon
createur j'ay comis et faix dont je me rent coupable, en luy demandant que
par ce humilité li plaise avoir pitié et mercy de ma cheytive arme qui
atant sa grace et sa misericorde avoir, lequelle sur moy par son beau
plaisir vueille espandre a le fin de mes jours, j'ay entrepris ou l'eyde
de Dieu, de le glorieuse Vierges Marie et de mon seigneur saint George
et expousé tout mon cuer entierement a fere le saint passatge d'outremer
en Jherusalem visiter le saint Sepulcre Jhesu Crist ou son precieux corps
fu mis. [22V] Et est ainxi que le cas puet avenir que aucuns auront
ceste mesme entencion que au present j'ay, et vourront enprendre de aler

20   et fere le voyatge susdi comme le plus digne et le plus souverein que soit,
mes pour ce que aucune foix l'en delaisse aler dehors en maintes pars par
deffaute que l'en ne scet quel chemin l'en doit tenir, a celle fin que
nullz ne puissent avoir telle excusacion et ne perdent si honnorable ne si
prouffitable voiatge, je leur ay mis en cest livre par escript tout le
chemin que je ay fait alant et retournant afin qu'ilz soient mieulx en-
dressés, ont sont compris toux lez royaumes, principês, ysles et païs et
toux les noms dez cités, villez, chasteaux et autres lieus et plasses, tant
dessa la mer que par dela, et le nombre dez lieues[1] et combien je demouray despuis le jour que je parti de Caumont que estoyt lundi xxvii

30   jour du moys de feuvrier l'an mil ccccxviii, lequel voyatge plaise a
Dieu, Nostre Seigneur par le merite de sa sainte passion que soie fait a
sauvacion de mon arme et que celle parfette amour que par sa digne
grace nous demoustra en nostre comensament nous vueille par son bon
plaisir demostrer a nostre fin,* [19R] ainxi qu'il scet que mester avons.
En priant cellez et ceulx qui cest livre liront ung pater noster pour l'arme
de moy, Caumont, vueillent dire: ce leur vient a plaisir que Dieu leur
dont paradis au finir.   Amen.

Ensuit ce le dit chemin et voyatge d'outremer comenciê pour le gracie
Nostre Seigneur et de monseigneur saint George a Caumont en Guasconhe

40   au mois de feuvrier le xxvii[e] jour en l'an de l'encarnacion mil ccccxviii.

---

*   demostrer a nostre fin. Folio 22 ends at this point and is follow-
        ed by Folio 19 ... ainxi qu'il scet ...

GUASCOGNE

[19V]   Premierement de Caumont je m'en allay couchier a le ville du Port sainte Marie ou il a iiii lieues.

AGENOIS

Du Port sainte Marie a la cipté d'Agen ii lieues.

De Agen parti lendemain que fut le premier jour de mars et de careyme et me allay disner a la ville de Moissac en Carssin que est a vi lieues et couchier part dela la riviere de Tarn davant Chasteau Sarrazin a Nostre Damme d'Allem ou il ha i lieue.

[20R] LANGUEDOC

De Nostre Damme d'Allem au lieu de Grizolles v lieues.

De Grizolles je tiray ver la cipté de Tolouze pour veir le saint suzaire de Jhesu Crist Nostre Seigneur[1] iiii lieues.

De Toulouze au lieu de Avinhonet vi lieues.

LAUREGUÉS

[20V]   De Avinhonet a le ville de Chastel Nef Darri ii lieues.

De Chasteau Nuef Darri au lieu de Saint Martin i lieue ou je trouvay monseigneur le conte de Foiz[2] que avoit pris ledit lieu de combatemant et mon entente estoit d'aller a Venize[3] moy mettre en mer et ledit monseigneur de Foiz me conseilla que je ne feisse point celuy chemin par cause dez guerres que ou païs estoient.[4] Si que m'en fit tourner vers Barcellone en Cataloigne et celluy jour je m'en revins aveques luy a le ville de Masieres ou il a v lieues et au chef de le ditte ville a ung tres beau chasteau et fort sur une rivere bien enmurré et de grosses tours machacollees tout autour et par dedens est tout depint merveilleusement de batailles et y troverés de toux les generacions crestiens et sarrazins ung pareill mascle et femele chacun sellon le poureture de son païs.

LA CONTEE DE FOIZ

[21R]   De Masieres a la cipté de Pamies ii lieues tres belle cipté et riche en le quelle a ung hault chasteau mot fort.

De Pamies a Foiz ii lieues. C'est une moult souvereyne place de fourteresse asize sur ung hault roc de toutes pars sens nulle venue et le

chasteau par dessus bien basti de bons murs et de tours et au pié d'icelluy
a une grosse ville de mille feux bien enmurree tout autour et une rivere
que li passe pardevant et ce dit communemant par tout que l'en nesset
une plus forte place a une tiel ville au pié comme celuy.

De Foiz a le ville de Tarascon ii lieues et passe l'en par davant une tres
forte plasse que l'en laisse a main senestre que se nomme Mon Gallart
grandemant hault de montaigne et de roche et plus avant on [21V] ne
veoit une autre a la main destre qui s'apelle Calemes qui aussi est sou-
vereynement hault que n'a garde de null engein ne d'estre pris afforce,
10   tant qu'il hi auroit vitailles.

De Tarascon a le ville d'Ax en Savartes iii lieues au dehors de lequel
ville a ung chasteau rochier assis en tres bel avantatge et fort.

D'Ax a l'Ospital de sainte Suzanne ii lieues.

De l'Espital ou Chasteau de Carol ii lieues et entre deux a une montaigne
appellee Pimorent que dure une lieue et demye chargee de grans nefs par
lequel est moult perileux a passer.

[23R] LE PAÏS DE SARDAIGNE

De Carol a la ville de Puich Sardain i lieue.

De Puch Sardain a la Borguade de Das i lieue.

20   De Das au lieu de Bagua iii lieues et passe l'en a une moult grant et
haulte montaigne que s'apelle Coll de Yau lequel dure une bonne lieue
demontant et une autre de davallant de tres mal port et perilleux chemin.

LA CONTEE DE CATALOIGNE

[23V] De Bagua a le ville de Bergue iii lieues.

De Bergue a Casserras i lieue.

De Casserras a Balceran iii lieues.

De Balcerein ou lieu de saint Pierre d'Our iii lieues.

De saint Pierre d'Our a la cipté de Menreze mye lieue.

De Menreze a Chasteau Guallin i lieue.

30   De Chasteau Gallin a Nostre Damme de Monserrat ii [24R] lieues lequelle

fet moulx de grans miracles; y est en une chapelle bien devote et riche
et defice en unes roches moult estranges et sur une d'icelles roches au
plus hault ha ung chasteau ou l'en ne puet monter que par ung chemin
estroit par escalons faitz de la roche mesme a grant dangier le montee
et de male venue et au pié de celluy est bastie le abbaye [1] de Nostre
Damme ou le ditte chapelle est, en le quelle fis*(i) chanter toux les
moynez du monestir messe haulte de Nostre Dame solempniaumat aveques
les orguines.

De Monserrat au lieu de Coll Beton i lieue.

10   De Coll Beton au lieu d'Espareguieres i lieue.

De Espareguieres a le ville de Mertorell i lieue.

De Mertorell ou lieu de Molin de Rech ii lieues.

[24V] Et entre ceux deux lieux ha une rivere que l'on appelle Lobregat
le quelle je passay a une barque et jouste le dit port a ung vilatge qui
s'apelle saint Andrieu.

De Molin de Rech a la cipté de Barcellone port de mer ii lieues ou je
arrivay le xxi jour de mois de mars et demouray en la ditte cipté jusques
ou quart jour du mois de may après suyant l'an mil ccccxix, le quel jour
je me mis en la mer ou plaisir de Nostre Seigneur en une nef de le quelle
20   estoient patrons Ramon Ferre et Fransois Ferrier de la ditte cipté de
Barcellone.

LA MER

Quant je fuy parti de Barcellone bien alevant en la mer que l'on ne veoit
que siel y eue, cy comensse a venir grant vent que de tout nous [25R]
cuyda pourter en terre de Barberie. [2] Mes Dieu que ne veulu nostre
domatge nous donne grace de ariver a ung port au royaume de Mallorque[3]
a une vila qui s'apelle Alcudie, le quelle est a cc milles de la ditte
cipté de Barcellone et content v milles par une lieue et la ditte ville est
environee de mer excepté devert l'une part bien la montance de deux
30   treitz d'arbalestre. Et ce disoit qu'en toute celle ille du royaume de
Mallorque n'avoit de nulle condicion de beste se n'est que serfs et
lapareux.

*(ii) Item après que le bon tamps fut venu, je parti dudit port d'Alcudie

---

*(i)   fis.   The ms. reading is fist, but fis makes better sense.
*(ii)   This paragraph is headed Le Reaume de Malhorque, which has
           been inserted in a different hand.

et tiray alavant,* passant pour davant l'isle de Menorque ou l'en conte lx milles.

Item d'icelle ditte isle de Menorque entray [25V] en le guolf de Lion que est unne mer ou l'en ne trouve fons, le quel guolf dure cclxxx milles, ains que l'on ne soit dehors sens veoir terre de nulle part.

Item saillant d'icelluy guolf de Lion il avint ung jour de dimenche a eure de midi le xiiii jour de may pluseurs dalfins vindrent pres de la nef et le patron d'icelle lez tira d'une lance a ung fer branqu liee a ung cordell et en ferut ung qui fut mis dens la nef et d'illeques fut departi a une dez
10 deux nefs que alloient en nostre compaignie, et come nous ajustions pour en donner a l'autre, se leva ung vent fort que fist ferir nostre nef du chasteau d'avant a l'autre sur le chief derrier si grant cop qu'il enporta les chambres secretes¹ en la mer et pluseurs autres tables de l'une nef et de l'autre et elles si entrelacees que l'on ne les povoit dessoupartir, et ce gastoient l'une l'autre en telle maniere que la mer entroit dedens. Si que les patrons dez dittes nefs voiant le menchief que ainssi estoit avenue pour celluy poysson furent grandemant esbaïz et toux ceulx qui estoient [26R] dens moult descomfourtés, qu'il en y avoit que ce despulloient et sautoient de l'une nef en l'autre si espaventés estoient; et croiyent a
20 haulte voix lez uns et les autres a Dieu et a le Vierge Marie que nous voulsist par sa pitié aider et secourrir de cell perill ou estiomps. Et croiy fermement que ce ne fussent lez bonnes oraysons que chacun luy faisoit de bon cuer, que nous estions en voie d'estre peris et noiés en la mer que autre que Dieu ne nous en povoit garder, don estoit grant pitié de veoir et ouyr lez cris et lez complains que lez bonnes gens faisoient, don loué soit Dieu Nostre Seigneur toutz jours qui nous ha bouté hors de cell grant perill et luy plaise par sa pitié nous en vueille garder et deffendre d'essi avant.

Item après que Dieu nous eut fait celle grace, parti dudit guolf de Lion
30 et passay pardevant l'isle de saint Pierre qui dure 1 milles ou il n'a nulle habitacion de nulle riens.

Item de l'isle de saint Pierre ha une grant roche [26V] reonde que s'apelle le Toro xx milles, lequel Toro est bien alavant dens la mer tout autor revironé et dedens ne demeure nulle personne ne beste se n'est que oyseaux.

Item de celluy Toro a xx milles plus avant passay davant une grant montaigne que l'on appelle le Chef de Taulat et illeques nous prist ung vent que fut force que nous alassons ariver ou port de Boutes, que est en l'isle

---

* alavant. The ms. reading is alanant.

du royaume de Sardeigne,[1] ha x milles du dit Chief de Taulat plus en arriere.

Item davant le dit port de Boutes ha une isle appellee Palmesolz bien grant que tient de tour xx milles et x d'ample environee de mer tout autour en le quelle isle demeurent chevaux, eques, motons, cervis et chiens sauvatges, qui y naisent dedens de leur nature, et sur l'entree de celle isle ha ung pont de [27R] pierre ou il ha vii arxs fais de mein d'ome lequel pont ha de large quatre brasses et c de lonc et par nulle autre part l'on ne puet entrer meyns de bateau y en le dite isle se recueill-
10   ble deux foix l'annee.

Item quant le bon vent fut venu je parti du dit port de Boutes et retournay ariere au Chief de Taulat et de la tiray au Chasteau de Caille, port de mer et siptê que est en le ditte isle de Sardeigne du quel lieu de Taulat au dit Chasteau de Caille content lx milles et le chasteau est en avan-tatge de roche et trois villes asson piê pousees a maniere de ung landier et sont bien grosses et fermes de mur et la premiere quant l'on prent terre s'apelle la Napolle ont je estoie lotgiê et l'autre que est a la main droite quant l'on entre a nom Ville Nove et l'autre de la par senestre Estampaig, le quel chasteau et villes tient le roy d'Aragon.[2]

20   *   Item partant dudit Chasteau de Caille passay [27V] pardavant sainte Marie de Carbonaire que est a lx milles de Caille.

Item de sainte Marie de Carbonaire en Trapena ou royaume de Cessile clxxx milles et trouve l'on une ille qui s'apelle Marempne ou il ne abite riens fors que sauvoizines.

Item apres l'on trouve deux ylles, l'une s'apelle la Yuisse et l'autre la Fonhane en le quelle a ung chasteau du roy de Cessille et cestes deux ylles sont pres et pres l'une de l'autre et de la susditte ille de Marempne a cestes deux ylles ha xx milles.

Item apres l'on trouve une autre ylle que se fet nompner la Pantanallee,
30   le quelle ille est toute poblee de sarrazins fors tant que il y a ung chasteau de [28R] Crestiens que se tient par le roy de Cessille[3] y est a lx milles dez dittes deux ylles de la Yuisse et de la Fonhane.

Item de la ditte ylle Pantanallee a une ille en la couste de Cecille que s'appelle Marsalle lx milles.

---

   *   This section is headed by the words Le Reaume de Sardeigne, which have been inserted in a later hand, the same hand as inserted Le Reaume de Malhorque on p.25, l.33.

Item de Marsalle a une autre ylle que l'on appelle Matzare xv milles.

Item de Matzare a la cipté de Chaque xxx milles.

De Chaque a le cipté de Gergent xl milles.

[28V] De Gergent ou Chasteau de le Lieuquate xxx milles.

De le Lieuquate a le ville de Terre Nove xxx milles.

De Terre Nove ou Chief de Ressequaram xl milles.

De Ressequaram ou Chasteau de Chicle xv milles.

De Chicle au Chasteau del Poussaillo x milles.

Del Poussaillo a ung chief de ille que s'apelle Capoupasseur,*(i) [30R]
10   xxx milles et ou mi lieu est une tour deserte, la tour de la Marcee ont ha ung port que ce nomme le Port de Pals ou il ha une chapelle.

Item de Capoupasser a le ville de Cuille que est sur une montaigne xx milles et au port de la mer est une tour*(ii) que s'apelle le Tour de Bendique ou l'en tient garde par lez sarrazins.

Item d'icelle tour a la cipté de Saregosse ou royaume de Cessille xx milles, sur l'entree de le quelle qui vient pour mer ha ung tres beau chasteau hors de le ditte sipté ung triet de pierre nommé Termeniaig et est quaire. En chascun quayre une tour reonde et par dedens tout vouté de pierre sans null ovratge de fuste et la fontayne d'eue fresche
20   liens au fons du chasteau ou l'en dessen par ung degré bien lonc. Le mur ha d'ample deux grans brasses au plus [30V] estroit. La entree de la porte est faite de grans pierres de marbre. Le mer le va autour ce n'est devert la cipté, laquelle aussi le mer environne de l'un costé et de l'autre, nessen fault la montance d'un giet de dart. Illeques ha ung autre chasteau loing de le cipté bien ii traitz de pierre, le quel s'apelle Marquet et a chacune part du dit chasteau ha unne murrete que vient ferir a la mer ou nulx de le ditte cipté ne puet saillir ni entrer ne nulle beste, ce n'est que au pié de celluy ha ung portel ou convient a passer a grant dangier du chasteau qui par mer nessen veult aler, et le ditte
30   cipté est entre ceulx deux chasteaus bien enmurree et bastie sur bonne roche tout autour et tient grant perprise.

*(i)   Capoupasser.   Folio 29 is out of position.   The scribe has indicated that it should follow Folio 32.

*(ii)   ... au port de la mer est une tour ...   The ms. reading is ... au port de la mer est a une tour.

(i) Item dehors toute le cipté a deux treitz d'arballestre ha une eglize de sainte Lussie¹ pres de lequel a une petite chapelle soubz le quelle ha une caverne de roche ou l'en dessent par xxxii eschalons en le quelle le beineuree(ii) sainte demouroit en devocion et faisoit penetance, et lez mescreans li mirent serpens par [31R] la fere mangier. Mes onques ne ly firent null mal; mes puis lez mescreans la tuerent a une dague et fist sepellir*(iii) illeques en ung bars de roche ou misrent son corps lequel ha esté amblé par lez Genevois² de lx ans enssa.

Item plus avant deux treitz d'arbalestre est la eglize ou saint Jehan
10   evangeliste escript ung livre et desoubz le ditte eglize ha une chapelle de roche faite en croix ou l'on dessent par deux degrés et l'un est de xxvi eschalons et l'autre de xxxi, en lequelle chapelle est le pilier ou fut flagellé le dit saint Jehan, lequel est de marbre et ha x palms et demy de gros et bien autre tant de lonc.³ Et sont vi autels en le ditte chapelle ou le dit saint Jehan chantoit messe et venant d'icelluy lieu a la cipté est l'ostel ou sainte Lucie nesqui et par le vertu de Dieu y est naissue unne fonteyne et maintenant hi ont fait unne chapelle.

[31V] Item partant de celle ditte cipté de Saragosse a x milles en la mer en celle mesme partie l'on veoit le chasteau et ville d'Aguoste, chief
20   de contee.

Item après l'on entre en le guolf de Cret, lequel guolf dure vii milles et passe l'en pardavant le royaume de Calabrie⁴ et de Calabrie pour davant le duchié de Cheffallenie⁵ que est une ille pour soy a cccc milles d'Agoste de le quelle ylle sus ditte a la ylle du contee de Jassenton⁶ xl milles.

Item du Jacenton a les deux ylles que ont nom lez Tamsphanies xxx milles.

Item de les Tamphanies a la cipté de Modon⁷ que est en terre ferme ou principé de le Moureye⁸ l milles, devant lequel est le ille de Sapience
30   a iii milles du di Modon.

[32R] Item de le ditte ylle de Sapience ou lieu de Corron⁹ en cell mesme païs xviii milles.

---

*(i)   This section is headed by the words LE ROYAUME DE Cessille which are added in a later hand.

*(ii)   beineuree. The ms. reading is beimeuree. He uses the word beneuré with other saints, so it is probable that here there is a scribal error.

*(iii)   sepellir. The ms. reads sepellie which makes little sense.

Item de Corron au chief de Maleye Matapain lxxx milles dens lequel est
le Port de lez Cailles ou ce dit qu'elles vont prendre port quant passent
le mer.

Item du dit chief de Maleie Matapain au chief de saint Angel que est le
derrier chief du principé de le Moureie lx milles. Entre les quels est
le guolf du Chasteau Raupa et le guolf de le Levetique devezint ces
deux le ylle du Semy en lequel Jhesu Crist se demostra cruciffié a saint
Estassi¹ et de cest païs fut antiquemant seigneur le roy Menelaus, mary
de le belle royne de Gresse qui avoit a nom Heleyne, le quelle par
10   force s'en apourta Paris en Troye.²

Item du dit chief de saint Angel jusques [32V] a le ylle de Setvilh x
milles lequelle antiquemant fut nompnee Sitaree dens lequel ylle est le
temple de le deesse Venus ont la dessus ditte Helleyne stoit vennue fere
oreison ou sacriffice quant le di Paris la prist et lassen mena comme
dessus est dit.³

Item davant selluy dit Setvill a ung petit roc en la mer desert que a nom
Lou et au plus hault est l'eue fresche et si est abondons en bestiars comme
sont motons et chieuvres; et pres de cest dit roc a trois autres rocxs desertz,
aqui disont Tria, Deux et As, en celluy lieu comence l'on entrer en
20   l'Arcepellec, lequel est une partie de mer moult copieuse de ylles
pobleez*(i) et desertes, que antiquemant se appelloient les ylles Ciclades,
que estoient jus la seignorie dez rois dez Grecx et aujourduy est de
divers seigneurs,⁴ et le dit Arcepelec est partit par iii escheles. Le une
si ha nom de Tresmontane, l'autre a nom eschelle Meyane et l'autre
eschelle de My jour,⁵ par lequel je passay allant en le dit pellegrinatge
ou trouvay lez ylles cy desoubz escriptes.

[29R] *(ii) Item partant de le ditte ylle del Setvill trouvay le ylle du
Sequillo que est loing xxx milles, le quelle ylle fut par tamps poblee et a
present est deserte. Toutes foix y a moultz bestiaux sauvatges, come sont
30   chevaux, asnez, motons, porcx, chevres, serfs et d'autres bestes sauvaizines.

*(iii) Item au partant de la ditte ylle du Sequillo ha xxx milles trouvey
le grant ylle de Candie que huy est jus le seignorie de Venessiens,⁶ le
quel antiquemant fut appellee le ille de Cret et pour ceste raison est
ainssi appellé le guolf de Cret. Et furent seigneurs et rois antiquemant
de ceste Saturnus et Jupiter et les deesses Venus et Juno, que fut suer et

---

*(i)   pobleez. The z is added in a later hand, similar to that used
          in the other additions.

*(ii)   This is the first line of Folio 29 which is misplaced in the manu-
          script as it should follow Folio 32.

*(iii) This section is headed by LE ILLE DE CANDIE, inserted in a
          different hand.

fama de Jupiter,[1] les quelles antiquemant lez gentilz colloient pour
Dieux et de le ditte ylle fu roy ycelluy just et docturer Minus que
en son tamps ne après en excerssisse de justice n'en eut per, de le
moiller [2] duquel fu nee celle merveilleuse et orrible beste*(i) que fut
appellé Minotaur, [3] que fut enfermee y enclouse dens celle entriquade
meson faite par Dedelus, merveilleux maquanit, [4] lequelle meson fut
[29V] nompnee Lebarinte et aujourduy par moultz est vulguelmant
apellé le cipté de Troie [5] en le quel meson estoient condampnés a
estre mis lez jeunes filz dez Hetenesiens par vengance de le mort
10   des Endrogeux, [6] filz du dit roy Minus jusques tant que par sort y
fut tramis le proux et vaillant Tezeu, filh de Egeu, [7] roy de Attenes,
condampné a estre devoré par le dit Minotaur; lequel Tezeu par consseill a ajude de Adriane, [8] fille du dit roy Minus, oussit ledi Minotaur et eschapa du perill de le ditte meson Nabarinte. [9]

Item du chief de le ditte ylle de Candie jusques a la cipté de Candie
c milles en le quelle cipté font les nefs et les carraques des Sipres
devant lequel a x milles ha une ylle appellee l'Escandeye ou demeurent
auquns hermitens.

Item plus avant de le ditte Escandeye loing v milles dens la mer ha
20   unne roche reonde appellee Lou en le quel demeure une hermite.

[33R] Item a xx milles plus avant ha une ylle qui a nom la Plane le
quel est deserte sens nulle habitacion.

Item de la ditte ylle de le Plane a la ylle de Scarpento c milles et
celle ylle est poblés et est en la seignorie du grant mestre de Rodes.[10]

Item de celle ylle de Scarpento trouvay le ylle du saint Nicolas du
Carqui ha lx milles le quelle est poblee et de le seignorie du dit
grant mestre. Et se dit que pour preguieres du benneuré saint Nicolas nesun fer*(ii) en la ditte ylle pour labour que l'on ne face n'en
se puet rompre ne uzer.

30   Item de la ditte ylle de saint Nicolas jusques a la ylle de le Piscopeie ha x milles le quelle est poblee et de le seignorie sus ditte.

[33V] Item de le ylle Piscopeie a le ylle de lez Semies l milles
ille poblee et en le dite seignorie.

    *(i)   ... de le moiller duquel fu nee celle merveilleuse et
              orrible beste ... Ms. reading: de le moiller duquel fu nee
              a celle merveilleuse et orrible beste ... which does not make
              sense.
    *(ii)   nesun fer. This is the ms. reading which, as it stands, does
              not make sense but there is no amendment which clarifies the
              meaning.

Item de les Semies a les ylles nompnees Escuells de saint Paul v
milles et ce sont ylles desertes.

LE ENPIRE DE GRECE [1]

Item dez ylles sus dittes a la cipté de Rodes [2] xxx milles ou je arrivay
le jour du corps de Dieu [3] le quelle cipté est pres le mer et en une
grant ylle pour soy mesme en le Enpire de Grece, [34R] et c'est le derriere ylle du sus dit arcepellec et le chief de le religion de saint Jehan
ou toux tamps continuement demeurent grant nombre de chevalliers qui
toux dis mayntienent le guerre contre les sarrazins pour mer et pour terre
10 que me semble font aussi bien comme les autres crestiens que font la
guerre entre eux mesmes et ont plus le cuer a destruire l'un l'autre que
aler contre les mescreans de le foy Nostre Seigneur. En le quelle cipté
avoit ung jeune chevallier bon et sage de grant lignee du royaume de
Navarre que s'apelloit messire Sancho de Chaux [4] et estoit frere de messire
Jehan de Chaux, Visconte de Vaiguier. Et pour ce que a moy estoit
necessaire avoir ung chevallier aveques moy a me fere chevallier au saint
Sepulcre, je pris celluy pour lez choses sus dittes et pour lez bonnes
meurs et costumes que je cognoissoye en luy et le bonne renommpee qu'il
avoit, lequel chevallier en heut tres grant joye et de tres bon taillant
20 s'en vint aveques moy en Jherusalem ou il me fist chevallier devant le
saint Sepulcre Nostre Seigneur ung samedi le viiie jour du moys de julhet
l'an que l'on comptoit mil ccccxix.

[34V] Item partent de la ditte cipté de Rodes passay en ung chief qui a
nom Seticaps et c'est au païs de Turquie ha lx milles loing de Rodez ou
il ha une generacion de gens qui s'apellen Turcx, [5] les quelz sont contre
le foy et la loy de Dieu Nostre Seigneur.

Item de Seticaps a xl milles plus avant trovay ung chasteau pres de mer
du dit grant mestre de Roddes qui s'apelle Chasteau Rog, le quel est dedens le païs de le ditte Turquie.

30 Item de celluy Chasteau Rog plus avant xxx milles a une ylle deserte appellee Cacomo et entre celle et la terre ferme ha ung port moult bell et
grant, lequell en tamps passé solloit estre cipté que s'en entra a fons et
encores aujourduy aparent grant partie dez hostels et mesons en le fons
de le mer. Et devant ledi port en terre ferme de Turquie deux milles
dedens terre ha ung chasteau que s'apelle saint Nicholas de Mirree pres
duquel ha une cipté deserte que en tamps ...* [35R] appelee Mirree, de
le quel fut evesque le benneuiré saint Nicolas. [6]

* There is a gap in the manuscript. The missing words are
probably ... passé fut ...

Item de le ditte ylle de Cacomo ha 1 milles en terre ferms de Turquie est
le chief de Seridoines davant le quel ha une mille sont deux illes desertes, le une appellee saint Pierre et l'autre Seridoine en les queles ne
croist riens se ne sont choux sauvatges.

Item du chief de Seridoines ha clx milles c'est le chief de saint Piphani,
le premier chief de le ylle du royaume de Chipre.[1]

Item du chief de saint Piphani jusques a la cipté de Baffa xxx milles ou
dit royaume de Chipre, le quel cipté fut jadis la mestre sipté dudi royaume et fut par les gentils conssacree a la deesse Venus en temps* ou tout
10   le dit royaume et ylleques ediffierent ung grant temple.

[35V] Item de celle ditte cipté de Baffa au chief du Guavata en Chipre
1 milles, en le dit chief ha ung monestir de calogeres grex que s'apelle
le monestir dez guatz, par se car y tiennent moultz dez guatz par des-
truir lez serpens aspis que demeurent alentour d'eux.

Item ha cclx milles plus a l'avant du dit chief de Guavata est la cipté de
Japha[2] en terre de sarrazins devant le quelle lez autres deux nefs furent
mises, la vespre de saint Pierre et de saint Paul ung poy d'avant midy le
xxviiie jour du moys de juing; en le quelle sipté l'on dit que fut premierement tractee la mort de Nostre Seigneur Dieu Jhesu Crist; et au tamps
20   passé le ditte cipté fut conquistee pour les crestiens[3] et destruite que a
present n'y a nulle habitacion, et devant celle je demouray en la nef
sans saillir en terre deux jours que furent venus devers moy ung des freres
meneurs de ceulx qui gardent le saint Sepulcre et ung autre home de trois
que sont qui demeurent par della consols pour les crestiens;[4] les quells me
portarent sauf conduit du Soudain de Babiloyne,[5] [36R] que tient toute
celle terre de mescreans en sa main.   Alors je sailli hors de la nef et
pris terre a le dite cipté de Japhe le premier jour du moys de juyllet et
furent venus au dit port le lieutenant du Soudeyn et pluseurs autres sarrazins et mescreans aveques luy que s'en allerent en moy en Jherusalem.

30   LA SAINTE TERRE DE JHERUSALEM

Item en ycelle ditte cipté de Japhe saint Pierre le postre aloit peschier
pour le mer[6] et encore y est ung houstel de pierre reont fait a maniere
de ung colombier de soubz terre ou il demeuroit. [36V] En lequel hostel
Nostre Seigneur se aparut ally et la ledit saint Pierre resuscita une femme
que avoit nom Tabita qui estoit servente dez apostres[7] et de cousté cell
ostel en ha ung autre ung poy plus mendre fait de celle maniere ou saint
Paul demouroit et après ung autre petit ostel ou saint Andrief[8] estoie et

---

*   en temps ...   The ms. reading is ... en semps ...

en toux ceulx lieux ha pardonances comme porrés veoir plus avant en cest livre.

Item de toute celle nuyt que je fuy arrivé a le ditte cipté de Japhe ne m'en parti jusques lendemein entre mydy et eure none que m'en allay ha une ville merchande que s'apelle Ramès[1] que est ha xii milles plus avant en le quele se dizoit que nasquit le glorieux saint monseigneur saint George[2] et aussi saint Marssal[3] duquel, ce luy plest, j'ay azouré sa prescieuse teste a le cipté de Lymotges en le duchié de Guyeine. Et en ceste dy terre de Jherusalem l'on compte trois milles par une lieue.

10   Item ha ii milles de Ramès a le [37R] senestre main a une cipté que l'on appelle Lidie[4] et est dissipee et desfaite excepté le grant eglize que aussi bien est le majour partie rompue en lequelle monseigneur saint George fut marturizé et decollé pour lez hennemys de le foy davant le grant autel ou present ha ung aultre autel ou je fis dire messe de monseigneur saint George presens pluseurs sarrazins que n'avoyant guieres devocion, dont je avoye grant despit de leur contenance que faisoient au precieux corps de Nostre Seigneur qui nous ha toux fourmés et resemus, et les faulx chiens n'en tenoient compte, ains s'en moucoyent en ceste ditte eglize a grant pardonance, le quelle tiennent lez Grex, tant
20   come se monte sez deux autels sus dis et le plus de l'autre partie les Mouros; et haut sur le clochier ha ung petit houstel reont ont les ditz Morous crient de lassus hault a leur Baffomet de Meque en leur lengatge seguont leur mauvayse ordenance nuyt et jour a sertaynes heures; et alant a le ditte cipté de Lidie pres du chemin a main destre l'on trouve ung figuier que l'on dit est de ceulx de Faraon,[5] le quel figuier porte son fruyt au corps de l'albre.

[37V] Item après que la ditte messe de monseigneur saint George fut ditte je m'en tournay a Ramès en le quelle ville demouray pour quatre jours et après que lez iiii jours furent passés, je me mys a chemin sur le
30   mye nuyt pour ce que lez challeurs de seu païs sont se grandes et males que a paines mit que gens ne demeurent mourtz sur lez chemins; et m'en allay le droite voye[6] a le sainte cipté de Jherusalem ou grant desir et voulenté avoie d'estre. Lequelle est plus avant de Ramès xxxv milles en le quele je arrivay ung jour de geudi a heure none le vi^e jour du sus dit moys de juillet et la fuy logié en ung grant oustel[7] que est davant l'eglize du saint Sepulcre.

Item a le mye nuyt lez freres meneurs que gardent le saint Sepulcre me vindrent querir et moy menerent ou grant lumiere par toute la cipté de Jherusalem en toux les sains lieux ou Nostre Seigneur Jhesu Crist avoit
40   esté entre lez faulx Juifs, quant le menoient si cruelmant et puis me menerent hors le ditte cipté en [38R] la vail de Josaphat ou est le saint Sepulcre ou le precieux corps de Nostre Dame fut mis et pousé après

qu'elle fut trespassee, du quel sepulcre lez angels le prindrent et l'en
pourterent au siel, et la passarent par unne fenestre haulte que est au
cuer derriere le dit sepulcre, au quel sepulcre ha une grant eglize ou
l'en dessent pour xlix degrès de pierre et la clef de celle ditte eglize
tiennent les sarrazins et fault payer argent ha eux qui entrer y veult; et
en celle ditte vall Josaphat se dit que Nostre Seigneur venrre fere le
jutgemant, plaise a luy que soit bon pour nous et par toux fielx crestiens.
Et partant de le ditte vall Josaphat allay au Mont d'Ollivet, du quel
lieu Nostre Seigneur s'en munta au siel et lessa le fourme desson pié en
10   une roche dens une chapelle que est au my lieu de l'eglize, le quelle
est en unne monteigne faite en reont: et monta l'en par xix degrès de
pierre, en lequelle aussi fault apaier[1] qui dedens veult entrer. Et de
celluy Mont d'Ollivet je tiray en Galilee[2] ou lez apostres furent en-
voyés par l'angel et la Jhesu Crist se aparut a eulx; et d'equi en hors
m'en allay a Montession ou Nostre Seigneur fit le cene a cez apostres,
du quel lieu m'en retournay en la cipté de Jherusalem.

[38V] Item celluy mesme jour que fuy arrivés en Jherusalem et venu dez
sains lieux ou part dessus avez oÿ, et estoit venrredi, le gardien et lez
diz freres meneurs me vindrent serchier a l'eure de vespres par aller a la
20   sainte eglize du saint Sepulcre Nostre Seigneur. Si que je m'en alay
aveques eulx et quant fuy davant le ditte eglize a ung grant pavemant
que est davant ycelle je trouvay le ditte place pres que pleyne de sarrazins et a le porte du saint Sepulcre avoit ung grant hofficier d'eux avec
sertains autres que gardoient la ditte porte: et par avant que null en-
trasse dedens prenoient de chascun sertain treuvatge et puys lez metoyent
dedens l'un aprés l'autre toux par compte; et quant je fuy liens, eulx
fermerent la porte en bonne clefs et le scellerent; en tel maniere demouray
toute celle nuyt davant le saint Sepulcre, lequel est en le ditte eglize
bas loing du cuer par soy mesmez environé d'une chapelle tout au tour en
30   reont faite de voute que n'est pas guieres grant; et celle mesme nuyt je
comfessay, et quant se vint lendemain, que estoit samedi et du mois de
juillet le viiie jour l'an mil ccccxix, je entray en celle ditte chapelle
ou le saint Sepulcre estoit ouyr ma [39R] messe de mon seigneur saint
George sur l'autel du saint Sepulcre Nostre Seigneur; et aprés qu'elle
fut chevee et moy receu Nostre Seigneur, celluy plaist, le bon chevallier que dessus vous ay nommé me donne l'ordre de chevallerie et moy
signe l'espee et lez esperons dourés et me frape v coups ha honneur dez
v plaies Nostre Seigneur et ung a honneur de monseigneur saint George.
Et puis le frere religieux, qui la messe avoit chantee, que encores estoit
40   revestu, entre luy et ledit chivallier me baillerent ladite espee toute
nue en la main, moy estant a genoulx, disont en ceste maniere que je

prenoie celle espee* en honneur et reverence de Dieu et de monseigneur
saint George et pour garder et deffendre sainte eglize et encontre les
hennemix de le foy, et en cell point je la mys en la gueyne que j'avoie
cintee. Toutes foix paravant me firent promittre et jurer vi choses sur
ledit autel du saint Sepulcre, ainssi qu'il est acoustumé de faire a toux
ceux que en cell saint precieux et digne lieu prenent ordre de chivallerie, les quelles dittes chouses s'ensuivent.¹

[39V] Ci ensuivent les serements que font les chivalliers ou saint
Sepulcre Nostre Seigneur en Jherusalem lequel je Nonper, seigneur de
10   Caumont, de Chasteau Nuef, de Chasteau Cullier et de Berbeguieres,
ay fait pour le plaisir de Dieu le viii^e jour du mois de juillet en l'an de
l'incarnacion mil ccccxix.

Premier il promettent garder et deffendre sainte eglize.
Secondemant de aidier a toute sa puissance a conquester le terre sainte.
Tiercemant de guarder et deffendre son pueple et fere justice.
[40R] Le quart de garder saintemant son mariatge.
Le quint de non estre en lieu ou place ou soit faite nulle traizon.
Le siseme de deffendre et garder les veufves et orphelins.

Item après que Nostre Seigneur Dieu Jhesu Crist m'eut fette le grace
20   d'avoir fait et comply les chouses sus dittes, je fie mettre le baniere de
mes armes toute desplee en la ditte eglize du saint Sepulcre. C'est
assavoir ung esqu d'azur a trois lieuparts d'or onglés de gueulles et
coronnés d'or, lequelle fut mise au costé dez armes du roy d'Angleterre;
et quant ce vint l'eure de prime lez sarrazins furent venus a le porte de
la ditte eglize sainte et moy acheve entieremant par le grace Nostre
Seigneur ce que je voulloie et moult desiroie, ne fis autre [40V] demeure,
mes que m'en alay vert la ditte porte pour saillir dehors ou trouvay les
sarrazins que estoient venuz par la obrir et a la yssue nous conterent et
nous firent paier par la maniere du jour davant, et fait cella je m'en
30   tournay a mon lotgemant en la cipté disner.

Terre de Judee

Item quant je fuy disné, je parti de Jherusalem et m'en alay en Bellem
que est une cipté dissipee a x milles de Jherusalem, en le quelle cipté
ha une grant eglize bien gente;² et la nesqui le filz de Dieu de le pucelle vierge Marie, auquel lieu a ung autel ou je ouy messe de la nativité et davant cest lieu est le greppe³ du buef et de le mulle ou Nostre

---

*   The ms. reading is ... et puis le frere religieux qui la messe
         avoit chantee que encores estoit revestu entre luy.   Et ledit
         chivallier me baillerent laditte espee ... This is clearly wrong
         as entre is used here to introduce a compound subject for bailler-
         ent while luy refers back to le frere religieux, now separated
         from its verb.

Dame rescondit [41R] son chier enfant Jhesu Crist par doubte du roy
Herodes que faizoit tuer les Ignocens: et aussi davant cest lieu ha ung
autre petit autel ou je ouy autre messe de la nativité et demouray tout
celluy jour et toute la nuyt en la ditte cipté de Bellem.

Item lendemeyn haulte eure je parti de Bellem et m'en alay vers la montaigne de Judee ou est la meson de Zacaries ha v milles, et a la main
senestre a ung lieu que s'appelle Capharneum lequel estoit de centurion [1]
ou ce dit que fut fait l'encluge ou lez cloux de Nostre Seigneur furent
fargés, en le quelle mezon de Zacaries sainte Helizabet porta escondre
10   son fillz saint Jehan Babtiste, quant les Juifs le serchoient et le mis en
une roche laquelle sitost come l'enfant y fut pousé se alla obrir et lez
Juifs qui le serchoient ne le purent onques trouver. En cest lieu ha une
chapelle et pres d'icelle en ha une autre ou Nostre Dame fist le Magnificat; en le quelle demeurent sertains Herminis qui chascun jour y font
l'office cellon leur ordenance. Et pres de ceste ditte meson de Zacaries
est le meson ou le dit saint Jehan Babtiste nesqui, [2] de le quelle je m'en
retournay en le [41V] cipté de Jherusalem ou l'en compte iiii milles et
entre ceste meson de saint Jehan Babtiste et le ditte cipté de Jherusalem
en my le voie est l'albre duquel se dit fut faite une partie de le crois
20   Nostre Seigneur. [3] Et celle mesme nuyt que je arrivay en Jherusalem,
entray autre foix au saint Sepulcre ou demouray toute le nuyt jusques
lendemein haulte prime, en le quelle sainte eglize sont vi manieres de
ordes de vi generacions. Et premierement sont les freres meneurs qui
gardent le Sepulcre; aprés lez Grexs qui tiennent le grant autel du cuer
de le eglize, lez Indiens qui ont une chapelle derrier le saint Sepulcre,
les Hermines au Mont de Calvaire en le chapelle ou est le lieu ou fut
cruciffié Nostre Seigneur, lez crestiens de le centure [4] et lez Jacobins
tiennent lez quatre chapelles qui sont en le place devant le ditte sainte
eglize, le quels chascun d'eux si font leur office nuyt et jour sellon la
30   maniere et usatge de leur paiis que est moult estrange. [5] Et ceste eglize
du saint Sepulcre est bien grande et belle et est fette d'une guize moult
estrange, et il y a ung beau clouchier et hault de pierre mes il n'y a
nulle campane car lez sarrazins ne le veullent. [6] Aussi le ditte cipté est
bien grande et devers l'une part est la vall Josaphat que est bien longue.
[42R] Et d'icelluy cousté est le ditte cipté plus haulte que de nulle autre
part et par de dens sont quatre rues principaux, toutes d'un renc et longues
tant comme ung home pourroit tirer la pierre en deux traitz et par dessus
sont toutes voutees de belle pierre bien gentement et au chief de ceste
cipté devers le Mont Dession est le chasteau du roy David. [7]

40   LE DESERT DE GERICO

Item ores avint quant je huy visité le saint Sepulcre et lez autres sains
lieux dens la cipté de Jherusalem et ceulx de hors, je fis mes ordenances
pour aller au desert de Jerico et au fluvi Jordain. Car en celluy païs

ne ha nullz vivres ne eschessement de l'eue, et pour ce je fis porter
aveques moy de vitailles celles que a moy estoient necessaires, et pour
ce que ceu païs est perilleux pour le maulvaize gens qui liens habitent,
que ne vivent que de [42V] rouberie et de ce de autruy, ¹ je fis tant
que j'eu le nepveu du seigneur d'eulx qui vint a moy acompaignié de
quelques xx personnes aveques luy, lequel fut mon conduit par tout cell
païs aller revenir, et ainssi parti de Jherusalem et fis mon chemin droit
a la cipté de Betanie que est a ii milles et est destruite que poy de gens
y demeurent, mes il y a une eglize en le quelle est le tombe ou Nostre

10   Seigneur ressuscita le lazer qui avoit esté mort iiii jours; ² de le ditte
cipté m'en alay au desert de Jerico ou il ha xviii milles, ou quel desert
est le grant montaigne ou Nostre Seigneur Dieu Jhesu Crist jeune le
caranteyne dens unes cavernes de roche que sont au mylieu de le montaigne ³ et au bout dez xl jours Nostre Seigneur commensse avoir ung
poy de fain, et le diable vint a luy pour le tempter que ne savoit pas
que fus celluy serteinemant et le pourta toute sa faude pleyne de pierres
et luy dit; Si filius dei es, fac ut isti lapides panes fiant. ⁴ C'est a
dire; ce tu est filz de Dieu, fay que cestes pierres soient faites pain; et
Nostre Seigneur luy respondit; Non in solo pane vivit homo sed in omni

20   verbo quod procedit ex ore Dei. ⁵ Que veult tant dire; No tant sole-
mant vif l'on de pain mes de le parolle que procedisse [43R] de le bouche
de Dieu.   Puis le diable le prist et Nostre Seigneur se lesse porter a
luy au plus hault de le monteigne et de lessus le diable li moustra toux
lez regnes de monde et le dit que l'en faroit seigneur s'il le voloit asourer
et Nostre Seigneur li respondit; Unum solum deum adorabis et illi soli
servies. ⁶ C'est a dire; Ung seul Dieu azoraras et ycelluy suel serviras.
Après le diable le monta sur ung hault pinacle de roche et le dist; Si
filius Dei es, mitte te deorsum quia escriptum est in psalmista angelis
suis mandavit de te ut custodiant te in omnibus viis tuis. In manibus

30   portabunt te ne forte offendas ad lapidem pedem tuum. ⁷ C'est a dire;
se tu est filz de Dieu, lesse te cheoir de bas car escript est en le psalm-
iste que Nostre Seigneur a ordenné *(i) aulx siens angels que toy gardent
en toutes tes voyes car porteront *(ii) en les meyns pour ce que par aventure ne te faisses null maul a tes piés.   Auquel diable Jhesu Crist respondit; Vade retro Satana, non temptabis dominum deum tuum. ⁸ Que
veult tant dire; Va t'en derriere, Sathanas, no temptaris le seigneur,
ton Dieu. Et lors le diable le lessa et les angels le vindrent aministrer
et après ce que j'eu esté au dit lieu ou avoit feit le jeune, je m'en descendi bas au pié de le ditte monteigne a ung monestire de saint Jehachim

---

*(i)   a ordenné. In the ms. there is no translation for mandavit
(l.29). As it must have been omitted by mistake, this seems
the most likely translation.

*(ii)   porteront. The ms. reads porter tout, which is an impossible
translation for portabunt (l.30).

ou le nuyt davant je avoye lotgié.*[1]

[43V] LE FLEUVE JOURDEYN

Item d'icelluy monestire de saint Jehachim je m'en allay vers le fleuve Jourdayn qui est a x milles. Et premieremant l'on trouve part dessa ledit fleuve une mylle ung lieu que s'apelle saint Jehan ou est le premiere eglize que fut faite,[2] auquel fleuve Jourdeyn Nostre Seigneur fut babtizé par saint Jehan Babtiste et dit Nostre Seigneur dessa bouche que toute persone que dens le dit fleuve se lavaist qu'il fusse lavé de toux ses pechiés, et pour ceste raison et honneur et reverence de luy je m'i baigney et me mis tout liens, ce fut le xii jour du moys de juillet, pres du quel fleuve est une mer ont soloient estre ediffiees les ciptés de Sodome et Gomorre et trois autres qui fondirent en abisme par le pechié de luxure, et a present s'apelle le Mer Morte, dens la quelle le dit fleuve Jourdein s'en entre et passe pour le mylieu sens soy mescler avec le ditte mer. Et devés savoir que c'est au pays d'Arabie ou [44R] il ha une generacion de gens qui s'apellent Alarebs qui ne portent vestu que lez chamizes longes jusques a terre et sur le testu ung chapeau lié a une toille; et vont toux a pié fors que aucuns qui vont a chevau sobre meschantes bestes que le plus grant partie sont asnes et petitz soumiers, et eulx ne portent nulle armeure fors que une petite berge en le main a ung petit fer qui no vaut guieres tout, et si vont piés deschaux et sens esperons et en telle maniere se abillent quant eulx se vuellent bien arreer ne vont en guierre.

Item quant j'eu ensuites se saintes peregrinacions, je parti de ceu pays et m'en retournay en Jherusalem par le chemin que je avoie fait ou grans chaleurs que faizoie et mal tamps de chemyner et que lez pelegrins ne trouvoient a boire ne a menger et tant pour cella que pour les chaleurs mouroient par lez chemins; et la que je fuy retournés en Jherusalem celle mesme nuyt entray autre foix au saint Sepulcre. Car il est a coustume a toux pellegrins qui par della sont de hi veiller deux [44V] nuytz he trois au mais que soit. Toutes foix hi ay je entré quatre et cest avantatge dizoient que ne avoient plus fait ha autres que yffussent esté et pour chacune entree et yssue avez a paier argent aux sarrazins. Ores ay je mys en cest livre tout ensequent les pellegrinacions cy desoubz escriptes a celle fin que plus clarement chescun les puisse mieux veoir et entendre, les quelles pleise a Nostre Seigneur que j'aye ensuites assauvacion de mon arme et en emandemant de ma vie.

Ci ensuivent les peregrinacions, endulgences et pardonances de peine et de coulpe de toute le terre sainte que je, Noper, seigneur de Caumont,

---

*   The ms. reads: je avoye lotgié i. The i, however, is a very doubtful reading.

de Chasteau Nuef, de Chasteau Cullier et de Berbeguieres, ay ensuites[1] par le grace Nostre Seigneur, les quelles endulgences furent concedees de saint Silvestre, papa, a le requeste de l'Empereur Costantin et de sainte Hellene, sa mere,[2] et furent escriptes en la cipté de Jherusalem le xiiie jour du mois de juillet l'an mil ccccxix.[3]
[45R] Les peregrinacions de la cipté de Japhe jusques en Jherusalem. En la cipté de Japhe est le lieu ou saint Pierre resussita de mort Tabite, serviteure dez apostres auquel lieu ha vii ans et vii carantenes de vray pardon.

Item de lieu ou saint Pierre peschoit vii ans et vii carantenes de endulgence.[4]

Item pres de le cité de Ramés a main cenestre est le cipté de Lidie ou monseigneur saint George fut marturizé et decolé vii ans et vii carantenes de endulgence.

[45V] Item la cipté de Ramés ou fut né Josep qui descendit Jhesu Crist Nostre Seigneur de le croix vii ans vii carantenes de pardon.[6]

Item le Chasteau Hemaux ou est le lieu ou lez deux diciples cogneurent Jhesu Crist en le fraccion du pain aprés sa resureccion vii ans vii carantenes de pardon.[7]

Item en ycelluy chasteau est le sepulture de Cleophas qui fut ung dez diciples de Jhesu Crist vii ans vii carantenes de pardon.[8]

Item le sepulture de Samuel le prophete vii ans vii carantenes de pardon.

[46R] Les peregrinacions du pavemant davant l'eglize du saint Sepulcre. Devant l'eglize du saint Sepulcre ou my lieu de le place ha une pierre pour signe et est dit que en ce lieu Jhesu Crist se repousa pourtant le croix vii ans vii carantenes de indulgence.

Item en ycelle place sont iiii chapelles, le premiere est fondee de le Vierge Marie et saint Jehan evangeliste. Le segonde est fondee dez angels, le tierce de saint Jehan Babtiste, le quatre de sainte Marie Magdalene et en chascune d'icelles ha vii ans vii carantenes de pardon.[9] Les peregrinacions du saint Sepulcre.

[46V] Et premieremant je dyray du Mont de Calvaire ou Jhesu Crist Nostre Seigneur fut cruciffié et espandit son sanc et morut pour nous, ou quel lieu ha pleniere endulgence de payne et de coupe.[10]

Item aprés se trouve davant le porte de le ditte eglize le pierre ou Jhesu Crist fut mis aprés qu'il fut despendu de le croix et la fut oynt et envolupé d'un linseul de Josep et Nicodeme, ou il ha pardon de peyne et de coupe.¹

Item auprés se trouve le sepulcre ou Jhesu Crist fut mis aprés qu'il fut oynt et la repouse trois jours et de la ressuscita glorieusemant, ou quel lieu ha pleniere endulgence et vray pardon a peyne et coupe.²

Item aprés le saint Sepulcre ha une chapelle [47R] de le Vierge Marie en le quelle se aparut premieremant Jhesu Crist assa mere pres sa resurreccion vii ans vii carentenes de pardon.³

Item en la ditte chappelle ha une fenestre en le quelle ha une partie de le columpne ou Jhesu Crist fut turmenté en le meson de Pilate vii ans vii carentenes de vray pardon.

Item en le ditte chapelle a main cenestre a une autre fenestre en le quelle fut par lonc tamps le moitié de le croix ou Jhesu Crist fut cruciffié vii ans vii carentenes de vray pardon.

Item ou my lieu de le ditte chapelle a une pierre reonde et en ce lieu fut esprové le quelle dez trois crois estoit celle de Jhesu Crist par ung corps mort qui en ce lieu fut resussité tantost que touche le croix de Jhesu Crist vii ans vii carentens de pardon.⁴

[47V] Item au dehors de le ditte chapelle au pié du degré a une pierre reonde et en ce lieu se aparut premier Jhesu Crist a Marie Magdalene le querant en fourme d'un ortolen vii ans vii carentenes de pardon.

Item a la main cenestre est une chapelle que est apellee le chartre de Jhesu Crist ou il fut enchartré tant comme on disposet le partus de le croix, l'eschelle, lez cloux et les autres inturments convenables par le mort de Jhesu Crist vii ans vii carentenes de pardon.⁵

Item en alant autour du cuer de le eglize se trouve le chapelle ou lez chevalliers diviserent lez vestiments de Jhesu Crist vii ans vii carentenes de pardon.⁶

Item se trouve aprés une chapelle ou fut [48R] trouves le croix, le lance lez cloux, le coronne en lequelle ha vray pardon de peyne et de coupe.⁷

Item auprés se trouve le chapelle sainte Hellene vii ans vii carentenes de endulgence.⁸

Item est une autre chapelle en le quelle est ung autel soubz le quel est une columpne a le que'le fut lié Jhesu Crist et coronné d'espines vii ans vii carentenes de pardon.

Item ou my lieu del eglize a une pierre qui se appelle le my lieu du monde vii ans vii carantenes de endulgence. [1]

Les peregrinacions dedens la cipté de Jherusalem. [2]

[48V] Premier se trouve le meson du mauvês riche qui les miques du pain de sa table ne veullent donner au pauvre lazar vii ans vii carantenes de pardon.

Item le meson de Pilate ou Jhesu Crist fut tourmenté et jugié a mort yl y a vraie endulgence de peine et de coulpe. [3]

Item le lieu ou Simeon le Sirenen fut prié que yl aidaist a pourter le croix a Jhesu Crist et en ce lieu se tourna devers lez fillez de Jherusalem leur disant que ne plouracent point sur luy mes sus elles et sus leurs enfans vii ans vii carantenes de indulgence.

Item le meson de Herodes ou Jhesu Crist fut vestu de blanc en signe qu'il estoit fol vii ans vii carantenes de indulgence. [4]

[49R] Item le meson de Johachim et Anne ou fut nee le Vierge Marie pardon de peyne et de coupe. [5]

Item le meson ou estoit le Vierge Marie quant les Juifs menoist son enfant en le meson de Pilate et quant elle le vit ainssi mener, elle cheit toute pasmee et come morte vii ans vii carantenes de indulgence. [6]

Item le lieu ou Jhesu Crist perdona lez pechiés a Marie Magdalene vii ans vii carantenes de pardon.

Item auprés sur unne arche sont deux pierres blanches sus les quelles il est dit que Jhesu Crist se repousa portant le croix vii ans vii carantenes de indulgence. [7]

[49V] Item le temple de Nostre Seigneur ou la Vierge Marie fut presentee, marié,* ou Simeon receput l'enfant Jhesus entre les bras le jour de le purificacion il y a pardon de peyne et de coupe. [8]

Item le porte saint Estienne par ont il passa quant on le menoit lapider vii ans vii carantenes de indulgencie.

Item a destre est le porte doree par ont Jhesu Crist entra en Jherusalem le jour de rams ou il ha vray pardon de peine et coulpe. [9]

---

*   marié presumably a scribal slip for ... mariee

Les peregrinacions de la vall de Josaphat.

Item de hors le ciptê jouste le ruiseau de [50R] Cedron est le lieu ou saint Estienne fut lapidê vii ans vii carantenes de indulgence.

Item le ruiseau de Cedron ou fut par lonc tamps l'albre de le croix ou Jhesu Crist fut pendu vii ans vii carantenes de indulgence.[1]

Item ou my lieu du vall de Josaphat est le sepulture ou le Vierge Marie fut enterree et il y a vray pardon de peyne et de coupe.[2]

Item en ycelluy vall est une caverne ou Jhesu Crist la nuyt de sa passion ala ourer et la sua sanc et eue par nostre redempcion vii ans vii carantenes de indulgence.[3]

Les peregrinacions du Mont Olivet.

[50V] Premier y est le jardin ou Jhesu Crist fut pris vii ans vii carantenes de indulgence.[4]

Item le lieu ou saint Pierre coupa le oreille a Malcus vii ans vii carantenes de indulgence.[5]

Item le lieu ou saint Pierre, saint Jacques et saint Jehan furent separês dez autres et ou il se adormirent vii ans vii carantenes de indulgence.[6]

[51R] Item ung poy plus hault est le lieu ou saint Thomas receput la sainture de la Vierge Marie vii ans vii carantenes de indulgence.[7]

Item ou my lieu du Mont Olivet est le lieu dont Jhesus voyant le ciptê de Jherusalem se print a plourer vii ans vii carantenes de indulgence.

Item ung poy plus hault est le lieu ou la Vierge Marie receput le palme del angel et la luy fut notifiê le jour de sa mort vii ans vii carantenes de indulgence.[8]

Item plus hault a main senestre est Gallilee ou lez apostres furent envoyês par l'angel et la Jhesu Crist se aparut a eux vii ans vii carantenes de indulgence.[9]

Item de l'autre part a main dextre est le Mont d'Olivet et de cest lieu monta Jhesu Crist aux sieux ou il ha vray pardon de peyne et de coupe.[10]

Item en retournant du Mont d'Olivet est le lieu ou lez apostres composerent le credo vii ans vii carantenes de indulgence.

Item auprès est le lieu ou Jhesu Crist fist le pater noster vii ans vii
carantenes de indulgence. [1]

[51V] Item au piê de le montaigne est l'eglise de saint Jacque le minor
qui fist veu que ne mengeroit ne beuroit jusques que Jhesu Crist seroit
resuscité vii ans vii carantenes de indulgence.

Item auprès est le sepulture de Zacharie le prophete vii ans vii carantenes de indulgence. [2]

Item auprès est le vallee de Siloe ou est le fonteyne ou le Vierge Marie
lavoit les drapellez de son enfant vii ans vii carantenes de indulgence.

Item auprès est le fonteyne de Siloe ou Jhesu Crist envoya le veugle se
laver et tantost recrouva le veue vii ans vii carantenes de indulgence. [3]

Item auprès est le place ou fut seê Ysaye le [52R] prophete par le my
lieu du see de bois vii ans vii carantenes de indulgence. [4]

Item en montant ou Mont de Sion est le meson ou se miserent lez apostres quant Jhesu Crist fut pris vii ans vii carantenes de indulgence. [5]

Item ung poy plus hault est le camp de Alchedemar qui fut achaté dez
xxx deniers don Jhesu Crist fut vendu vii ans vii carantenes de indulgence. [6]

Les peregrinacions de Mont Dession.

Premier en venant est le lieu ou [52V] lez Juifs voulurent ravir le corps
de le Vierge Marie quant lez apostres pourtoient le dit corps en sepulture vii ans vii carantenes de indulgence. [7]

Item auprès est l'eglize de saint Sauveur que jadis fut le meson de Cayphe,
en le quelle meson est le grant pierre qui fut mise davant l'uis du monument de Jhesu Crist vii ans vii carantenes de indulgence. [8]

Item en le ditte meson est le chartre ou Jhesu Crist fut mis tant que
Cayphe tenoit le consseill avequez lez Juifs et que il examinet les faux
tesmoings vii ans vii carantenes de indulgence.

Item auprès en alant ou Mont Dession se trouve le lieu ou saint Jehan
dizoit messe a la Vierge Marie après la mort de Jhesu Crist vii ans vii
carantenes de indulgence. [9]

[53R] Item après est le lieu ou la Vierge Marie trespassa et il y a vray
pardon de peyne et coulpe. [10]

Item auprès est le lieu ou saint Mathias fut esleu ou lieu de Judas et saint Jacques le minor evesque de Jherusalem vii ans vii carantenes de indulgence. [1]

Item le lieu ou fut enterré premier saint Estienne aveques Gamaliel et Abibon vii ans vii carantenes de indulgence. [2]

Item auprès est l'oratoire de le Vierge Marie vii ans vii carantenes de indulgence.

Item auprès sont deux pierres ou Jhesu Crist aucune foix preschoit a ces apostres vii ans vii carantenes de indulgence. [3]

[53V] Item derriere l'eglize est le lieu ou fut chaufee l'eue de quoy furent lavez les piés dez apostres et rosti l'aignel paschal vii ans vii carantenes de indulgence.

Item de soubz l'eglize est le cepulture de David et Salamon et pluseurs autres roys vii ans vii carantenes de indulgence.

Item dedens l'eglize ou est le grant autel est le lieu ou Jhesu Crist fist le cene et ou il sacra son precieux corps et dona a ces apostres et il y a vray pardon de peyne et de coulpe.

Item auprès est le lieu ou il lava lez piëz a cez apostres vii ans vii carantenes de indulgence.

Puis se trouve dehors l'eglize le senache [54R] ou les apostres recepurent le saint esperit yl y a vraie indulgence de peyne et de coupe.

Item descendant au claustre se trouve le chapelle ou Jhesu Crist s'aparut a saint Thomas et ou il fut certifié de sa resurrexcion vii ans vii carantenes de indulgence. [4]

En s'en alant vers le Chasteau de David est l'eglize de saint Jacques et la fut decolé vii ans vii carantenes de indulgence. [5]

Item plus outre est le lieu ou Jhesu Crist s'aparut aux trois Maries disant; Avete vii ans vii carantenes de indulgence. [6]

Les peregrinacions de Bellem.

[54V] Premier en le voye a deux milles est le lieu ou s'aparut le stelle aux trois roys vii ans vii carantenes de indulgence. [7]

Item auprès est l'eglize ou fut né Helie le prophete vii ans vii carantenes de indulgence. [8]

46

Item dedens l'eglize est le lieu ou Jhesu Crist fut né et il y a vraie indulgence de peyne et de coupe. 1

Item auprès le greppe ou il fut mis entre le buef et l'asne ou il ha pardon de peyne et de coupe. 2

Item a la main destre est le chapelle ou Jhesu Crist fut circuncis al viiie jour de sa nativité et il y a vray pardon de peyne et de coupe. 3

Item a la main cenestre est le chapelle ou [55R] le stele se desparut aux trois rois et ou il preparerent l'offrende que il firent a Jhesu Crist vii ans vii carantenes de indulgence. 4

10 Item dehors l'eglize ou cloistre est l'escolle de saint Jeronime ou il translata le Bible vii ans vii carantenes de indulgence. 5

Item plus outre est le chapelle ou furent mis une partie dez Innocens que fist ossire Herodes vii ans vii carantenes de indulgence. 6

Item au dehors de le cipté en alant en le montaigne de Judee est le cepulture de Rachel vii ans vii carantenes de indulgence. 7

[55V] Les Peregrinacions de le montaigne de Judee.

Premier se trouve le meson de Zacharie ou entra le Vierge Marie et salue Helizabet et la composi Magnificat vii ans vii carantenes de indulgence.

20 Item en l'entree de le ditte meison ha unne chapelle ou sainte Helizabet musa saint Jehan par Herodes que faisoit tuer lez Innocens et la se trouve le pierre que se fondit par le musier vii ans vii carantenes de indulgence.

Item dessus en le ditte meison est le lieu ou Zacharie escript quant saint Jehan fut né Johannes est nomen eius et adonc luy fut rendue le parolle vii ans vii carantenes de indulgence. 8

[56R] Les Peregrinacions de Jerico.

Item pres de Jerico est le lieu ou se seet le veugle jouste le veugle que Jhesu Crist enlumina vii ans vii carantenes de indulgence.

30 Item ainsies que on vigne au desert de Jerico a la senestre main a une grande montaigne ou Jhesu Crist ou mi lieu jeuna xl jours et xl nuytz et il y a vray pardon de peyne et de coupe.

Item au chief de le monteigne est le lieu ou le diable pourta Jhesu Crist et ly mostra toux lez regnes du monde vii ans vii carantenes de indulgence.¹

Item le cipté de Jerico ou se trouvent*⁽ⁱ⁾ lez serpens [56V] de quoy est fait le tiriaque vii ans vii carantenes de indulgence.

Item a le dextre mein est le monestire saint Jeroime vii ans vii carantenes de indulgence. ²

Les peregrinacions du fleuve Jourdeyn.

10 Item jouste le fleuve de Jourdain a ung tret d'arbalestre est l'eglize de saint Jehan Babtiste ou il est dit que Jhesu Crist estoit quant saint Jehan dist trois foix; Ecce agnus Dei etc. vii ans vii carantenes de indulgence. ³

Item le fleuve Jourdeyn qui divise Judee et Arabe ou il ha vray pardon de peyne et coupe.

[57R] Item de l'autre partie du fleuve est le lieu ou saint Jehan babtizoit Jhesu Crist et en ce lieu estoit Betanie le segonde vii ans vii carantenes de indulgence.

Item aprés se trouve la Mer Morte que fut cree de pluye et de feu quant Sodoma et Guomorre et lez autres ciptés fondirent et en ycelle entre le
20 dit fleuve de Jourdain vii ans vii carantenes de indulgence. ⁴

Item outre celle mer est le cipté de Segor ou se sauva Loth du feu dez dites cités vii ans vii carantenes de indulgence. ⁵

Item jouste le ditte cipté en le voye est le estatue de seel en la quelle le fame de Loth fut convertie vii ans vii carantenes de indulgence.

(ii) Ci fenicent lez peregrinacions, [57V] indulgences et pardonances de le terre sainte, et comence a parler de le divize de le eschirpe d'azur que je prins a pourter au dit voyatge Jherusalem.⁽ⁱⁱⁱ⁾

---

*(i)   trouvent. The ms. reads trouvet but a plural verb is clearly called for.

*(ii)   This is followed in the ms. by the following insertion written in a different hand. Somme xix remissions a peine et coulpe. Item sis c ans item xix ans. Item vi c quarantaines Item xix quarantaines tous les pardons dessus scriptz montent la somme desus scripte.

*(iii) This is followed by an addition in a third hand. C'est le devize de l'eschirpe d'azur que le seigneur de Caumont a levé au voyage Jherusalem.

Noper, seigneur de Caumont, de Chasteau Nuef, de Chasteau Cullier
et de Berbeguieres fais assavoir*(i) que j'ay enpris de porter sur moy en
divise une eschirpe d'azur qui est une couleur que signifie loyauté a
memoyre et tesmoign que le vueill maintenir.*(ii) Et en icelle eschirpe
a une targe blanche a une croix vermeillie pour mieux avoir*(iii) en
remembrance le passion Nostre Seigneur, et aussi en honneur et sou-
venance de monseigneur saint George*(iv) par tel qu'il luy plaise moy
estre en toute bonne ayde. Et hault en le targe ha escript FERM.*(v)

*(vi) [58R] Se Dieux faisoit son comandemant d'aucun de ceux de le
10 ditte eschirpe, sceu qu'ilz l'aient,*(vii) chacun fera chanter trois
messes, deux de requiem et une de monseigneur saint George pour
l'arme d'ycelluy et moy xx. Et oultre ce*(viii) ay establi et ordonné
que se null de le ditte eschirpe perdoit son heritatge et n'avoit de quoy
vivre, suy tenus*(ix) la que par luy seray requis ly donner*(x) et tenir
son estat sellon qu'il l'appertiendra.*(xi)

Le Retour de Jherusalem

Le retour que je fis de le sainte terre venant en terre de Crestiens a mon
pays partant de le sainte cipté Jherusalem ou moys de juillet le xvii^e
jour. [58V] Premieremant de le cipté de Jherusalem je m'en revins
20 en Ramés xxxv milles ou je demouray jusques le xxe jour du dit moys.

Item de Ramés je parti et m'en alay en Japhe xii milles ou lez nefs qui
m'avoient porté me demouroient et celluy mesme jour que je y arrivay,
je m'enbarchay et lendemain ferent voyle et la voye vers le royaume de

*(i)   fais assavoir. The words which originally followed have been
         erased. a toux ceulx qui sont et advenir seront.
*(ii)   que le vueill maintenir. The word je has been inserted in a
         different hand between que and le.
*(iii)   pour mieux avoir ... ce que has been erased between pour and
         mieux. aye has been erased in favour of avoir.
*(iv)   saint George. The following words have been erased. come
         le plus souverain chevallier que onques fust ne jamais sera.
*(v)   FERM. Followed by En which has been erased. En is follow-
         ed by sig which has been erased more completely than en.
*(vi)   Le item has been added in a different hand to begin this section.
*(vii)   sceu qu'ilz l'aient replaces et qu'ilz le saurront que.
*(viii) oultre ce replaces Après ces choses sus dit. ay establi. j' has
         been inserted in a different hand in front of ay.
*(ix)   suy tenus. suy replaces je soye.
*(x)   requis ly donner. de has been erased between requis ly.
*(xi)   qu'il l'appertiendra. l' has been inserted in a different hand.

Chipre.[1] Et la pris port en une cipté que s'apelle Famagoste[2] ou l'on compte cccc milles et la cipté est hedifiee a rive de mer en le quelle ha une mot belle eglize. Et en ceu pays content a lieues.

Le Royaume de Chipre

Item de Famagoste je m'en alay pour terre [59R] vers le roy de Chipre,[3] le quel estoit a xii lieues en une cipté grant qui l'on appelle Nicossie. Mes premieremant ou partant de Famagoste je passay par davant ung chasteau en terre playne que s'apelle Chasteau Franc a iiii lieues, le quel le roy de Chipre avoye fet fere, n'avoit guierres et me sembloit estre ben basti et fort sellon le lieu playn ou il estoit assis; de celluy chasteau sans rescansser je tiray plus avant iiii lieues a ung lieu del Espitel de Rodes qui s'apelle Mores ou je couchay celle nuyt.

Item de Moures a le cipté de Nicossie iiii lieues ou le roy estoit pour le quel j'eu mot grant chere et feste et estoie logié a ung grant houstel de saint Jehan de Roddes que est comanderie en le quel houstel ha une chapelle ou il ha de belles reliques les quelles me furent mostrees. C'est assavoir le bras de monseigneur saint George, le chief de sainte Anne, mere de Nostre Dame,[4] et le corps tout entier de sainte Heuffemie[5] et le fer de le lance ou quel monseigneur saint George ossist le serpent et pluseurs autres saintes reliques. Ores quant j'eu demouré avec [59V] le dit roy deux ho trois jours je m'en retornay par celluy mesme chemin que je avoie fait a le cipté de Famagoste d'ou je estoie parti ou lez nefz me demoroient. Si devés savoir que c'est ung païs grandemant plein de chaleurs tant que les gens a peynes hy ousent chivaucher de jours fors que de nuytz pour le grant ardeur de solliel, et gens estrangiers a paynes y puent durer longament en sanité. Et en cest pays sont communemant lez arrayzims noirs et lez vins sont toux blancs.

Item a Famegoste me mis en la mer et fis le voye pour le couste de Chipre au chief de saint Andrief ou il ha lxx milles.

Item de celluy chef de saint Andrief a le vile du Carpas xxv milles.

Item du Carpas ou Chasteau de la Candera xxx milles.

[60R] Item du Chasteau de la Candera au Chasteau de Leonde autrement dit Buffavent xxx milles.

Item de Buffalvent au chasteau et vile de Cherines x milles, le quel est port de mer et la mestre fors de Chipre.[6] Et celle hediffie selluy magnanimo Hechilles que fut roy de Tessallie.[7]

Item de celluy Cherines au Chasteau de saint Hellarion v milles. Ores laixe le royaume de Chipre et* viens ou pays de Turquie qui par avant solloit estre nommé Hermine[1] et a present sont Turcx mescreens.

Le païs de Turquie qui par avant solloit estre Hermine.

Premieremant le cipté de Tersson pres du quel est [60V] le grant cipté de Entioche que est loing du dit chief saint Andrief c milles, le quelle cipté de Tersson se tient ou jour duy par le roy de Chipre, davant lequel ha une ille que s'apelle Colquos[2] ou demouroit le moton en le leyne d'or que conquista Jeson, roy de Tessaillie.[3]

10 Item de le ditte cipté de Tersson jusques au chasteau du Qurc l milles.

Item du Qurc a une ylle que se nomme l'Esquellh Provenssal que pour tamps solloit estre poblee lx milles.

Item de l'Escuelh Provinssal au chasteau et vile de Sachim c milles.

Item de Sachim au chasteau et vile de Hastilimurre xv milles.

[61R] Item de Hastilimurre ou chasteau et ville de le petite Antioche xxxv milles.

Item de le petite Hentioche au chasteau et vile del Escandeleur xl milles, le quelle est le mestre force du grant Caramanh, chief de Turcxs[4] pour qui les forces sus dittes se tiennent. Est vray que devant
20 le dit Escandeleur le jour de saint Lorens[5] nous trouvames en le mer sus le point de jour une gallee armee de Turcxs qui venoit d'Alexandrie ho de Damiate, chargee de marchandize que valloit sellon que l'on disoit plus de lx mille ducatz et estimoient que dedens povoit bien avoir deux cens et xx combatens avant plus que meins; et comme nous le vimes, chascun se arma et se vist a point et tirames droit a eux, cuydans celluy jour abesonher aveques eulx et pour ce car ilz feizoient contenence de venir aussi escontre nous. Mes si tost come nous fumes bien pres pour lez ferir, ilz virent tout a cop leur gallee et s'en fuirent vers le dit port d'Escandeleur qui se tient pour eulx et nostre nef après lez va suy-
30 ant, si que lez gardames d'arriver. [61V] Mes ilz avoient grant avantatge que se ajudoient de deux voylles e d'avirons ou se dizoit que en avoit lxxx que toux tiroient a ung cop. Et pour ce ilz, voyant que nous leur fumes au davant, prindrent autre chemin et nous a l'enchaux. Mes le vant nous va faillir au plus grant besoing que ne povions aler plus avant et ainssi nous eschaparent lez Turcxs mescreens don estions toux malemant corrossiés, et dura l'enchaux du point de jour jusques pres d'eure nonne.[6]

---

*   et is added in a different hand.

Item de l'Escandelour a la cipté de Satallie xc milles le quelle cipté
est de Creissi, enpereur ho roy de Turquie, [1]devant le quel cipté a ung
grant guolf que s'apelle le guolf de Satallie, en lequel ou tamps passé
toutes lez nefs que par illeques passoient perizoient en jusque tant que
sainte Helleyne mere de l'enpereur Costantin hi bouta ung clou de ceux
en que fut encloué Jhesu Crist Nostre Seigneur en le croix.

Item de Satallie au Chasteau de Fer et d'Au [62R] cc milles, lequel
chasteau est au dit paiis de Turquie et se tient pour le grant Mestre de
Roddes a mau gre dez Turcxs.

* Item du dit Chasteau de Fer et d'Au a la cipté de Roddes xxv milles
ou je fuy de retour au moys d'aust le xviiie jour et hy demouray pres
que de deux moys. Ceste cipté est en une ille bien grande et complie
de toux biens et y a de belles fortalesses, qui sont bien guardees pour
gens autres que Grecxs, et aussi faut il mester pour chouse du pays de
le Turquie qui confronte avec le ditte ille chiere pour chiere de le
ditte cipté de Roddes ou il n'a que ung poy de travers de mer, a le
quelle cipté le mer bat au pié dez murs et droit ont lez nefs prendent
port ha une grant chaussee faite de grans pierres de massonerie cran-
allee aux bors qui se tient en le mur de le cipté et entre dedens le mer
bien iiii tretz da dart et tout au lonc d'icelle sont assis xvi molis de
vent, toux d'un ranc qui nuyt et jour molent yver et esté, et a paynes
l'on les voit toux ensemble molir ne toux a ung cop cesser. [2]

[62V] Item de Roddes je me levay ung bon matin et m'en aiay pour
terre a une haulte montaigne qui est pres de le ditte cipté v milles que
l'on appelle le puy de Philermo [3]on jadis solloit estre le cipté de Roddes
hediffiee et en ceu tamps se solloit apeller Colossensses ou saint Paul
feysoie lez Epistoles; [4] et c'est une place moult avantatjose mes est
tout despasti fors que d'un chasteau qui est sus l'entree de le venue et
en toute l'autre partie de le montaigne n'a riens fors que une chapelle
de Nostre Dame bien devote, le quelle fet de grans miracles et pour
cause d'icelle mon voulloir fut de y aller pour oÿr messe après le quelle
je m'en retournay le jour mesmes en Roddes.

Item pres de le ditte cipté de Roddes ha une petite chapelle ou est le
lieu ou premieremant fut trouvee le teste de saint Jehan Babtiste qui
au present est en Rome et pour miracle de Dieu audit lieu s'est fette
une fonteyne de le quelle chacun boit voullentiers qui liens entre, en
le quelle chapelle ha de grans pardons he je y estoie le feste de saint
Jehan decollacé et la fis chanter messe. [63R] Et si ay je esté depuis
et celle chapelle tiennent lez Grecxz. [5]

---

*   This section is headed by Le Ille de Rodes which is added in a different hand.

Item devers l'autre partie de le cipté entre le chasteau et la mer ha une
eglize qui s'apelle saint Anthoni en le quelle ha pardon a peyne et
coupe iii jours de le setmaine,[1] c'est assavoir le lundi, le mecredi et
le venrredi; et la suy esté, si plest a Dieu, pluseurs foix et faytes dire
dez messes; et aussi dedens le chasteau de le ditte cipté ha ung beau
houstel expressement pour recevoir toux mellades. Et toux ceulx qui
dedens fenicent sont absoluz de peyne et de coupe comffés et penitans
et ceste grace ha esté ottroyee et conformee pour lez sains peres de
Rome; et pour cause d'icelle pluseurs grans seigneurs et autres quant
10   sont mellades s'i font porter, et la sont servitz de messes et bien pens-
sés de myres et d'autres bonnes viandes et de bons lis a le despensse del
Espital de Roddes; et cest houstel appelle l'on le enfermerie et toux
ceulx qui dedens entrent visiter lez mellades guaynent aussi sertains
jours de indulgence.[2]

[63V] Item devés savoir que en le ditte cipté de Roddes ha ung chasteau
a l'un chief de le ville bien grant, fort et bien basti de murrs et de
tours tout autour, et dedens ycelluy en le chapelle de liens ha une dez
espines de quoy Nostre Seigneur fut coronne, le quelle devient toute
florie le jour du venrredi saint en tel eure comme Nostre Seigneur pris
20   passion; et dit l'on que nulle dez espines ne flourissent fors que celles
qui ont touché au propre test de Jhesu Crist, et celle ditte espine ne se
mostre que une foix l'annee au dit jour du saint venrredi et lors chascun
le puet veoir. Et toutes foix en celuy tamps je n'y estoie mye mes par
le grant devocion et affeccion que j'avoye de la veoir le lieutenant du
grant Mestre de Roddes et lez seigneurs freres chivalliers de le religion
la moy mostrerent secretament en disant que le cas pareil n'avoit esté
plus fet a nul autre, ne n'eussent rompu leur costume et ordenance ce
ne fust pour l'amor de moy a qui ilz vourroient fere plaisir et toute
honneur et furent par moy remerssiés grandemant. Le quelle espine
30   estoyt encloustree en ung beau veessell d'or et après moy mostrarent le
bras de madame sainte Cathelline[3] et pluseurs autres reliques, lez
quelles toutes asouray en reverence de le passion Nostre Seigneur.

[64R] Item le xxe jour du moys de septembre je me mys en mer au port
de le ditte cipté de Roddes pour m'en revenir au bon paiis de Guasconhe
en ma terre et fis le voye par davant le couste de le Turquie a ung chief
que entre dens la mer que se nomme lez Escuelhs de saint Paul ou l'on
compte xxx milles. Et pres d'icelluy chief a une ille que l'on appelle
lez Semyes et de l'un a l'autre n'a que ung poy de través de mer.

Item après l'ille de les Semyes est le chief du Crieu ha xl milles et
40   c'est le derrenier chief de le Turquie.

Item du dit chief du Crieu ha une ille que est del Hospitel de Roddes
que s'apelle le Languo x milles, le quelle ille est bien poblee et grandemant complie de toux biens.

53

Item du Languo a ylle deserte que l'on apelle Viro xv milles.

[64V] Item du Viro passay entre deux ylles; le premiere est a main senestre que l'on apelle le Piscopie et l'autre de main dextre se nomme Nitzere, qui sont a xv milles l'une de l'autre et a v de la ditte ille de Viro et sont toutes deux poblees et de le senhorie de Roddes.

Item aprés les illes sus dittes l'on trouve deux autres illes desertes que l'on appelle l'une Caloquirane et l'autre Quirane, les quelles sont a v milles plus avant a main cenestre.

10   Item aprés celles dittes illes Caloquirane et Quirane l'on trouve deux petis rocxs pres l'un de l'autre que se nomment lez Coffres ou il n'abite riens et sont a xx milles dez illes sus dittes.

Item aprés les Coffres est une ille assés grande que s'apelle l'Estampaleye ou il ha ung chasteau hault sur une roche au bout de le mer le quel aussi s'apelle [65R] l'Estampaleye et celle ille est a xv milles dez Coffres.

Item de le ditte ylle Estampaleye a une ille que l'on appelle Pipi x milles, en le quelle naist le greyne de l'escarlate et est de le seignorie du duc de Nixie.[1]

20   Item de celle ille Pipi a l'ille que se nomme Namphi xv milles que aussi est du sus dit duc de Nixie ou il appert ung chasteau et se fet le coton en le ditte ille.

Item de Namphi a une autre ille poblee que s'apelle Marguon xxx milles, au pié de le quel sont calloigeres grexs. C'est a dire monges de leur loy qui demeurent en ung monestire jouste le mer, le quelle ylle est pres du duchié de Nixie xii milles duquel le ditte ille est.

[65V] Item del Marguon a l'ille du Nyeu ou l'on voit ung autre chasteau sur le montaigne le quelle ille est du sus dit duc.

30   Item de l'ille du Nyeu a l'ille Senturion xx milles, le quelle ille est de le ditte seignorie de Nixie et est bien grande et poblee de gens et de bestiaux, et aparent iii chasteaux en le ditte ille esquels se requeill foizon de coton.

Item de le ylle Senturion a deux petites ylles desertes jouste l'une de l'autre que ont nom le Crestiane x milles.

Item de le Crestiane assicandron ylle deserte xxx milles.

Item de Sicandron a Poliquandron, ille deserte xv milles.

[66R] Item de Poliquandron a Polymo, ylle deserte x milles.

Item de Polymo a une ylle poblee que se nomme Nyl xx milles.

Item de Nyl a le ylle de Panaye x milles, en le quelle n'a nulle habitacion de nulle riens se n'est que asnes sauvatges.

Item de Panaye a une tour en une ille deserte que l'on apelle Serffine v milles.

Item de Serfine a Intimil xv milles, ille deserte.

Item de Intymil a Ormonyl, ylle deserte, x milles.

[66V] Item de Ormonil a Nuye v milles, ylle deserte.

Item de Nuye a Falconayre, ylle deserte, xxx milles.

Item de Falconayre a Caram xx milles, ylle deserte.

Item de Aquaram au Chief de saint Angel xv milles, le quel chief est en terre ferme sur le plus hault de une monteigne a ung hermitatge ou demeure ung hermiten.

Item du Chief de saint Angel a le ylle du Setrilh xx milles, le quelle ylle est poblee et se demostre en ycelle ung chasteau hault sur une roche.

Item du Setrilh a l'ille del Servo x milles, le quelle est deserte.

[67R] Item del Servo al Matapain que est terre ferme lx milles.[1]

Item du Matapain au Chief de Maynes aussi terre ferme x milles au quel chief a deux chasteaux.

Item de Chief de Maynes al Venetiguo xl milles, ylle deserte. Mes hy demeurent iiii hermittes en une eglize haulte sur un puy.

Item del Venetiguo a Courron x milles. C'est une bonne ville en terre ferme au pays de le Moureye mes les Venessiens le tiennent.

Item de Quorron a Cappoguailh, terre ferme x milles.

Item de Cappoguailh jusques a Cabre x milles, ylle ou il ne demeure nulle gens dedens. [67V] Ce n'est que pastours que y vont garder bestiaux.

Item de Cabre a le ylle de Sapience v milles, une petite ylle deserte ou il ne abite riens fors que hermitens que demeurent pres de le
mer au pié de le montaigne en une eglize que l'on appelle sainte
Marie de Sapience, et une guayte que tiennent hault sur ung puy le
quelle avize les nefs que viennent par mer et fet seignal a unne cipté
que est davant la ditte ylle de Sapience a ii milles que l'on appelle
Modon en terre ferme en le principé de le Moureye.*(i)

*(ii) Item de Modon au Port de Jonx x milles au quel port avint une
foix ung miracle que une nef chargee d'eulle passoie par davant et la
ont si grant tourmente que deffait aloye ferir en contre le dit port en
une grant montaigne de roche que nullz ne l'en povoit garder fors que
Dieux. Ainssi que le patren et lez autres que dedens la nef estoient
voyant qu'ils estoient toux peris feirent veu et promission a Dieu et a
la Vierge Marie que s'ilz povoient eschaper assau-[68R] vemant qu'ilz
metroient toute le merchandize de le nef*(iii) a hediffier une eglize a
prier Dieu a toux jours et quant celluy veu fut fet par miracle de
Nostre Seigneur le tout puissant et de le benoyte Vierge Marie, encontenant celle roche se ala obrir et partir en deux pars par le quelle
oberture le ditte nef passa, car desye estoient par donner dessus,
seyne et sauva sans null mal avoir et ainssi eschaparent de selh perill.
Et mayntenant que le dit patron de la nef et lez autres furent arivés
en terre, ne eurent pas oblié le veu qu'ilz avoient fait ne le grant
grace que Nostre Seigneur leur avoit fette qu'ilz vendirent toute le
ditte merchandize pour bastir le ditte eglize, le quelle firent fere pres
d'icelluy lieu sur ung hault puy et s'apelle le ditte eglize sainte Marie
de Pitié.

Item a celluy Port de Jonx ha ung chasteau hault sur une montaigne
que se nomme Chasteau Navarrés et d'icelluy l'on entre en ung grant
guolf que l'on apelle le guolf de Cret que dure cccclxxx milles sens
veoir terre et quant je fuy dedens, nous prist ung vent contraire que
fit retourner le nef [68V] a Modon que j'avoye passé de xl milles et la
pris port et hi demouray par quatre jours attendant le bon vent. C'est
une cipté en terre playne au pié de le quel vient le mer devers l'une
part, le quelle est bien emmurré tout autour et se tient pour les Gene-
voys.[1] Et la moy fut dit que a une mille et demye en une eglize avoye
ung corps saint qui s'apelle saint Lion[2] qui fut sabatier au temps qu'il
estoit en vie et venoit du saint Sepulcre et au retour maledie luy pris

---

*(i)   Moureye.   This is followed by ont je arrivay which is added
         in a different hand.

*(ii)   This section is headed by Le Principé de le Moureye which is
         added in a different hand.

*(iii)   de le nef.   dite has been inserted after le in the same hand
         as the rest of the manuscript.

en le nef de le quelle morut et fut geté en le mer dans une caisse et
la mer le alla porter a terre pres de le ditte cipté de Modon et aucunes
gens le trouverent si se merveilloyent que c'estoit et cogneirent que
c'estoit ung home et vont le enterrer en une fosse que ly firent. Si
que chascune nuyt dessus ycelle foce ou il estoit enterré, l'on veoit
trois brandons de feu alumés par miracle de Dieu, et si avint une nuyt
en avizion al evesque de la ditte cipté que en ceul lieu avoye ung
corps saint et que il alasse part della et le fist desenterrer et tenir en
celle honnour comme il apertenoyt d'un corps saint qu'il estoit; lors
10   lendemeyn quant le dit evesque fut levé, il revela le chouse et firent [69R] ordenance d'aller part della et menerent evesques et pluseurs chapellens et autres gens aus grandes processions. Et tantost la
ou il comenserent a le serchier, le trouvarent et ilz le desenterrerent
et le mirent sur une charrue, tiree aus buefs; et ainssi le porterent,
et quant ilz furent pres la cipté au lieu ou a present est, cuydant le
porter dedens ilz ne puirent onques passer plus avant et comvint que
illeques le leissacent* et fut la fette une eglize ou il demeure
depuys, ens se que l'on dit a bien lxxx ans et la fet de grans miracles
par le vertu de Nostre Seigneur. Et quant il est tamps de guerre en
20   cell pays ou ilz ayent en le cipté ausques savances que mal leur doye
venir pour dobtance de le perdre ilz le vont querre et le porter en la
cipté sus ditte. Mes se il n'est voir, ilz n'on puissance pour riens
qu'ilz facent de le movoir de son lieu. Et en ycelle eglize je fuy
pour veoir le dit corps saint, le quell tiennent lez Grexs au derrier le
grant autel du cuer de le ditte eglize en une caisse ferree ou je le vi
tout entier, se luy plest, et retournay par ung autre chemin ou il ha
ung lotgis ouvert que s'apelle saint George de les Tribulleye, out il
ha une chapelle de monseigneur [69V] saint George que les Grexs
tiennent, de le quelle m'en alay a la cipté de Modon d'ou je estoie
30   parti.

Item de la ditte cipté de Modon je parti et m'en alay faysant le voye
que premieremant j'avoye commencee quant le vent m'en fist retourner
du guolf de Cret a Modon. Et trouvay une ille deserte en le mer que
l'on appelle Predent, que est sur l'entree du dit guolf de Cret et ha xv
milles du sus dit Port de Jonx, et voulloye tout droit aller en le royaume de Cecille a une cipté que est en le mer que se nomme Saragoce
ou je estoie passé venant audit voyatge comme part dessus est plus a
plain declaré, en le quel guolf de Cret me vindrent deux tres males
fortunes et perilleuzes. Le premiere est assavoir que ung jour de
40   samedi le viie jour du moys d'octobre environ eure de prime ainssi
come je fuy bien a l'avent en la mer, presque de la moytié du susdit

*   ... leissacent ... ms. reads ... leissatent ...

guolf de Cret, que l'on ne povoit terre veoir de nulle part soubdaynement se leva une grande obcurté avec ung fort vent*(i) et puis apres
aqui mesmes hault en l'ayre ung si tresque grant bruyt [70R] espaventable qu'il n'est ou monde bombarde ne canon eusse puissance de le
fere tel ne sy grant comme celluy fut, car il sembloit que ce fust que
siel et terre s'encontrast si grant estoit le cry qu'il fist, avec le quel
descendi tout a cop une chose, que l'on ne savoit que c'estoit dedens
nostre nef et donna tiel cop au grant albre qui lez voiles portoit qu'il
le rompi en pluseurs piesses et y mist le feu et trenqua une grant partie
10   du chasteau que sus le dit albre estoit et volla en piesses pour le mer
et du grant espavant qu'il fist a la dessendue, tombarent plus de xxviii
parsones, et en y eut nuef de blecés et ung mort que fut geté en le mer.
Et puis la ditte chose s'en entra de soubz le couverte de le nef ou
rompi le fust d'une grant ancre de fer qu'il y avoit et encores ne estions
assertanes s'il avoye passee le nef d'outre en outre par de soubz que
nous dobtions moult.   Si que toux ceulx de le ditte nef estoyent
grandement effrees et mot esbaiis et descomfourtés come ceulx que
avoyent bien de quoy du grant accident et espaventable chose que
ainssi soubdaynement estoit venue, la quelle nullz n'en savoit que
20   povoit avoir esté, fors tant que dizoient ausquns qu'ils avoyent veu
dessendre une chose noire [70V] chargee de feu et de flama, et dizoit
l'en que c'estoit le fulgre, et lez autres prousomoyent que c'estoit le
pechié enfernel que ainssi nous avoit mallement abatus, en tele maniere que ne*(ii) n'y avoit nul que ne cuydast que la nef et toux quans
estions dens fussions perilz et noyés et que jamais penssace eschaper a
vie, et gens, que eussent peu veoir le maniere comment nous alloyt,
ne eusse pancé du contraire, et c'estoit grant pitié alle veoir et a oÿr
lez cris et lez complains que toux les bones gens foysoient comme
ceulx que veoient le mort davant eulx et ne regardoient l'eure que le
30   nef s'en entrost affons, et estoient toux despuilliez et avoient pris de
tables qui povet pour ce donner le meilleur conssseilh qu'ilz pourroient
par le mer ha alongier le vie jassoit qu'il estoient mal apparelliez
d'eschaper et c'estoient toux comffessés l'un a l'autre, ainssi que tout
bon crestien doit fere majorment, qui est si pres de le mort comme a
celle eure nous estions.   Car ne n'y avoyt null que dessoy tenist plus
compte ne que cuydast jamés veoir terre, voyant que le grant albre
qui la nef menoit estoit en piesses et le feu en le nef, et ne nous en
povions aydier et estions au my lieu de le grant mer ou l'on ne veoit
que siel y eue et ne savions nulle nef en nulle part pour nous aydier
40   et secorrir.   Et ainssi en telle maniere alions sa et la pour le mer
[71R] comme esperdus avec grande paour et doubtance, attendant
piteusement le misericorde de Dieu Nostre Seigneur.   En cest propoux chascun de tout son cuer se comandoyt a luy bien souvant et a la

*(i)   Ms. reading ... avec ung fort vent. Et puis ... This would
        leave the second sentence without a main verb.
*(ii)   ne has been added in the same hand.

benoyte Vierge Marie, sa chere mere pleyne de pitié, en lez faizant chascun pluseurs veux et promissions que leur pleust nous fere celle grace de nous sauver lez viez et nous donast venir a quelque bon port assauvement. Si que faiz lez veux dessus dis Dieu et le Vierge Marie nous donna emendemant de bon tamps et toute celle obscurté et grant vent qui part davant faysoit, cessa tout a cop et se converti en beau solleilh par le vertu de Dieu qui cheremant estoit reclamé, et lors le dit albre qui cheÿ n'estoit du tout fut tantost recorru par lez mariniers et lié de grans tables et le dit feu escanty et descaint aveques de
10   l'eue et de l'eulle d'ollive du vinaygre; et voyant le miracle de Dieu qui ne voulloyt nostre perdicion furent grandemant recomfourtés trestoux et le louvant et regrassiant de le grace qu'il nous avoye fette de garder de mort a le quelle estoit a nous impossible d'eschaper se sa misericorde ne fust que eut pitié de nous en luy priant qu'il nous voulsist dessi avant deffendre et guarentir de tout meschief, et ainsi nous eschapames de ceu perill et tirames a levant vers la ditte cipté de Saragoce ou je estre voulloye.

[71V] Item le samedi après venant nous eumes tant allé pour le mer que je fuy a la vehue de le ditte cipté de Saragoce ou je ne pance
20   qu'il eusse plus de x milles et penssoie y estre a disner lendemain que estoit dimenche le xve jour du mois d'octobre.   Et droytemant quant vint sur le mye nuyt, le vent se comensse moult mallemant a refresquer et quant fut le jour nous eumes tant de tourmente que par force nous fit retorner   jusques au royaume de Calabrie et d'illeques nous porta a le cipté de Cathanie ou royaume de Cecille, et de Catanie nous fist courrir a une autre cipté au dit royaume de Cecille que l'on appelle Messine mes nous avions si tres malle et outregeuze fortune de vent et de mal temps que par puissance que le patron de le nef ne lez mariniers eussent ne puirent onques prendre port en nulh de ces lieux dessus dis,
30   ains allions sa et la par la mer a la mercy du vant a pleynes voilles, les quelles n'avion peu dessendre de l'albre par le force du grant vent que soubdaynemant tout a cop estoit venu de nuyt; le mer estoit si haulte que lez ondes entroient pour le plus hault de dens la nef et se tribailloit tant de l'un costé sur l'autre que n'estoit homme liens se puisse tenir de piés ne assigié, s'il n'estoit bien afferré aux bors de [72R] le ditte nef ou aillors par lez chambres en quelque autre chose bien lié, ne arque ni tablc ne riens que liens fusse ne povoit se tenir en son lieu, ains alloye per la nef a través de la gent tant se tourmentoyt la nef, et chescune foix nous penssions qu'elle versse* par l'un
40   bort ou pour l'autre.   Car le voille du grant mast touchoit en le mer et faisoit encliner la nef, tant que les ondes entroyent de dens et lors cuydions du tout qu'elle s'en entrast et que l'albre qui rompu estoit par

---

*   versse.   The ms. reading is veusse which does not seem to have any meaning in this sentence.

devant, comme dit est par dessus en l'autre article, s'achevast du tout
de rompre et cheïsse en le mer et tirast le nef aveques luy, et aussi
avions ung grief vent terriblement mallecieux et le plus fort que je
veysse onques que nous portoit a contre une grant roche en le mer, et
les mariniers et autres voyant nostre perdicion et que la nef se alloye
toute debrisier se comencerent a despullier et a deschausier, car ilz
veoient que fait estoit de nous; et moy avizant leur maniere ne faut
mye a demander se jeffuy recomfortez.   Toutes foix je me conffessay
prestemant et comandey a Dieu et a la Vierge Marie mon arme, priant
pour leur misericorde en eussent pitié et mercy.   Et que vous en
diroie je?   Le fait estoit en tel parti que de mon corps ne faizoie je
plus compte.   Car si nous avions esté en grant perill de mourir [72V]
par davant, nous en estions a present en aussi grant ou plus, et toux
se estoient pourveus de ce lyer bien fort a tables et a fustes et s'estoient toux comffessés par le maniere que davant, voyant chascun la mort
davant sez yeulx.   Dez veulx et de les promissions se il se n'y faizoient pluseurs a Dieu et as sains, ne fault a demander.   Car je crey
qu'il ne n'y avoit nulh que a une autre foix le savast ^{1} a fere.   Mes
Dieu et le Vierge Marie qui desemparé ne nous avoye nous donna grace
que, ainssi comme nous estiomps a ung trait de pierre de le ditte roche
et la cuydions encontrer tout au travès, que selluy fort vent nous
estrema ^{2} et vint ung autre qui soffla tiel cop le ditte nef que l'en
porta long hors toute celle montaigne de roche; bien avions mestier
si prestemant le soccors.   Car autrement la nef estoie toute debrizee
encontre le ditte roche.   Ainssi alla la nef raddant par le mer a le
mercy du vant et de la tormante que dura du dit samedi a mye nuyt
jusques le dimenche par tout le jour sans cesser le mal tamps, et le
mardi venant arrivay en le ditte cipté de Saragoce a grant peyne.
En le quelle cipté demouray*(i) pres de ung mois jusques tant que le
dit albre et la nef fusse adobee que en avoie grant besoing et moy
estant en ceste fourtune fis a Nostre Seigneur le ourayson que s'en
suyt.

[73R]*(ii) Dieu, le tout puissant, mon createur et mon souverein
seigneur qui mon arme as formé a le toye semblance et m'as redempt de
ton precieux sanc, lequel voulsist eschamper pour moy et pour toute
humayne nature ouster de le mort et dampnacion perpetuelle, gustes
et voys claremant le tres grande fourtune et orrible tourmente et
coment je suy a grant perilh en ceste nef et a grant dangier de le mer
moult endignee que me veult fere noier et perir liens, si que entre ma
vie et ma mort n'a nulh moyen ne remede coment je puisse eschaper
ne saillir hors, ce n'est pour ta misericorde que je atant et espoir avoir,

---

*(i)   Ms. reading: En le quelle cipté a demouray ... a is
redundant.
*(ii) This section is headed by Le Oreïson, added in a different
hand.

en le quelle du tout ay ma parfette confiance et mon entier recours
comme avoir doy. Et pour ce mon souverein Dieu que je croy ferme-
mant sens nulle erreur voyant que tu as apliqué moy en cest monde
pour toy servir et que tant chieremant je t'aye cousté, je te prie umble-
mant et supplie piteusemant a ta haulte magnificence que de moy ta
petite creature ayes pitié et merci a moy trere de cest perill que je
n'aye affiner mes jours en ceste mer malecieuse contre moy et que ne
le vueilles donner povoir de moy desfere si soubdaynement et [73V] me
vueilles guarder et deffendre du terrible torment et engoice ou quel je
10 suy a present et estre ne puis aquitté se par toy non. Et mon createur
que feray-je en cestuy cas, se ne me fais par ta bonté de ta grace
auqun abondonemant? Pleise toy par ta humilité de le faire et de
obrir tes yeulx de misericorde vers moy et pour ta haulte puissance
avoir compassion de moy a me delivrer briefmant de ceste grief peni-
tance en que je suy. Et vray Dieu Jhesu Crist, bien say que je t'ay
failly en pluseurs manieres et suy vil pecheur contre toy don ne
vueilles pas regarder a mes grans deffautes et maulx fais que sont in-
numerables. Car mestier je n'ay mie que me doyes punir sellon que
j'ay desservi, ains ay necessité de ta misericorde et mercy que moy
20 donnes tamps et espace de me corregir et de amender ma vie affin que
je puisse faire auqune chose par tamps a venir que soie pleisante et
agreable a ta devyne magesté par le quelle me faces digne d'avoir ta
benigne grace et amour que grandemant desire. Et beau sire Dieu
regarde coment je suy desconceillé que ne say que fere et suy du tout
pardu se tu ne moy aydes, se ne moy soustiens et ne moy deffens de
ceste malle fortune [74R] que contre moy court et ne puis resestir sens
ta bonne ayde. Car je sans toy ne puis vievre ne avoir nulh bien et
say serteynemant que se tu me desempares, le mort est yssi appareilee
par me prendre. Pour quoy te prie, ne moy laixssier ne desemparer
30 ores ny autre foix; fay moy vievre lonc tamps toy louant toy glori-
ffiant que je te puisse rendre grace dez grans biens, honneurs, que m'as
donné en cest monde, dez quells puisse fere biens et aumosnes par les
quels tez bons mandemans soyent par moy acomplis. Et vray Dieu de
paradis ou quel j'ay ma ferme esperance et tout mon recomfort, aies
pitié de moy ta pourre creature et entent mon orayson et te prie a
juyntes mains par le merite de ta sainte passion que de non ne moy
vueilles dire a ma priere. Car tu sces que je suy tout tien corps et
arme et a present le toy comferme et le te donne entieremant sans fin.

Item quant le ditte nef fut adobee et l'aubre [74V] bien reparé je me
40 mys en la mer a la ditte cipté de Saragoce et comensay de fere le voye
ou royaume de Cerdeigne et quant je fuy xl milles en la mer a ung
chief que l'on appelle Capoupasser, ung vent nous prins que nous fist
torner arriere davant le ditte cipté. Mes ne y fis nulle demeure, ains
tiray a l'avant a une aultre cipté long d'icelle c milles, le quelle
s'appelle Messine, et passay tout le lonc de le coste de Cecille, et

veoyt l'en auprès de le mer deux chasteaux que sembloyent estre mot
fortz, l'un avoyt nom le Molle et l'autre Tabermine, et x milles plus
bas en avoyt ung autre que se appelloit l'Eschallete et de l'autre bande
estoyt le royaume de Calabrie ou il avoit sur le coustiere de le mer
ung hault chasteau que se nommoyt Pintodatol et après celluy une
bone ville qui avoit a nom Rejols a rive le mer, et sont ces deux royaumes de Cecille et de Calabrie droit et droit l'un de l'autre qu'il n'y
a guieres de travês de mer. Mes Calabrie est en terre ferme et Cecille
est une ille le quelle est bien grant, et cuydoye passer entre ceulx deux
10 royaumes par ung pas, le quel nomment les mariniers Bouque deffar, et
quant je [75R] fuy a l'entree, autre vent contrere nous prist que nous
en fist tourner et en alant sa et la roddant par le mer cuydans encores
passer le dit pas, demourames quelques viii jours, mes onques ne
puymes le passer, ains nous en fist le vent retourner arriere au dit
Capoupasser ou premier avions estê. Mes puis eumes si bon vent pour
aller nostre chemin que c'estoit merveille et passames celluy Capoupasser de plus de cc milles a l'avant en la mer, et ainssi alant par le
voye s'en devint ung venrredi vers le mye nuyt que estoit le xe jour
du moys d'octobre qu'il se lieva fourtune en le mer si grant que c'estoit
20 merveille et a paynes lez voylles se puirent abaissier par le force du
vent qu'il faizoit et pleuvoyt et tomboit pierre et faizoyt une nuyt si
obscure que a paynes en le nef se povoyt veoir l'un l'autre, tant que
le patron et les marinyers a paynes povoient guoverner le nef pour le
mal gracieux tamps que faizoie et aussi par le grant obscurtê de la nuyt;
atant avions de trevailh et estions en grant perill que nullz ne pansoie
estre quite de le mort, mes tres toux eumes recours a Dieu, Nostre
Seigneur et le feymes priere que pour sa pitiê ly pleut de nous amender [75V] le tamps et sauver les vyes et puis criant a haute voys trestoux aux sains et saintes de paradis, chascun pour ourdre l'un après
30 l'autre.   Et tenant ceste maniere Nostre Seigneur nous envoya ung
glorieux saint que voullontiers lez mariniers invoquent, lequel s'appelle monseigneur saint Helm[1] et se vint mettre sur le panell que les
marynyers tiennent au chasteau derriere le nef pour conoistre le vent
de quel part vient. Et puis se alla pouzer hault au chasteau du mast
et eumes par deux foix celle nuyt ceste tourmente et a chacune dez
deux il vint et estoit qu'il sambloit ung torchon alumê que getoit grant
resplendeur, le quel par se grace je vy a chacune foix qu'il vint bien
cleremant et si firent pluseurs autres de la nef et lors dessa venue fut
chascun recomfourtês et subitement toute celle fortune nous estrema et
40 fist retorner le nuyt que estoit escure comme dit est si clere, que l'on
povoit veoir bien long et la mer appaisimee, mes avions le vent contre
nous que nous tourna en le ditte ille de Cecille a ung chief que l'on
appelle Port de Pals ou prymes port et pousemes les ancres a grant
payne pour le grant vent et marour qu'il faizoit.

[76R] Item voyant toux cestes tres grandes, malles fourtunes que
estoient diversses et malvaizes et trop plus perilleuzes et espaventables

que je n'ay compté et venoient bien souvant, et regardant le mal
tamps del yver par ou nous entroions le plus contraire que estre povoit
ha aller pour mer et les fortunes plus prestes de croistre que de amend-
rir, et aussi que la mer est deffendue d'aller pour le saint pere de Rome
certains moys de l'an, je vous fis ajouster, mes escuyers et serviteurs.[1]
Et voys mettre le chose en consseilh si regardant les choses sus dittes
et les grans perills que avions passé, leur sambloit que je ne deusse
plus aller avec celle nef ne avec tiel tamps d'yver pour le mer, si que
conclusi toutes choses ilz avizerent et cogneurent pour le sauvacion de
ma parssone que le meilleur estoit par moy de me demourer en le ditte
ylle de Cecille par le present et aqui attandre le bon tamps et laixssier passer cel yver et celles malles fourtunes et puis au tamps novel
je me pourroie mettre en mer et tenir mon voyatge seuremant en la
grace de Dieu. Et encores je fis venir le patron de le ditte nef en
ma chambre et luy demoustray toutes cestes choses, [76V] lequel aussi
me dist toux les grans perills que se povoient ensuir et me consseilla
du tout le demouree comme les autres mes escuyers avoient fait. Et je
qui oÿ dire toux jours que bon consseill l'on doyt croyre et eu bien en-
tendu tout se qu'ilz dizoient que c'estoit le meilleur par moy et le fait
du patron que bien se entendoit en tels faix de mer, voix les croire et
par leur conceill que moy sembloit estre bon par eschiver a tout mal,
je me demouray en le dit royaume de Cecylle et pris terre a ycelluy
Port de Pals, le xiiii jour du moys de novembre, au quel port n'a nulle
habitacion, ce n'est ha xviii milles ung chasteau que l'on appelle
Espacaforno au quel je envoyay premieremant davant pour serchier dez
chevaux, et si tost qu'ilz furent venus, je montay a cheval et m'en
allay pour terre au chastel sus dit. Car mon entente estoit de tirer
vers le cipté de Palermo que est port de mer ou toux jours vont et
vienent de les nefs.

Le Royaume de Cecille

[77R] Item d'icelluy Espacaforno je m'en allay au chastel et ville de
Modique, que est ha x milles, le quel est chief de conté et une tres
forte place de chastel et grande a[re]chevoir* grans gens d'armes.

Item de Modique au chastel et ville de Arragoce iiii milles. C'est une
moult grande ville le quelle est assize soubre une bien haulte montaigne que me semble estre grandemant forte.

Item de Arragoce au lieu de Cheremant viii milles.

Item de Cheremont a la ville de Calatagironne xviii milles.

Item de Calatagirone au chasteau et ville de Chatsse xii milles.

---

*   ... a[re]chevoir. This is a conjectural emendation of
            achevoir.

[77V] Item de Chatce a le ville de Calassivete xii milles et cousté
du chemin a main cenestre l'on trouve un lac d'eue que tient de tour
xviii milles, [1] le quel au tamps passé se dist que soulloy estre ville
que avoit a nom Castroy Anuy et par ausquns pechiés qu'ilz faizoient
encontre Nostre Seigneur, le ditte ville fondi et s'en entra en abisme
et est en une vallee revironee de puys et la ditte ville leur solloit toux
surmonter de haultesse, et mayntenant lez diz puys le surmontent. En
cest lac d'eue n'a nulh poyssion de nulle condicion que soit ayns ceulx
que l'on y boute par norrir ni puent vivre, et aussi le lyn que l'on y
porte mettre liens par apparellier depuys qu'il y a esté ne vaut affere
riens, si que se dit que nulle chouse que soie ne s'i puet aproufiter.
Et le ditte ville de Calassivete est en ung fort puy; adroit de ceste
ditte ville en une tres grande et haulte montaigne ha une grant ville
avec deux chasteaux, le quelle se nomme Castrojohan, et a l'un chiest
de le ditte ville est l'un dez chasteaux en tres grant avantatge assis,
le quel est moult fort de toux costés sans nulle venue que par une
eschine de montaigne [78R] devers le part de le ditte ville, sus le
quelle venue ha bonne tranchee de roche et une grosse tour davant et
celluy chastell appellent le Chasteau dez Lombars, au quel chastel le
roy de Cecille tynt lonc tamps le siege et onques ne le peut avoir par
force.

Item de la sus ditte ville de Calassivete a une grande ville que a nom
Pollissi xxiiii milles, le quelle ville est en grande montaigne et haulte
de toutes pars fors que devers ceste entree que ha une venue que n'est
pas trop grant et en ceste part ha ung chasteau et environ le ditte ville
n'est pas tout autour environé de mur, mes l'avantatge de le place est
assés grant et fort.

Item de Pollissi au chasteau et ville de Termes xxiiii milles. C'est
une tres forte place bastie en haulte roche tout au tour et bien enmurré et le chasteau acéz grant, et le ville au pié du roc devers l'un
costé, et de l'autre part ha une ville overte [78V] et se tient au bout
de la mer et venent a ceste ditte place passe l'on par davant deux
fors chasteaux pres l'un de l'autre que on lez laixsse a mayn cenestre,
et le premier chasteau que on trouve s'appelle Calataboutero et l'autre
que es aprés Esclafena, et cestuy est chief de conté et toux deux sont
de ung seigneur. Et de ceu chemin voyt l'en en le mer le montaigne
de Volquam en le quelle ha ung grant partus que nuyt et jour geta
grant fumee et auqune foix grant flame et tira grandes pierres de dehors
et de pres celluy partus oyt l'en mener grant bruyt liens, si que l'on
tient que c'est une dez boques d'enfer; et les nefs que vont par mer
et sont ver celles parties voullontiers se retraynt a celle ditte montaigne par le tourmente fouyr et la ne ousent pauzer nulle ancre de
nef qu'en chascune n'ayt une croix. Car autrement seroit perill que
celles malles choses que liens sont les levassent et feissent perdre le
naville et toux ceux que dedens seroient.

Item de Termes m'en allay tout au lonc de rive le mer a la cipté de
Palermo et quent j'eu chevauchié [79R] xii milles, trouvay a main
destre au bort de le meryne ung beau chasteau et fort en terre pleyne
que s'appelle Sollento et d'icelluy chasteau a le cipté de Palermo
compte l'on autres xii milles. En le quelle cipté ha une tres belle
chapelle et grande dedens le palays que l'on appelle le chappelle de
Santo Petro,¹ le quelle l'enpereur Fedric² fist fere au tamps qu'il
vivoyt, et dit l'on que c'est une des belles qu'on aye veues ou monde
et par dedens toute fette d'art de musique de menue pierre soubredorees
de fin or et a trois voutes par dessus et deux renx de pilliers de marbre,
entre les quels en ha deux que sont de jaspe, que est une pierre precieuze, et davant le cuer de le chapelle ha une grant pierre carree encloustree ou mur que est si clere que toute le chapelle en puet l'en
veoir qui regarde liens et aussi clerement si puet l'en veoir come en
ung myroer et nulle poynte de dague n'i puet pendre, car davant moy
s'est assayé. En celluy mesme palays a une autre chapelle que l'on
dizoit solloit estre aussi belle mes l'ont lessee*(i) toute dechoir,³
et en le ditte cipté en ha une autre que l'on appelle le chapelle de
l'Almyrail,⁴ que est obree de celle mesme manyere de pierres bien
gentemant fette. [79V] Mes est de grant partie plus mendre et n'est
pas aussi gente come l'autre est. Aussi l'eglize du arcevesque de le
cipté est moult belle, grande et longue. En le quelle eglize est ense-
velis le dit empereur Fedric que fist fere*(ii) lez dittes chapelles sus
dittes et le emperiere sa fame, et sont en unes sepulturas d'une pierre
moult estrange ou il n'a que deux piesses, celle de dessoubz et celle
de hault, et sont bien grandes et cleres que l'on s'i puet veoir et en y
a vi de tel manyere, lez quelles si soustienent chacune sobre piliers
de pierre marbre hault dessus terre demye brace,⁵ en lequel cipté
j'estoie lotgié au chastel du roy qui touche en le mer. Ceste cipté
est en une belle playne au bort de le mer et devert le part de terre est
revironnee de puys et de montaignes et la cipté est bien grande et bien
enmurree de bons murs espés tout autour, et dit l'en que c'est le meilleur cipté de celluy royaume et se fet en ycelle grant foizon de sucres.
Et come je venoye a ceste cipté de Palermo en my le voye je trouvay
pour tiel encontre ung bon chivallier du païs de Bearn que avoyt a
nom messire Arnout de sainte Coullomme, le quell aussi bien alloit
part devers le ditte cipté et eut tres grant [80R] joye de ma venue et
de ma encontree car il cognoissoit tout mon pays qu'il c'estoit norri en
ma terre ou monseigneur mon pere, cuy Dieux absoille, a Caumont.
Ainssi nous alames alavant parlant pour le chemin et moy comensa a
domander de mon voyatge Jherusalem coment j'avoye esté de ma parsone, ne quiel tamps avoye eu, et je luy respondi que de ma parsone
avoye je esté bien sain la Dieu mercy et quant au tamps, celluy m'avoyt

---

*(i)   lessee. Ms. reading is lessea, presumably a scribal slip.

*(ii)   fere. Ms. reading is f..., but fere is the obvious reading.

esté contrere en le mer et voys luy compter lez fortunes que j'avoye
eues ainxi comme par dessus est declaré et coment mes escuyers et
aussi le patron de la nef m'avoyent conceillé le demouree en cel pays
de Cecille celluy yver en jusques tant que le bon tamps novell fusse
venus; et il me dist que j'avoye esté bien conceillié. Car le tamps
estoit moult perilleux; ainxi nous en alames celle nuyt couchier au
dit lieu de Termes et quant se vint au soir ung poy davant souper le
dit chivallier me prya que je luy vouzisse donner ung don, je luy respondi que s'il estoit chouse que je puisse fere que se faroye je moult
voullentiers, et lors il me dist qu'il me prioyt chieremant que je vouzisse fere ma demouree de tant qu'il me plaizoit estre en Cecille asson
houstel, car il en avoit tres grant plaisir [80V] et honneur. Je luy
merciay de son bon voulloir et voys luy dire que encores n'avoie je
bien avizé que je devoye fere, mes, desso qu'il me dizoit, j'auroye
mon aviz ou mes escuyers. Si que a le parffin ains que je partisse
d'icell lieu voulsist que je feisse sa voullenté ainxi que je luy avoye
outroyé au comensament et ainxi fu fait. Ores lendemain au matin
nous tirames nostre chemin vers le ditte cipté de Palermo en le quelle
demourames par viii jours et puys nous en partimes ensemble le premier
jour du moys de desembre et tournames couchier celle nuyt a Termes
que part dessus ay nommé pour aller droit asson houstel.

Item celle nuyt je couchay au dit lieu de Termes come dessus est dit
et puis lendemain au matin je m'en parti aprés disner ensemble ou le
dit chivallier tenant nostre chemin droit asson lieu, et quant j'eu chi-
vauchié xix milles passay par davant ung chastel et ville au bort du
chemin a main cenestre, chief de conté que avoit nom Guolizano, du
quel chasteau a l'oustel du dit chivallier n'en avoit que v milles, le
quel se nomme Lazenello ou je arrivay celluy jour que estoit le ii jour
de desembre, et c'est ung [81R] fort chasteau rochier aveques une bone
ville au pié desoubz luy de cccc feux et estoit basti sur une haulte
roche de toutes pars et a l'un costé avoyt une haulte montaigne que
surmontoit de haultesse celuy roc et tout le chasteau de plus de la
moytié qu'il seroit avis que de lassus hault l'on puisse grandemant
domatgier le dit chasteau et ville que est asson pié, et ne feroit l'en
point. Car il est assayé que de la hault une arbalestre de tour[1] ne
puet encore pourter a ung petit rieu que passe au pié du roc ou le dit
chastel est basti tant est grande la haulture de celle ditte montaigne
de roche qu'il en est trop plus lung que ne semble estre. Cest chasteau est en païs de montaignes et y croist le regalice. Et le roy de
Cecille l'avoit donné au dit chivallier par les bons, agreables services
que le dit chivallier li avoye faix en cez guerres au dit païs, et de
cestuy chastel voyt l'on deux places que sont de ung seigneur et
s'apellent l'une Poleno et l'autre santo Mauro qui bien semblent estre
fortes ambedeux; lequel chastel est en belle veue et en beau desduyt
de chasses sellon le païs ou il est poblé et souvante foix yssuy allé
chassier et esbatre en moy donnant [81V] de bon tamps allegremant le

meilleur que je povoie. Combien que sans penssemant estre je ne
povoie quant il me souvenoit de ma tres chere et bone amye ma loyal
compaignie que j'eyme tant, le quelle souvant par moy estoit desiree
de veoir comme celluy que lonc tamps en avoye esté moult loingtain
et le grant amour sertayne que je ly ay me faizoit souvante foix le
journee d'elle avoir le souvenir, tant que par celluy panssemant
m'estoyt avis propremant que la nuyt en moy dormant la veoye, dont
estoye aillors en si grant plaisir que pas revellé estre ne vouldroie,
tant avoye de joye et de solas. Mes si j'avoie esté bien a mon ayse
au reveller que je fis, je me trouvoye en aussi grant desaise plein de
douleurs, vuyt de liesse et garni de souspirs que plus je ne povoie,
quant je veoie que tout cella que j'avoie veu estoit par le contraire.
Hellas, que tant estoie en grief peyne quant il m'en souvenoit pour ce
que mon vouloir ne povoie acomplir et que nullement de elle aproi-
chiar ne me povoie. Car se pour chevaux ou par mes piés moy puisse
ajouster, peyne et treveil, tout me seroit neant. Mes je suy yssi en
ces ylles de mer environees a le merci de Diey et du vant le quel ou
present plus je vouldroye que ung chastel plein d'or.

[82R] En telle maniere souspirant me demouroie priant a Dieu qui
toute grace donne* que a moy voulzisse donner le vent que j'avoie
necessaire pour mon retour, a celle fin que je puisse assauvament aller
la ou le ditte tres chiere et bone amye demouroit et que ce fust brief-
ment. Ores quant j'estoie parti de Palermo pour venir a cestuy chastel de Lazinello, je avoye ordonné ou le chastelain du chastel de le
mer que si tost comme il veusse nulle nef en Palermo après que le moys
de jenier fust passé qu'il encontinent le me fist assavoir la ou j'estoie.
Après que le dit moys fut passé arriva une grosse nef au dit port qui
venoit de Napols, le quelle voulloit aller en Cataloigne a la cipté de
Barcellone, et comme ella fu arrivee, le dit chastelain ala parler ou
le patron d'icelle qui avoit nom Michel Buguere disant li que je voulloie passer vers celles parties ou elle vouloit aller et qu'il moy attend-
isse jusques a ma venue, le quel patron en fut bien content de le fere;
et tantost le dit chastelain le me fist assavoir ainssi qu'il estoit ordonné par avant et je, voyant que celle malle yvernee estoit passee
et le bon tamps de le primevere venoit qui toute douceur de tamps
ameyne, eu grant joye de ces noelles et [82V] parti du sus dit chasteau
ou j'avoie demouré le moys de desembre et de genier et du moys de
feuvrier jusques le xe jour, le quel je en parti pour torner a le ditte
sipté de Palermo et fis celle mesme voye que davant avoye fette ou
venir quant j'estoie parti, le quelle nuyt m'en alay couchar a Termes
et lendemain matin après le messe me alay disner a ungs houstels qui
sont pardella une eglize que l'on appelle saint Michel que est en my
la voye; et après que je fuy disné je montay a cheval et tenuy mon
chemin tout droit vers le ditte cipté de Palermo en le quelle je arrivay

---

*   donne replaces donnoit.

celle nuytee, et la ordonay de achater toutes mes provisions que me
faizoient besoing pour bouter en la nef sus ditte ou je devoye aller.

Ore quant je fuy arrivé en le ditte cipté de Palermo lendemain après
disner je chevauchay pour terre pour aller a une cipté que l'on appelle
Mont Real que est au pié d'unes grandes montaignes ha v milles long
de ceste ditte cipté pour se que j'avoie oÿ dire que la eglize du arcevesque, disoit l'on qu'estoit une dez belles que fussent [83R] ou monde
et ou il avoit de plus soutils et estranges ouvratges.¹ Et par icelle
regarder et veoir s'il estoit ainsi come l'on disoit je me mis en le voye
10   droit a le ditte cipté ou l'eglize estoit que l'on appelloit l'eglize de
sainte Marie: et quant je fuy arrivé par della je allay tout droit vers
le ditte eglize et trouvay que les portes d'icelle estoient fermees: et
tantost je vi venir ung moyne de ceulx de liens que encontinent qu'il
me vy me ouvry toute le porte que estoit en clef fermee, et je entray
de dens et allay tout droit au cuer de l'eglize ou le grant autel estoie;
et la que j'eu fette mon oraÿson je m'en alay tout autour de le eglize
avizer le maniere et condicion d'icelle et coment estoie faite. Si
moy sembloit estre moult belle et riche et de estrange maniere ouvree.
Car premierement elle est grande et large par dedens et tout autour de
20   grans pierres de marbre obree a belle rengue sutilement pousees que
ont bien ung aste de lance de longueur et environ v palmes d'ample
bien gentilles et sont mizes de chief en amont; et au cuer de le ditte
eglize a d'autres pierres belles et moult estranges et roluysans que l'on
se puet de dens cleremant veoir, et les appellent porfedo et en y a de
trois manieres de couleurs, l'une est vert, l'autre est blanc et l'autre
de violle; et de dens ceste eglize dehors le dit cuer a une [83V]
petite chapelle ou il a x piliers reons de ceste ditte pierre porfedo
toux de couleur violle assès lonx et du cuer en bas est le ditte eglize
a deux rengues de piliers de marbre toux reons bien lonx et assès gros
30   et sont faitz moult soutilmant et tout les coustès de haut. En leditte
eglize de l'une part et de l'autre est toute faite part dedens de menue
pierre come ung dé et la plus greigneur partie soubre dourees de fin
or et d'autres de diversses couleurs et cest ouvratge l'on appelle ouvre
de musique; et de celle est le ditte eglize toute estoriee de belles
ystories du fait de Nostre Seigneur et de Nostre Damme et dez sains et
saintes de paradis sens autre couleur qu'il n'y a fors que celles que les
dittes pierres ont.² Lequel ouvratge est moult riche et soutil et bas
au seul de le ditte eglize est tout fait et ouvré de menues pierres
carrees a petites piesses de pluseurs manyeres de couleurs et aussi il y
40   a de celles pierres sus dittes du porfedo reondes et de carrees que est
tres beau a veoir coment le solle de l'eglize est tres honestemant et
richemant ouvree; et par dessus hault elle n'est pas de voute de pierre
mes autremant elle est couverte d'estoys de grans [84R] chevirons bien
gentemant ouvrès et depyns. Et liens ha une sepulture de ung roy qui
s'appelloit le roy Guilhem que ou tamps qu'il vivoit fut roy de celle
ylle de Cecille et de Naples, le quelle sepulture est mot belle et

riche voyant lez estranges pierres que en ycelle sont. Le ditte sepulture est de une grande pierre toute entiere de celle ditte pierre que
l'on appelle porfedo de couleur violle, et par dessus ceste tombe est
le covercle tout d'une autre piesse de celle mesme pierre et couleur
et sont si soutilmant joyntes que eschassemant l'on le puet conoistre.
Ceste sepulture se soustient hault sur terre soubre piliers de celle
pierre et a l'environ ha vi piliers reons que aussi sont toux du avant
dit porfedo violle, les quels soustienent une couverture de ung porfedo
blanc que trespasse toute le sepulture gentement fait a maniere d'une
10   couverture de chapelle;[1] et davant ceste ditte sepulture ha une tombe
de pierre ou le filz de cestuy roy est ensevellis que avoit a nom le roy
Guilhem ainssi comme son pere, lequel fist fere ceste ditte eglize, le
quelle tombe n'est my si belle ne fette si richemant ne encore quant
il trespassa, il ne n'y voulloit point pour ly. Car il dizoit sellon
qu'il dient que celles ondrances [84V] ne vayneglories du monde assa
mort n'avoit il cures.[2] Toutes foix les moynes de liens y ont faite a
celle que je dy a memoyre de ly et de l'autre cousté est le sepulture
du roy saint Loys qui fut roy de France ont il fu mis après qu'il fu trespassé don me disoit le moyne qui le porte de l'eglize m'avoit ouverte
20   qu'il morut os parties de Barberie tenant assigié ung roy sarrazin davant
Tonys et la en cell lieu finit de sa maledie et puis fu pourtés son corps
a ceste eglize et mis en ceste ditte sepulture;[3] et le roy de France,
qui par le tamps estoit, envoya prier au roy Guilhem de Cecille qu'il
ly voulsisse envoyer le corps et qu'il luy trametoit une dez espines de
Nostre Seigneur et ung chaperon de Nostre Dame, et le dit roy Guillem resseu le present et ly envoya le corps de saint Loys excepté les
ventrailles que demourerent par reliquies en le ditte tombe; et encore
je demanday au dit moyne coment il estoit allé du sietge qu'il tenoit
au roy de Tonys sarrazin. Il me dist que quant il fut mort, sa gent
30   demoura toute au dit roy Guilleaume pere d'icelluy que fist le ditte
eglize et le roy de Tonys, qui assigié estoit, luy donna une somme
d'or par tiel qu'il se levast du [85R] sietge et s'en allast avec toute
le gent, et ainssi il le fist et se departi du sietge et par celle cause
le appelloit on depuis ensa le mal Guillem; et asson fill l'on appelloit le bon Guillem par se qu'il avoye fait fere et bastir le ditte
eglize et fist porter le corps de son pere et celluy deu dit saint Loys
de France, qui aillors estoient sevelis, en le eglize sus ditte,[4] le
quelle en sen tamps, qu'ilx morirent, n'estoit mye achevee; et les
portes de celle sont de boys mes par dessus sont toutes couvertes de
40   metal, le quel est tout ouvré et pourtrait de ymatges ystorié honneste-
mant;[5] et davant le grant porte de ceste eglize a une plasse assés
grande couverte de boys gentemant, et soustiennent le ditte couverture
viii piliers de marbre reons et bien haults et plain fais, et toute celle
paroy davant celle entree et les coustés tant comme tient le ditte
couverture, que est tout de belles tables de marbre joyntes couste et
couste, mises au lonc le chief an amont, moult belles et playnes, et
toute le place de bas est ouvreede belle violete de pierre et de

grandes pierres de porfedo et de marbre.   Et est mot beau a veoir le
entree de ceste ditte eglize.   Et au cousté de celle a une claustre
carree le quelle ha lxiii pas de lonc par chacun caire.   En chacun
dez [85V] trois caires a ung griffon par ont gete l'eue fresche nuyt et
jour; et devert le porte par ou l'en entre en le ditte claustre n'en ha
poynt mes a l'autre caire devers celle part a main droite en a deux,
l'une saill par ung grant griffon, l'autre par ung petit pillier reont
que est de celle pierre d'un porfedo vert, et l'eue saut pour le chief
d'amont sans cesser; et tout autour de ceste claustre sont les piliers
10 de deux en deux mot gentement ouvrés, l'un pareill de marbre tout
plain bien ouvré et entrelassé a chacun chief, et l'autre pareill tout
ouvré de ouvre de musique de celle menue pierre sus ditte soubre
doree et les chiefs soutilmant entrelassés en diversses manieres; et
par dessus la claustre sont lez deux caires couvers de voute de pierre
et lez autres deux non ains sont de boys par se qu'il ne fut achevé;
et au caire de le claustre ou sont les deux griffons de le fonteyne est
le porte du reffreteur, le quel est bell et gent, lonc et large assés,
et au my lieu de celluy a ung pillier de marbre fait tout en reont et
par le chief de haut saut l'eue et celle que tombe chiet asson pié et
20 s'en vet par conduys dehors.   Si que l'eglize et tout le monestir me
sembloit estre beau et puissant d'ouvratge et de notables hediffiamens
mes il ha si lonc tamps qu'il [86R] fu fait, qu'il se disenys tout et est
grant perdre de laixer ainsi decheoir ung tiel ouvratge.   En quore
demanday je au moyne com bien il avoit de tamps qu'il fut fait, il me
dist qu'il povoit bien avoir cclx ans[1] et souloit estre au comensemant
abbaye et y eut deux abbés et depuis fu fait arcevesquez,[2] car il est
au present, si luy dis s'il povoient savoir ni trouver par livres de celle
eglize quant pouvoyt bien avoir cousté de fere; il me respondi qu'il
ne le trouvoient par escripture mes il estoit dessi grant afere qu'il se-
30 roit grant fait a la somer ne estimer toutes celles grans pierres dessus
dittes, les quelles dizoit il estoient apourtés de Troye et de Costantinoble et c'estoit grant merveille a trouver tante belle et puissante
pierrerie comment il y a, ny de estre ouvrees par le maniere et si
richemant; et sus hault en le montaigne ha ung chasteau que l'on
appelle le chasteau de Mont Real et chere par chiere de le ditte sipté
non guieres long a une abbaye que appellent le abbaye de Loparto.
Ore quant j'eu avizé ceste notable eglize et m'en tournoye a Palermo,
je trouvay en le voye le chivallier messire Arnaut Guillem de sainte
Collome, guascon et filz du honorable chevalier que si grant compaignie
40 m'avoit fette en Cecille comme par dessus est dit, le quel venoit au
davant de moy, chassant en son oustour, si que je me mys a [86V]
chasser et ne trouvames fors que ung oiseau que appellent francolin
que ressemble une pardis et l'oustour le voulla et le pris, et après nous
en tournames en la sus ditte cipté de Palermo.

Or devés savoir que en le ditte cipté de Palermo se fait grant quantité
de sucres comme par avant j'ay dit dessus le quell voulloie veoir le

manyere comment ilz le faizoient, si que le dit chevalier moy mena
en ung houstel ou le dit sucre se faizoie. Le sucre il croist es champs
et ressemble que se soient chevenieres et oussi sont elles de celle
mesme maniere mes que elles ont dedens mesolle et croistent deux foix
l'annee sellon qu'il dient, et quant ilz lez ont culhiers, ils les des-
pessent a menues piesses et puis les mettent dens ung trueill de pierre
a ung cheval[1] que tourne une roc tout environ come l'on fet l'eulle
en nostre pays et quant il est bien molu et rompu, ilz le boutent en
ung petit trueill de bois et la le cugnent bien fort, et tout le sustance,
10   que de liens saut, ilz mettent dens grans chaudieres que sont sur ung
grant four alumé de grans piesses de boys que fortmant les font boillir
et quant il est bien cuyt [87R] et parboilli, ils le boutent en manches
de toille ou ilz le font couller, et après le mettent en petis cournes
de terre et la le leessent esfreir jusques tant qu'il se prent et quant il
est bien pris, il est fait sucre; et en telle maniere le faizent mes il y
faut pluseurs abillemans et choses a se fere que me semble soient de
grans coustatges.

Quant se vint le jeudi après venant que estoit le xve jour du mois de
feuvrier je me mys en mer en le sus ditte nef que du royaume de Naples
20   estoit venue, lequelle estoit belle et grande, et le patron de celle
estoit catalain et avoit nom Michel Boguere que voulloit aller en
Barcelone, en lequel je m'en barchay a eure de mydi et allions le
voye de Caille ou reaume de Sardaigne; et quant fumes bien a xxi^e
milles a l'avant veymes une nef, ne savyons don estoit, et entre les
Catalains et les Genevois estoient les treves qu'ilx avoyent entreux
rompues et avoient guerre,[2] si que penssa le patron de nostre nef et
lez autres que ceste nef fussent de leurs henemis genevois; et elle
venoit prendre port, a le cipté don nous estions parti a Palermo; et
nous tirons a l'avant nostre [87V] chemin, et quant fumes pres et pres
30   les uns dez autres envoya le patron une barque garnie de gens vers
elle savoir s'ilz estoient genevois, et ils nous trametoient en icelle
l'escrivain de leur nef;* et par avant que nostre barche fusse de retour
a nous passer, nostre nef avoyt ja eu le vent contraire que l'avoyt
fette revirer don nous estions parti, si que les nefs toutes deux tenoient
une voye, et come l'autre cuydoye passer par davant le nostre, nous
fumes aussi tost au pas come helle; je ne say se elle le faizoit par
s'en aller com bien que nous ne volumes per helle pas laixer nostre
voye en sel poynt, nous fumes si pres que nous fausit ahurter; sur ce
les dittes nefs ambedeux se entre fierent dez chasteaux davant telle-
40   ment qu'il sembloyt que toutes deux fussent debrisees, si que de le
nostre se rompi assés de fustatge et toutes les deux bonetes[3] que se
tenoient en le voille du grant albre en le quelle fist de si grans partus
que par le mendre pourroie bien passer une grosse pipe, et nostre nef

---

        *   de leur nef.   After this is added que ne savions riens.

le encontra tiel coup qu'il l'en pourta tout le chasteau davant et mist
en piesses l'aubre que dedens celluy estoit et pleusers autres tables
que voullerent pour mer; et par se que le fait fut ainssi avenu nous
cuydames toux qu'ilz fussent genevois [88R] que pendre nous voulsissent; getz de dardes et de lances se comenssent a descharrier sur
eulx tellement que null d'eux n'ouzoit demourer haut en couverte.
Car ils alloyent si espessement que null remembrament en eux avoir
ne pourient de riens que fere deussent per fere nulle deffensse. Ore
se aluignerent les nefs ung poy que l'on n'i povoit plus trere, et
10   nostre nef comence a pendre le tour par retourner sur eux et leur fu
crié abayssacent les voilles a bas; ils, que virent qu'il estoient pres
de recevoir autre hurt, tantost abaicerent come ceulx qui se veoyent
pardus, car nostre nef estoit assés plus puissante que la leur et mieux
garnie de gens; et quant fumes davant eux retournés, ilz mostrerent
une bandiere de Cecille, disant qu'ils estoient dez nostres et criant
par Dieu merci, que leur nef estoit toute ouverte et desjoynte et le
mer entroie mallement liens, que ne voulsissions fussent perdus; si
que le patron estoit constre moy et je luy diz qu'il n'y eust plus encontre car il seroit perill que a l'autre foix helle s'en entrast affons
20   mes que eussions pitié d'eux puis que mercy demandoyent. Ainssi
fut fait, car autrement ils estoient en voye d'estre peris en le mer.
Si leur demanda l'on pour coy avoyent eulx [88V] voleu hurter a nous
que veoyent bien que estions plus fors que eux. Ils distrent que ne
voulloient ils point mes le vent le leur fist fere a force maugré qu'ilz
en eussent. Après que ce fu fait arriva a nous le nostre barque que
encore n'estoit tournee avec l'escrivain de leur nef et a ly fut demandé
se le nef estoit genevoise ou secilliane coment helle dizoit. Il dist
que vrayement elle estoit de Cecille et venoyt de Alexandrie ou elle
avoyt chargié d'espisserie, et avoit passé pour Candie et aqui avoit
30   achaté clxxx pipes de marvezie que elle pourtoit a Palermo. En tant
le vent contraire se reffresque que ne puymes passer avant, ains nous
en fist tourner vers Palermo ou nostre nef alla arriver lendemain en
ung port que l'on appelle saint George ou il ha une eglize, la quelle
est entre le ditte sipté et une montaigne qu'eux nomment Monto Pelegrino; et la le patron me dist que je povoie aller en le cipté se je
voulloye. Car il failloit attendre le bon vent et qu'il me vendroit
querre quant il seroit tamps de partir et trouveroye que le nef seroit
adobee, et ainssi il me fist trere une barque dehors que me pourta
arriver a terre et je m'en tournay vers le sipté d'ou j'estoie parti le
40   jour davant. [89R] En telle maniere je demouray en le ditte sipté
tant que nostre vent venisse; et quant il vint, furent quatre jours
passés, après les quels je m'en retournay en le nef ung lundi le xix[e]
jour du sus dit moys et prymes nostre voye au pleisir de Nostre Seigneur par tirer avant; et quant j'eu allé lx milles, trouvay une ille

deserte que l'on appelle le Ostegue.   Et partent d'icelle plus alavant
trouve l'en trois ylles d'un renc, l'une devant l'autre. Le premiere
s'apelle la Yvisse, le quelle est deserte, le segonde a nom le Fonhane,
en icelle ha ung chasteau, la tierce, que est plus avant, appellent le
Maresme ou il n'a nulle habitacion, et de le sus ditte ille de l'Ostegue
a yceste ylle del Maresme comptent lxxx milles, lesquelles trois illes
laixe l'en a mayn cenestre qui vient en Sardeigne pour celle partie.

    Item partent de celles dittes illes je allay sy alavant que je fuy a le
veue de l'ille de Sardeigne bien pres que cuydions lendemain y arriver
10   et pour doubtance de le terre encontrer par cause de le nuyt que dessus
nous venoit, lez marinyers nous firent prendre place en [89V] le mer,
car la nuyt faizoit moult escure et ne feysoit point de lune, et quant
le nef fu al large de le mer, le vent la pris et l'en pourta si priont que
quant vint a lendemain, null de le nef n'eut puissance de veoir terre;
et si cuydions bien estre allés nostre chemin et furent toux esmerveillés
coment puyons estres si alongués de le terre que le jour davant avions
veue et come nous cuydions ajouster de le ditte ille et tout jour nous
en alloinyons, plus avant alames par retourner en le ditte ille que en
tournejant sa et la par le mer null ne savoit en quel part estoie tant
20   avions roddé et tournoié le mer.   Aprés vint ung soir que aucuns
mariniers monterent haut sus le chasteau du mast pour veoir si pourroient veoir terre et a une ille qu'ils virent, cogneurent que nous estions
en les parties de Barberie pres de Tonys ou le roy sarrazin demeure a
meyns de xx milles.   Si que toux furent merveillés grandemant que
povoit avoir esté que nous fussions ainssi tombés en celles marches.
Ore le vent estoit sessé et estions en calme et ne poyons aller avant ne
arriere, don chacun estoit bien en panssee et comensoyent a parler
l'un a l'autre leurs oppynions; disoit l'un ,Nous avons failly [90R] le
chemin pour deffaute dez mariniere qu'il n'ont priz plus haut nostre
30   voye.'   Disoit l'autre ,Il fait si grant obscurté la nuyt que l'on ne
puet veoir ou l'en doyt aler.'   Et disoye l'autre ,A nostre enbarchier
de nef devions avoir regardé que la lune fusse en bon poynt.' Et
l'autre dizoit ,Attant come celle famme que est en le nef soit allotgee
si pres du tymon que est guovern de le nef, nous ne pourrons aler avant.'
Se dizoit l'autre ,Il doyt avoir siens quelque malvaize chouse que nous
guarde de aller nostre voye.'   Et l'autre dist ,Il a pres de Caille sur
le mer une eglize de Nostre Dame que fait de grans miracles que l'on
appelle sainte Marie de Bon Ayre, ayons donné chacun de l'argent a
fere ung beau siri que arde davant le benoyte ymatge par tel que luy
40   plaise pour sa pitié nous donner grace que puissions tourner en nostre
chemin.'   La quelle chose si tost com elle fu ditte, la vindrent
demoustrer a moy; je leur fis responce que se que fait seroit par honneur et reverence de Nostre Dame ne povoit estre que ben fait; et
lors me dyrent que comensesse a donner premieremant, de le quel
chouse fuy content et comenssay par tel que le dit siri se feisse et puis
les autres aprés, et la que ce fu fait trestoux nous mesimes de genoils

a comensier le Salve Regina. [90V] Et quant l'eumes ditte jusques
a Hostende auqun ala comensier Ora pro nobis sancta Dei genetrix et
d'aqui avant comenserent a dir les oraisons. Après que ce fut dit,
demourames celle nuyt ou grant esperance d'avoir auqun bon vent et
que lendemain fussions en quelque part on l'on se cogneusse. Et
quant fut le jour nous regardames tout autour de nous et ne veymes que
siel et eue et fumes ousi loing de terre come jamais enquore plus,
chacun ne s'en tient mye content, bien aviont de quoy, car le Barberie estoit au davant qui toux jours avoyent fustes par le mer, jassoit
que nous avions plus grant navili qu'euxs n'avoient, mes nostre nef
n'estoit pas grandemant pourveue de vitailles par le longe demouree
qu'elle avoit faite que ne cuydoye pas tant tarder de estre en Caille,
et pour se celles que nous avions estoient pres que defaillies et de
busche n'avions ja point ains faizoient feu de cordes que en y boutoy-
ent de oussi grandes come est le bras d'un home; de l'eue fresche y
avoit il bien poy, com bien que le nef estoie bien avitaillee de vin
grec et quelques clxx pipes; et par cause d'autres vitailles qu'il n'y
avoit estoient les gens plus descomfourtees. Car dobtoyent alonga-
ment de tamps ou quelque mal exident que nous venisse de nuyt encontre quelque roche, [91R] pour ce que ne savions celles mers.
'Hellas' dizoient ils 'Que nous avons ainxi failli le chemin. Je croy
que c'est a nom enchantemant.' Et vont demander a moy que se
povoit estre. 'Je nessay' fi je 'Se n'est le voullenté de Dieu, mes
je vous diray se que moy semble. Nous comensames l'autre soir a dire
le Salve Regina et ne achavames pas de dire O clemens, o pia, o
dulcis virgo Maria, pour quoy je vouldroie bien que nous la comens-
assions de le dire autre foix et que la achevons toute; et la que se soit
fait ay esperance en Dieu et la Vierge Marie que nous trametra bon
vent.'¹ Distrent les ungs que ce seroit tres bon et autres que se prindrent a rire. 'Et riés vous?' en fi ge 'Vous prisiés poy se me semble
se que plus vous puet aydier.' Ainxi la chouse demeura par tel deux
jours passés que encores n'avions eu vent que nous puisse bouter avant.
Car nostre nef estoit grant navile et avoit besoing force de vant, et
après que les deux jours furent passés ils vindrent a moy et me distrent,
'Je croy' firent eux 'Que ce que vous aviés dist sera veoir que nous ne
pourrons partir dessi jusque se que le Salve Regine soit achevee.' Je
leur respondi 'Je le vous ay bien dit et pancés que se soient bourdés
mes la ou plus se tardera a dire et plus vous en pourrietz repentir, mes
ajoustés vous [91V] trestoux et encontinent que la ayons comenssier.'
Se dirent eux 'Nous le voulons bien et qu'il se faize.' Et c'estoit
ung mardi au soir et nous avions ja esté environ quinze jours en mer,
ainssi nous alames toux mettre a genoils et comenssier le Salve Regine
qui ne demoura a chevoir come l'autre foix avoie fait quant elle fu dite.
'Ore' fi je 'Ayons prié se que plus nous puet aidier a Nostre Seigneur
et ayons tres toux bone esperance en elle qu'elle nous aydera.' En
tant demourames celle nuyt et quant vint au jour ung petit vent fresquet
fut venu que poy a poy se refresqua et nous comensa a tirer vers le iile

de Sardeigne ou nous voulions aller. Et tout celluy jour feymes
nostre voye et a l'autre endemain le gueyt de nostre nef va voir liens
en le mer une nef, et eschessemant estoit jour cler et j'estoie ja levé
et hors de ma chambre et pres de ly quant il l'a veu; et lors chacun se
comensa a lever et monter haultsur le nef par la veoir, et fut ordonné
que une barque l'on boutest dehors le nef et qu'allasse savoir qui elle
estoit. Ainssi fu fait; tantost l'on tramist vers elle une barque, et
quant fu pres de le ditte nef ils parlerent ensemble [92R] et entrerent
ceux de nostre barque en leur nef, et trouverent qu'elle estoit ces-
10 silliane que partoyt de Trapena et avoyt esté sinq jours en mer roddant
comme nous autres feissions et voulloit aller a Caille en l'ille de Sardeigne come nous; et nous eumes grant joye d'avoir trouvé compaignie
et par savoir de novelles. Car nous ne savions com bien avions a aller
et elle dist a ceux de le ditte barque que nous estions bien a xxx milles
du Chief de Carbonayre que est en le ditte ille de Sardeigne a xxx
milles de Caille ou nous voullions estre et elle aussi. Quant nous
oÿmes ceste novelle nous fit grant recomfort, car nous en penssion bien
estre trop plus loing et avions doubtance de passer necessité si guieres
demourions plus. Toutes foix celluy recomfort nous fu joie sens profit
20 car nous coneumes bien après qu'il en y avoit enquore plus de cxxv,
mes tout jour nous suymes selluy vent que venu nous estoit, le quel se
revenu si fort que passames l'autre nef hors de toute veue, et ne nous
donames guarde que fumes pres du dit port de Caille et la arivames ung
poy davant mye nuyt le premier jour de mars. Et comme lendemain
j'eu pris terre sans rescansser en le ville [92V] ne en nulle part je tenu
mon chemin a sainte Marie de Carbonayre et pleusers autres de le nef
qui ainxi l'avoient empris, et la je oÿ ma messe en le chapelle qui est
bien devote et lendemain y fu pourté le brandon que avions donné a
Nostre Dame aveques mes armes en ycelluy, le quel pesoit xxviii libres;
30 et la regraciames Nostre Dame de la grace que faite nous avoit. Plus
bas de ceste eglize a ung chief que entre en le mer ha une eglize que
l'on appelle saint Hellie,[1] que puet bien estre a deux milles de Caille
en le quelle sipté je demouray viii jours.

Item de Caille je parti le noveme jour du dit moys de mars a heure de
terce et trouvames en le mer que le nef que premieremant avoit esté
en nous voulloyt arriver le quelle je croy n'avoit peu entrer par le
grant tourmenta qu'il avoit fette; et nous tenumes nostre voie au Chief
de Taulat ou l'en compte de Caille lx milles.

Item de Taulat au Port de Boutes x [93R] milles et davant celluy port
40 est le ylle que s'apelle Palme de Sols a viii milles, de le quelle ille
j'ay parlé au comensemant plus a plain, et davant ceste ille a v milles
en le mer ha une montaigne que l'on appelle le Vaque et de soubz
ycelle a une rochete souparee par soy que appellent le Vedell.

Item ha x milles de ceste montaigne que appellent le Vaqua d'entre
le mer a une grant roche reonde que s'apelle le Toro, et je passay
entre l'une et l'autre, le quelle roche du Toro est bien haulte et
droite et la fait beau veoir, et me semble que ung chasteau se y estoit
yffusse bien assis et moult fort y seroit tant qu'il y eusse de vitailles.

Item de celluy Toro a l'ille de saint Pierre xx milles, le quelle est
assès grande mes est sans nulle poblacion.

Item partent de ycelle l'on entre en le guolf [93V] de Lion que dure
cclxxx milles et au chef de celluy guolf est le ylle de Menorque en le
quelle ille pres de le mer ha une montaigne sus le quelle ha une
eglize que l'on appelle sainte Marie de Touron de Menorque; et plus
alavant a ung puy ou le quel ha ung chastel qui bien semble estre fort,
le quell s'appelle Fournelhs, et ceste ditte ylle de Menorque a de
tour c milles.

Item de l'ille de Menorque au royaume de Malhorque lx milles, le
quelle ylle ha cc milles d'environ.

Item du royaume de Malhorque a la cipté de Barcelone cc milles en
le quelle sipté de Barcelone je arrivay le xiiiie jour du moys de mars
l'an mil ccccxix.

Item le xxiiiie jour du moys de mars je parti de la ditte cipté de Barcellone et fis le voye vers [94R] Molin de Rech, une ville ou l'on
compte ii lieues, et a la moytié de cest chemin a une place a main
cenestre bien haulte que l'on appelle Cervellon.

Item de Molin de Rech m'en alay a le ville de Mertorell ii lieues, et
au my du chemin passay a une barche le rivere qui appellent Lobregat.

Item de Mertorell a saint Pierre de Breze i lieue.

Item de saint Pierre de Brese a l'Espareguiere mye lieue.

Item de l'Espareguiere a Coll Baton mye lieue et la a ung beau chast-
ellet en avantatge.

Item de Coll Baton a Nostre Dame de Monserrat 1 lieue, out je arrivay
le jour de Nostre Dame de mars que l'on comptoit mil ccccxx.

[94V] Item de Monserrat a Chastel Gualhin ii lieues.

Item de Chastel Gualhin a Manrese i lieue.

Item de Manrese au lieu de Torroelle i lieue.

Item de Torroelle au Chastel de Calus mye lieue.

Item de Calus au lieu de Surie mye lieue.

Le Contee de Cardone

Item de Surie a Cardone, chief de conté, ii [95R] lieues, le quel est ung fort chastel hault sur une montaigne, le quelle est toute de sal dont tout le pays de Cataloigne se provedis.

Item de Cardone au lieu de Solsone ii lieues.

Item de Solsone au Chastel de Cambrils iii lieues, le quel chastel est tres fort et en tres grant avantatge de roche de toutes pars fors que d'une petite venue qu'il ha dessus tantsolemant.

Item de Cambrils a Perles i lieue, et a main droyte voyt l'en ung chastel sur une pene de roche qui est moult grandemant haulte et droyte, le quel chastel s'apelle Liuyan, et partent du dit Parles l'on entre en le visconté de Chastelbon.

Le Visconté de Chastel Bon

[95V] Item partent de Perles passe l'on au pié d'un chastel que appellent Canelles et au pié d'un autre qui s'apelle le Roquete et ung autre qui appellent Pujol et a ung autre qui s'apelle Narago qui son tres toux moult fortz, et après on trouve le ville d'Orguenhe on l'on compte de Perlas en fora i lieue.

Item de Orguenhe au lieu de Sentis ii lieues.

Item de Sentis au lieu de Asfa mye lieue.

Item partent de Asfa trouve l'on ung chastel qui appellent Mont Ferrer et après l'on trouve ung beau chastel a une ville au pié, le quel chastel se appelle Ciutat, et puis après l'on trouve le cipté qui s'apelle le Seu d'Urgel out comptent de Asfa en fora mye lieue.

[96R] La Val d'Endorre

Item partent de la Seu d'Urgel entre l'on en le Val d'Endorre, et premieremant l'on trouve le Chastel de la Bastide et après saint Jolyon et après Endorre et après l'on trouve ung pont de pierre et pres de œl luy pont ha une fontayne de eue chaude, après y est ung lotgis que appellent Enquant et après autre lotgie qui s'apelle Canillo, on l'on compte de la ditte Seu d'Urgel en fora iiii lieues.

Item de Canilho a l'Espital de sainte Suzanne iii lieues et l'on passe ung grant port de neges et de males montees et d'avalhees moult dangereuzes de passer.

Item de l'Espital a Esmarencs i lieue.

Item de Esmarenx a Dax en Savartes i lieue, [96V] et aqui avans que l'on entre en le ville par dehors ha ung chastel que est moult grandemant fort a main droite, et a ceste place l'on sailh de le val d'Endorre et entre l'on en le conté de Foix.

Le Contee de Foiz

10   Item Dax a le ville de Tarascon iii lieues, en le quelle ville ha ung fort chastel et ung autre qui est par dehors le ville non guieres loing, et venant a yceste ville a main droite est le chastel de Lordat moult grandemant fort.

Item de Tarascon a Foiz ii lieues, et pour le chemin l'on voyt deux fortes places asizes sobre grans avantatges toutes deux et le premiere si est a main destre que l'on trouve aprés que se nomme Mongualhart.

[97R] Item de Foiz a Sadarcet i lieue.

Item de Sadarcet a la Bastida i lieue.

Item de la Bastida a Chastel Nuef i lieue.

20   Item de Chastel Nuef a Riumont i lieue.

Item de Riumont a l'Escure mye lieue.

Le Contee de Comenge

Item de l'Escure a Mon Joy mye lieue.

Item de Mon Joy a la cipté de saint Leser de Cosserons mye lieue.

[97V] Item de saint Leser a ung chastel qui appellent Caumont i lieue, et au pié du chastel passe une rivere qui s'apelle le Salat, part dela le quel rivere a ung chastel qui appellent Taurinhac.

Item de Caumont au Chastel de Pratz i lieue.

Item de Pratz a Poentis iii lieues.

30   Item de Poentis a Miramont qui est bien fort i lieue, et aqui passe le rivere de Guarone.

Le Païs de Nebesayn

Item de Miramont a une bone ville qui s'apelle saint Gausens a main cemestre du chemin a ung [98R] lieu qui s'apelle Valentin, et tenant le chemin a l'avant a main droite a ung chastel qui appellent Ville Navete, ont comptent de sent Gausens mye lieue.

Item de Ville Navete entre l'on en Lane de Boc jusques au lieu de Lanemesan ou il ha iii lieues.

Item de Lanamesan au lieu de Tornay ii lieues et voyt l'on a main cenestre ung fort chastel qui s'apelle Mal Voysin.

10   Item de Tornay a la sipté de Tarba ii lieues.

Le Contee de Biguorre

Item de Tarba a Ybos mye lieue.

[98V] Item de Ybos a Ger mye lieue.

Le Païs de Bearn

Item de Ger au Chastel de Pau iiii lieues, lequel chastel est pour le dit dez gens le plus bel du monde fait de main d'ome, car il est tournoié alentour desson pié d'un beau talu fait de bone massonerie de pierre carnelé tout alentour et est bien hault et au pié a ung molin a une grosse tour et forte et le rivere du Gave li bat au pié. Et au chief de cest talu
20   est ung beau jardin en le quel a une belle fontayne et de cestuy jardin puet l'on entrer sur le chief de le ditte tour du molin a une planche levadisse. Ore vint que de cestuy talu ont le jardin est a ung autre talu par dessus fait pour ceste maniere que cestuy mes non pas si haut: et dessus a une murrete tout entour, et par dedens celle murrete est le murralle du chastel a quatre quayres bien [99R] haulte et toute machacollee alentour; et par dedens ceste murralle a quatre grosses tours machacollees et par dedens notablement basti de sales, chambres, chapelles il n'y a pluseurs et le place du my lieu du chastel est toute faite de beau pavemant de pierre et la est le jeu de le palme; et au chief de
30   ceste place ha ung tres beau puis et qui veult entrer en cestuy chasteau ly faut entrer par v portes de fer, si que a mon avis c'est le plus bell que j'aye veu et mieux compli de toutes choses, le quel chastel fit fere ung conte de Foix qui nommoyent en celuy tamps Febus. [1]

Item de Pau a la sipté de Lescar i lieue.

Item de Lescar au Lac iii lieues.

Item del Lac a Hortès ii lieues ou il ha une puissante ville et riche et
au chief d'icelle a ung tres beau chastel et fort qui ha ung [99V] beau
fosse entour de pierre tallee a une grosse tour de dens le murralle tresque belle et forte; et au piè dudit chasteau devers l'une part a une grant
praerie a une forest, le quel est revironee de beau palenc et par dedens
demeurent de serfs et de daynes, et par de dens le dit chastel a l'entree
du tinel a ung beau porge en le quel sont figurees et pourtreytes de
toutes manieres de bestes, masle et femelle de chacun ung pareill, en
le quel chastel je tint feste de pasques ou le conte de Foix.

10 Item feste passé je parti de Hortès et m'en alay couchier a ii lieues a
ung chastel et ville qui s'apelle Saut de Noalhas.

Item de Saut a Urgon iiii lieues.

Item de Urgons a le ville de Durffort ii lieues.

[100R] Le Viscontè de Marssan

Item de Durffort je m'en alay disner a une abbaye qui est bien pres
d'aqui, lequelle s'apelle saint Jehan de le Castelle; et d'illeques passay a une ville pres de ceste abbaye que se nomme Caseres et plus avant
alay a ung chastel qui s'apelle Puyou et alay coucher celle nuyt a le
ville de Roquaffort ou l'on compte de la ont je estoie parti v lieues, en
20 le quelle ville a deux chastels et deux riveres, l'une se nomme le Lodose
et l'autre l'Escampon.

Item de Roquaffort je m'en venuy oÿr messe et disner a Chasteau Geleux
et puis a Caumont ou il ha de Roquafort ix lieues, ont je arrivay de (de)
retour de mon dit voyatge le xiiii^e jour du mois d'avril que l'on comptoyt
[100V] mil ccccxx, et estoyt le viii^e jour de pasques, au quel voyatge
complir je demouray ung an ung moys et xv jours.

Plaize a Dieu que ce soit assauvacion de mon arme.   Amen.

EXPLICIT LE VOYAT
GE DOUTRE MER

Johannes vocatur qui escripsit benedicatur
Et eius cognomen Ferriol esse dicatur.

[101R] Ce sont les joyes que sont en le huche de Sipres achatees en Jherusalem.

Premieremant ung drap de damas roge et ung autre douré.

Item une piece de camelot noir.

Item une piece de satyn blanc.

Item une piece de tele fine.

Item une piece de telle d'indie vetade. Et autre tant de telle blanche.

[101V] Item une piece de soye blanche.

Item ungs pater nostres d'evoyre blanc.

Item six pater nostres de musquet noir.

Item quatre cordes de pater nostres de cassidoine et de cristal et quatre cintes de soye blanche et de fil d'or que sont les mesures du saint Sepulcre Nostre Seigneur et de Nostre Dame.

Item troys borsses de soye et de fil d'or.

Item deux petis draps de soye et de fil d'or que sont pour couvrir le custode Nostre Seigneur.

[102R] Item xxxiii anels d'argent qui ont touché au saint Sepulcre.

Item xii croix d'argent surdourees et ung cassidoyne enclaustré en argent, les quels ont touché au saint Sepulcre et en les autres saintes reliques.

Item une pierre precieuze de trois manieres de pierre en claustree en or avec une perle, le quelle ha touché au saint Sepulcre Nostre Seigneur.

Item une pierre precieuze que est bonne pour les huilhs.

81

Item v serpentines les trois de coulleur jaune et l'autre de coulleur persse et blanche et l'autre toute blanche, les quelles sont bonnes contre venin et une grosse croix douree qui ha touché au saint Sepulcre.

[102V] Item xxvii croix de perles qui ont touché au saint Sepulcre.

Item vi anels de calssidoine vermeilhs qui sont bons pour estancher sanc et ont touché au saint Sepulcre.[1]

Item x anels de serpentine, les v vers et lez autres v pignaillez de sa mesme coulleur et ont touché au saint Sepulcre et a lez autres saintes reliques.

10   Item reliques de le terre sainte de Jherusalem ou il ha de le columpne sainte ou Jhesu Crist fu lié et batu et flagellé a le mayson de Pilat, du Mont de Calvaire ou Jhesu Crist fu crucifié.   Item de le grepie ou Nostre Seigneur fu pausé entre le beuf et l'ane.   Item du lieu ou fu trouvee le vraye croix.   Item du sepulcre madame sainte Caterine ou fut sevellie.   Item de le porte doree par le quelle Jhesu Crist entra le jour de ramps en Jherusalem.   Item de le osse saint Barnabé[2] et dez xi mille vierges.

[103R] Item une borsse de damas noire douree et brodee et escripte de fil d'or.

20   Item deux parells d'esperons dourés et l'un pareil ha touché au saint Sepulcre.

Item quatre rozes d'outre mer qui ont touché au saint Sepulcre.

Item vii pareils de gans blancs de camoix.

Item ung grin d'or et ung fermail d'or ou il ha ung robin et viii perles.

Item v qanivetz de Turquie.

Item xv cordes de pater nostres de sipres et une de fust d'aloe.

[103V] Item six borsses de fil d'or et de soye.

Item auzelles de Chipre par parfumer chambres.

Item troix caixons l'un de sipres et lez deux de fust pinte ou sont l'une
30   partie dez joyes susdittes.

Item une autre petite caixete de sipres ou il ha quatre targes de gorge de ma devise ouvreez de fil d'argent et de soye.

Item xii ganivetz de Turquie.

Item xxi borsse de soye.

Item une ambolle couverte de palme plaine d'yaue du fleuve Jourdein.

[104R] Item xiiii borsses de fil d'or et de soye.

Les quelles joyes de celuy païs je pourtay pour donner a ma femme et aux seigneurs et dames de mon païs.

Notes

Page 10

1. This is the motto of the family. Nompar de Caumont adopted the arms of the extinct branch and probably the motto as well.

2. This refers to his account of his pilgrimage to Compostella. His account of this journey follows the list of presents in the British Museum manuscript. There is no narrative, just a list of distances.

3. This poem is in the British Museum manuscript. There is another copy in the Bibliothèque Municipale et Périgueux, which has been edited by Dr. Galy. The two copies are identical, and the edition is absolutely accurate. It is a poor poem, illustrating the author's inability to handle metre and rhyme.

4. Berbeguières came into the family as the dowry of the grandmother of the author, Magne de Castelnau, the wife of Nompar the Seneschal.

5. Guillaume Raimond de Caumont had died very recently, so that he was unable to go on the pilgrimage. (The Author, his Family and his Work, p.134.)

Page 11

1. His family has possessed these territories for the previous two generations, about forty years. Before that there had been a disputed overlordship following the death of the last member of the senior line.

2. The name of his wife is unknown. The only children known are his two sons, Nompar and Brandelis.

Page 12

1. At this time his possessions were extensive. Caumont, Chastel Nuef, Chastel Culier, Berbeguières, Damazan, Samazan, Monpuillan, Bouglon, Gontaud, La Bastide de Castelamouroux, La Mote Verte, property in Bordeaux and presumably Bourg, seized by his grandfather. (Ibid., p.133.)

Page 13

1. John, 19, 38-39.

2. This is Nompar de Caumont who died in 1446 after losing his lands to the French.

Page 14

1. There is no evidence that Nompar de Caumont had any daughters apart from this sentence. If there was a daughter, she may have died young.

2. This remark indicates the low opinion in which jongleurs were held.

3. Jean de Grailly, Conte de Foix et de Bigorre (1415-1436), the son of Archambaud de Grailly and Isabelle de Foix, heiress of her brother Mathieu, Conte de Foix.

4. Arnaut de Caumont was probably the bastard of Anissant de Caumont, great-uncle of the pilgrim, or of Jean de Caumont, seigneur de Lausun. The families had close links, although they were only distant cousins. There seems to be no record of Galhardet de Tozeux.

Page 15

1. Luke, 23, 42-43.

Page 16

1. There are no other records of Bertran Chastel and Gonsalvo de Bonelles.

Page 17

1. Archambaud de la Mote might be a descendant of Bertrand, seigneur de la Mothe, who married Giraude d'Albret, daughter of Bernard Ezy d'Albret and Mathe d'Armagnac in 1370. (Le Père Anselme, Histoire Généalogique et Chronologique de La Maison Royale de France, Paris 1730, Vol.6, 210) Jehan de Taris is probably a member of the family of Taris en Bazadais. (Ibid., Vol.5, 742.) Any other identifications are very tentative.

2. Chasteau Cullier, brought into the family by the pilgrim's great-grandmother, Esclarmonde de Rovignan, was one of the first possessions lost by the pilgrim's son. It is frequently erased from the text which suggests that the text was written before 1432, date of the loss of Castelculier, and then corrected to take account of the new situation. The corrections may have been done by a reader unsympathetic to the family, which would not have regarded itself as having lost the right to the fief.

3. Genesis, 2, 17. Adam ate of the fruit of the tree of knowledge of good and evil. He did not eat of the fruit of the tree of life.

Page 18

1. This is a misquotation of Nullus tam fortis cui parcant vincula mortis, which is a medieval proverb. (H. Walther, Carmina Medii Aevi Posterioris Latina, II/3, Göttingen 1963, p.475, no.19, 133. Henceforth Walther.)

2. These lines refer to Luke, 12, 20.

3. In ignem eternum is found in Matthew, 18, 8. A closely related form of words is found in Matthew, 25, 41. Discedite a me maledicti in ignem aeternum.

4. I cannot trace this quotation.

Page 19

1. M. Maloux, Larousse Dictionnaire des Proverbes, Sentences et Maximes, Paris 1960, p.552. Qui a bon voisin, a bon matin. (Manuscrit du xiiie siècle sans titre, Oxford, Rawlinson.) The fable is not recorded.

2. Matthew, 19, 19 and 22, 39. The Vulgate gives 'Diliges'.

3. I cannot trace this proverb.

4. This is another medieval proverb. (Walther, II/2, 3, no.8635.)

5. The meaning seems to be 'we dared to make waxen eyes for Our Lord as he could not see a thing'. The idea is that people on earth pretend that Our Lord cannot see what they are doing because his images have wax eyes, and people do not have the imagination to see beyond this.

Page 20

1. I cannot trace this proverb.

2. I have not identified this quotation.

3. According to a Spanish folk legend the mole got his tail by trading his eyes for it. (Stith Thompson, A Motif Index of Folk Literature, Vol. i, A 2378.1.4.)

4. A medieval proverb. (J. Morawski, Proverbes Français Antérieurs au xve Siècle, Paris 1925, C.F.M.A. 47, p.79, no.2175. Henceforth Morawski.)

5. This is found in Ezekiel, 23. <u>Nolo mortem impii sed ut convertatur impius a via sua et vivat.</u>

6. A medieval proverb. (Walther, II/1, 591, no.4861.) Walther gives only: <u>Da tua, dum tua sunt; post mortem tunc tua non sunt.</u>

Page 21

1. A medieval proverb. (Walther, II/1, 532, no.4430.) Primo is a variant of primum.

2. There is no record of this proverb.

Page 22

1. Nompar travelled both ways in Catalan ships which meant that he had access to some of the best maps and charts of the period. '... les ordonnances royales d'Aragon prescrivirent, dès l'année 1359, que chaque galère devait avoir non seulement une mais deux cartes marines ...' (J. Lelewel, <u>Géographie du Moyen Age,</u> Vol.ii, 37, Bruxelles 1852.) Catalan charts for the western Mediterranean were of almost a modern standard, but the cartographers found the Levant difficult and were several degrees out. (Lelewel, loc.cit., p.44.)

Page 23

1. There is no mention of the saint suzaire among the relics at Toulouse, although in 1187 the body of St. George was given to the cathedral by Guillaume Taillefer. (<u>Catholic Encyclopedia,</u> New York 1911, Vol.14, 797.) It is strange that with his great devotion to St. George Nompar should make no mention of such a relic. The most famous shroud is the one at Turin, but despite its wanderings (Lirey 1360, Chambéry 1450, Turin 1578) there is no evidence that it was ever at Toulouse. (Ibid., 13, 762-3.)

2. See page 14, note 3.

3. The usual pilgrim route was through Venice where the pilgrimages were highly organized. It was unusual to go from Barcelona.

4. In Italy there were two wars along the route to Venice. The Duke of Milan was engaged in a war of conquest. (J.P. Trevelyan, <u>A Short History of the Italian People,</u> revised by D. Mack Smith, London 1956, pp.163-4.) Venice was at war with Sigismund of Hungary. (R. Lodge, <u>The Close of the Middle Ages,</u> London 1915, p.246.)

Page 25

1. Montserrat was famous for its ancient wooden statue of the Virgin and Child. The Benedictine community there had become an abbey in 1409.

2. Barberie was the general term for north Africa.

3. Majorca had been annexed by Peter iv of Aragon in 1344. (H.J. Chaytor, History of Aragon and Catalonia, London 1933, pp.170-2.)

Page 26

1. The chambres secretes were the privies, carried on beams over the sea, and thus easily knocked off.

Page 27

1. Sardinia had been part of the Kingdom of Aragon since its conquest by James iii of Aragon. (Lodge, loc.cit., p.480.)

2. The King of Aragon was Alphonso v (1416-1458), also ruler of Sicily and Sardinia.

3. See previous note.

Page 29

1. There is still a church of Santa Lucia in Syracuse, erected on the spot where she is supposed to have suffered martyrdom. 'A subterranean passage from the right transept leads past an entrance to the catacombs to the original Cappella del Sepolcro di Santa Lucia, the old baptist- ery which lies in front of the main church and is half underground.' (K. Baedeker, South Italy and Sicily, London 1930.) This corres- ponds to Nompar's description.

2. Nompar seems to have received a very garbled version of the legend of St. Lucy, whose accuracy is, in any case, doubtful. She was de- nounced during the persecutions of 303 by her fiancé, sentenced to prostitution, but God made her immovable. Her persecutors then tried to burn her, but God saved her, and they had to kill her with a sword. Her relics were eventually taken to Corfinium by the Duke of Spoleto and then in 972 to Metz by Otto i. Some relics were found at Constantinople and taken to Venice in 1204. (Catholic Encyclo- pedia, 9, 414-5.)

3. Presumably the church of San Giovanni alle Catacombe, incorporating all that is left of the early medieval building. It contains the tomb of St. Marcian, said to have suffered martyrdom bound to one of the granite columns. St. Marcian had been sent by St. Peter from Antioch in the year 44 and had founded the first Christian community there. (K. Baedeker, loc.cit., pp.458 and 447.) Nompar has confused the saints.

4. Calabria was part of the Kingdom of Naples ruled by Joanna ii.

5. Cephalonia belonged to the Tocco family (Dukes of Leucadia from 1357). The ruler was Carlo i (about 1377-1429). (Cambridge Medieval History, Cambridge 1936, Vol.iv, 455 and 475. Henceforth C.M.H.)

6. Zacynthos or Zante was part of the duchy of the Tocco family.

7. Modon, one of the chief strongholds of the Morea, was captured by Geoffrey de Villehardouin in 1204 and soon acquired by the Venetians. It fell to the Turks in 1499. (L. Polak, Le Pelerinage de Jehan de Tournay, unpublished Ph.D. thesis, London 1958, Vol.ii, 85. Henceforth Polak.)

8. The Morea was divided between the Venetians and petty princes such as the Despot of Mistra and the Prince of Achaia at this period.

9. The history of Corron is identical with that of Modon.

Page 30

1. St. Eustace, a famous martyr, was one of the fourteen Holy Helpers. His legend is worthless. (Thurston and Attwater, Butler's Lives of the Saints, London 1956, Vol.iii, 606-7. Henceforth Butler.)

2. Menelaus was King of Sparta. Helen, his wife, the most beautiful woman in the world, was promised to Paris by Aphrodite at the judgement of the Golden Apple. In the classical legend Paris did not use force to abduct Helen. Nompar may have used Le Roman de Troie en Prose in which Paris does use force. (Le Roman de Troie en Prose, ed. L. Constans and E. Faral, Paris 1922, C.F.M.A., 29, pp.40-41.

3. Cythera was a Venetian possession (1363-1797). It was famous for the worship of Aphrodite, here called Venus as Nompar only knows the Latin names for the ancient gods and goddesses.

4. The Ciclades had not been Greek since the Fourth Crusade in 1204. They were divided amongst various Italian rulers, mostly under the Dukes of Naxos. Most of these families had been Venetian. (Lodge, op.cit., p.495.)

5. Tresmontane is the north wind, Meyane is the middle and My jour is the south. The divisions are therefore north, mid and south.

6. Crete had been conquered by the Venetians in 1208.

Page 31

1. Saturn is the equivalent of the Greek god Cronos and has no particular association with Crete; Jupiter is the equivalent of Zeus who was closely associated with Crete, as he was born on Mt. Aegeon and then brought up secretly so that his father, Cronos, would not destroy him. Juno (Hera) and Venus (Aphrodite) have no close associations with Crete.

2. Nompar has confused two kings of Crete called Minos. The famous law-giver was Minos, son of Zeus and Europa who, after his death, became one of the judges of the shades in Hades. The second Minos was his grandson. He was the husband of Pasiphaë and the father of Androgeos. He was killed in Sicily pursuing Daedalus. Pasiphaë became enamoured of a bull, and from this union the Minotaur was born.

3. The Minotaur was half man, half beast and devoured the Athenians sent to Crete as tribute.

4. Daedalus, an exceptionally skilful craftsman, designed the wooden cow in which Pasiphaë had intercourse with the bull. He then designed the labyrinth for the Minotaur. Minos imprisoned him for this, but Pasiphaë freed him. He manufactured wings for himself and his son Icarus, but as they fled to Sicily, Icarus flew too near the sun, which melted the wax on his wings and he crashed into the sea. Maquanit is presumably from the Greek mechanetes.

5. This passage is cited by W.H. Mathews, Mazes and Labyrinths, London 1922, pp.156-63, The Dance or Game of Troy. He gives a description of an Etruscan wine jar with a labyrinth, labelled Truia, and armed men, possibly dancing, and then refers to Aeneid v, II.585-591. Iulus joins his companions in the 'Ludus or Lusus Troiae', also called Troia. According to Roman tradition it was introduced into Italy by Aeneas, and his son Ascanius imparted it to the Alban kings and thence to the Romans. The game consisted of a processional parade or dance in which some of the participants appear to have been mounted on horseback. Virgil draws a comparison between the complicated movements of the game and the

convolutions of the Cretan Labyrinth.

> Ut quondam Creta fertur Labyrinthus in alta
> parietibus textus caecis iter ancipitemque
> mille viis habuisse dolum, qua signa sequendi
> falleret indeprensus et irremeabilis error. (v, 588-91).

Nompar is repeating a misunderstanding based originally on Virgil.

6. Androgeos, son of Minos and Pasiphaë, beat all opponents at the Panathenaean Games and was then slain at the instigation of Aegeus. The Athenians had to send seven youths and maidens each year as tribute to Crete.

7. Theseus was the son of Aegeus and Aethra. He was brought up at Troezen by his mother and after going to Athens volunteered to go to Crete as one of the tribute victims, where with the help of Ariadne he killed the Minotaur. Aegeus was the son of Pandion and became King of Athens. He had arranged that if Theseus returned alive from Crete, the ship should carry white sails, if dead black. Theseus forgot to change the sails, and when Aegeus saw the black sails, he threw himself into the sea.

8. Ariadne was the daughter of Minos and Pasiphaë. She gave Theseus the clue of the thread which enabled him to retrace his steps in the Labyrinth. Afterwards she fled with Theseus but he abandoned her on Naxos where she was found by Dionysos who married her.

9. The source of Nompar's classical knowledge is uncertain. The Ovide Moralisé does not know the name of the Minotaur and always refers to it as a monster. (C. de Boer, Ovide Moralisé, Amsterdam 1915, pp. 34-35.) Nompar shares with the Ovide the belief that Theseus went to Crete by lot instead of voluntarily as in the ancient legend. The Ovide is clearly not his only source. As he seems to know some Latin, he may have drawn on Latin sources.

10. The Grand Master was Philibert de Naillac (1396-1421).

Page 32

1. The Greek Empire by this date was Constantinople and a few scattered possessions round the Aegean. The title existed until its fall.

2. Rhodes was seized by the Knights of St. John of Jerusalem in 1310, and they stayed there until 1523.

3. Le jour du corps de Dieu is the Thursday following Trinity Sunday. In 1419 it was Thursday 1 June. (L'Art de Vérifier les Dates, Paris 1818.)

4. Professor Lionel Butler, who very kindly examined the records of the Knights for me, could find no record of Sancho de Chaux or of Nompar de Caumont, but the records for this period are particularly scanty.

5. At this period he must mean the Ottoman Turks under Mohammed i.

6. St. Nicholas was Bishop of Myra and died in 345 or 352. He was a very popular saint, but little is known about him. His body was stolen in 1087 by the people of Bari who built a new basilica for it. (Catholic Encyclopedia, Vol.II, 63-64.)

Page 33

1. Cyprus was ruled by the Lusignan family, who had purchased it from Richard i of England in 1192. It reached the peak of its power under Peter i who established himself as overlord of Cilicia, but in the following reigns Genoa and then, towards the middle of the fifteenth century, Venice became the real power in the island. (C.M.H., Vol.iv, 469-70.)

2. Japha was derelict in the fifteenth century and only came to life with the arrival of the pilgrim galleys. (W. Heyd, Histoire du Commerce du Levant, tr. Raynaud, Leipzig 1885-86, Vol.ii, 466.)

3. It had been abandoned to the Crusaders in the First Crusade. (S. Runciman, History of the Crusades, Cambridge 1951, Vol.i, 282.)

4. The Franciscans were the official pilgrim guides. (Polak Vol.ii, xxxi.) Venice kept a consul at Rama to protect pilgims and in 1415 asked permission from the Sultan to establish one at Jerusalem where the Genoese already had one. This was granted despite the protests of the Genoese, and although the two states were on bad terms, the consuls worked amicably together for the next half century. The Knights of St. John also acted as consuls. (Heyd, loc.cit., Vol.ii, 466-7.) This reference is probably to the Venetian consul at Rama, as he would have been the nearest.

5. The Sultan of Cairo was Cheik Almahmoudi (1413-1421). (Ibid., 473.)

6. One of the venerated places at Japha. (Polak, Vol.ii, 104.)

7. Acts 10. Another of the venerated places. (Ibid.)

8. There seems to be no record of these houses.

Page 34

1. In 1494 Rama was described with its palace, mosque, bell tower, bazaar, noted for its fruit, and its tumbledown houses. (Canon Pietro Casola's Pilgrimage to Jerusalem in the Year 1494, ed. and tr. M. Newett, M.U.P. 1907, pp.239-241.)

2. St. George suffered martyrdom at or near Lydda before the reign of Constantine. He was supposed to have been put to death three times, but each time he was resuscitated by God. His remains were said to be at Lydda. He was surrounded by legend, and his cult was very early and very popular, especially after the Battle of Antioch in the First Crusade where he was seen assisting the Crusaders. (Catholic Encylopedia, Vol.6, 453-54.)

3. St. Martial was a third century Bishop of Limoges who did much to spread Christianity. Popular legend made him a first century apostle and then translated him to the period of Christ's lifetime. He was said to have been at the Last Supper. (Ibid., Vol. 9, 721-22.) This may explain why Nompar falsely associates him with the Holy Land.

4. Lydda was famous as the place of the martyrdom of St. George in the sixth century. Under Justinian a basilica was built over his remains. It became a bishopric during the Latin kingdom. By the fourteenth century it was destroyed. (Polak, Vol.ii, 157.)

5. Pharoah's figtree is presumably ficus egypta. (Isidore of Seville, Etymologiae, XVII, vii, Paris 1509.)

6. The usual pilgrim route was Rama, Beit Nuba, Kubebeh, Neby Samwil, the valley of Wadi Bet Hanina (mistaken for the valley of Terebinth where David killed Goliath) up to the plateau west of Jerusalem. (Polak, Vol.ii, 108.) Presumably Nompar followed this route but as there are few details it is hard to be certain.

7. This may be the Hospital of St. John, where pilgrims were usually put up. It was a large desolate house, part of the ancient Hospital of the Knights Hospitallers. It was not, however, directly in front of the Holy Sepulcre, although it was near it. (Ibid., Vol.ii, 109.)

Page 35

1. On the Mount of Olives was the beautiful Church of the Ascension. The Constantinian church had been restored by the Crusaders and was very impressive. It was circular with an aperture in the roof above the round central edifice which enshrined the actual place of the Ascension where traces of Christ's footprints in the rock were venerated.

It had become a mosque in the thirteenth century. (Ibid., Vol.ii, 113.)

2. See page 43, note 9.

Page 36

1. The Order of the Holy Sepulcre was the oldest of the religious orders, appearing in 1099. It only became an Order of Knighthood after 1187. It was the most esteemed of all the Orders and was a real brotherhood. A man had to be noble for four generations, sufficiently rich to keep his station without stooping to trade or servile work and of good repute. He had to promise to obey the Pope and the Emperor, to defend the Catholic Church, maintain her laws, protect the clergy, govern peaceably, render justice to widows and orphans, strangers and the poor. He was not to make pacts with infidels, he was to defend Christianity, to aspire to reconquer the Holy Land, to avoid vice and to go to Mass daily if possible. (Ibid., Vol.ii, 135-6.) As can be seen from the list of oaths which follow, the main omission is that Nompar does not mention the Pope or the Emperor. This may be deliberate as for some time it had been difficult to obey both the Pope and the Emperor.

2. The Church of the Nativity was the most beautiful in the Holy Land. It was built under Constantine and restored under Justinian. It had five naves separated by four rows of columns. In the fifteenth century there were still medieval mosaics and paintings. The walls of the nave were covered by mosaics on gold background showing on the right Christ's ancestors and above that the first seven ecumenical councils; on the left Christ's genealogy according to Luke. The south apse showed the Nativity in the Byzantine manner, the Adoration and the return of the Magi. The south transept had scenes from the Passion and the north transept other scenes such as the Ascension. The mosaics were dated 1165, and the columns were painted with the figures of saints. (Ibid., Vol.ii, 143-4.)

3. To the south east of the crypt of the Nativity down three or four steps is a recess covered in white marble where the crib stood. The pilgrims could kiss the rock through three holes. (Ibid., Vol.ii, 142.)

Page 37

1. This refers to Luke, 7,2.

2. Two churches were venerated corresponding to the two houses which Zacharias would have owned. The Visitation was located in the lower one and the birth of St. John the Baptist in the upper. In the former, to the left of the fountain, was the hole in which St. John was hidden, and some broken altars and traces of paintings were all that remained

of the Armenian monastery and church, still used in the fourteenth century.

Uphill from the fountain was a large church surrounded by ruins of the monastery. The church was adorned with paintings and had the chapel of the Birth of St. John the Baptist. The modern church of the Magnificat stands over the fifteenth century upper church of the Nativity. (Ibid., Vol.ii, 145.)

3. Although he does not say so, Nompar probably saw this relic in the fourth century Byzantine church and convent of the Holy Cross which had been in Georgian hands since the Crusades. (Ibid., Vol.ii, 146.)

4. These were Syrian Christians, called crestiens de le centure because their ancestors had been converted by the miracles done by St. Thomas with the girdle of the Virgin. (Ibid., Vol.ii, 102.)

5. In the Church of the Holy Sepulchre the Latins owned the Sepulchre, an altar on Mount Calvary, the Chapel of Our Lady and an altar in the Chapel of the Invention of the Cross. The Greeks had the choir, the main altar on Mount Calvary, the prison of Christ and the altar of the Dividing of the Garments. The Indians (better the Abyssinians) owned the altar of the Crowning of Thorns and a rush hut to the left of the entrance. The Armenians had once owned Calvary, but having lost it to the Greeks had bought a place on the upper ambit. The possessions of the Georgians varied from time to time. The Jacobites had the chapel behind the Holy Sepulchre, the Chapel of the Angels in the Courtyard and the stone of the Unction of Our Lord. (Ibid., Vol.ii, 152-4.) Nompar puts the Indians behind the Holy Sepulchre and the Jacobins in the courtyard but as he gives no details of the rites which would enable us to identify the sects to which he is referring, and as he does not mention all the sects, too many conclusions cannot be drawn from his description.

6. In 1187 Saladin had the cross surmounting the belfry removed and the bells broken. The tower remained intact until the middle of the sixteenth century. (Ibid., Vol.ii, 123.)

7. This is the Citadel (el-Kalia), containing the tower of Herod. (Ibid., Vol.ii, 126.)

Page 38

1. In the fifteenth century a band of Arab robbers had their headquarters in the former monastery of St. John the Baptist near the Jordan. (Ibid., Vol.ii, 151.)

2. In the fourth century a church was built over the tomb of Lazarus. Melissende, wife of King Foulques, built a convent there in 1138, which became the property of the Hospitallers in 1158. In the fifteenth century only the church remained. A marble sepulchre on the right was the tomb, and the high altar marked the spot where Christ stood when he called Lazarus forth. To the right of the stone where the sisters met Jesus Christ stood a ruined church which was shown as the house of Marie Magdalene. (Ibid., Vol.ii, 148.) Nompar does not seem to realise that le lazer is Lazarus, brother of Martha and Mary.

3. This is Mount Quarantina where Christ fasted. The site was half way up in a large cave turned into a chapel. It was kept by two Greek monks in the fourteenth century whose altars and paintings were still visible in the fifteenth. On the summit the ruins of a chapel marked the Devil's temptation of Christ. (Ibid., Vol.ii, 150.)

4. This is close to the Vulgate text in Matthew, 4,3. Si filius Dei es, dic ut lapides isti panes fiant.

5. Matthew, 4,4. Vulgate text ... de ore Dei.

6. This is close to the Vulgate, Matthew, 4,10. Dominum deum tuum adorabis et illi soli servies.

7. This is close to Matthew, 4,6. Si filius Dei es, mitte te deorsum. Scriptum est enim; Quia angelis suis mandavit de te et in manibus tollent te ne forte offendas ad lapidem pedem tuum.

8. This seems to be a combination of Matthew, 4,7 and 4,10 where the verse begins Vade satana. 4,7 is Rursum scriptum est non tentabis dominum deum tuum. It is possible that Nompar is quoting by memory.

Page 39

1. In the fourteenth century there was a monastery of St. Jerome, inhabited by Greek monks. In the fifteenth century the pilgrims found the church profaned and the monastery empty and in bad repair. This could refer to the Monastery of St. Gerasimus Abbot (d. 5 March 475), an anchorite of the order of St. Basil, who founded a monastery near the Jordan. (Ibid., Vol.ii, 151.)

2. The Monastery of St. John the Baptist, built in the fifth century and rebuilt in the twelfth. In the fifteenth it became the headquarters of a band of Arab robbers. It is the modern Kasr el Jehoudi, Convent of St. John. (Ibid., Vol.ii, 151.)

Page 40

1. He does not give a complete list of the pilgrimages to be made, which is partly explained by his saying that it is a list of the ones which he has visited. Even so he does not mention everything in the list of stations at Jerusalem, for example.

2. The indulgences actually originated in Jerusalem and the whole of this legend is a pious fraud conceived by the Franciscans just before 1345. This was the official myth. (Ibid., Vol.ii, xxxi.)

3. He claims to have written his list while he was actually in Jerusalem which would support the idea that the account is a sort of diary.

4. See page 33, notes 6 and 7.

5. See page 34, notes 1, 2 and 4.

6. This is probably Ramatha, three miles east of Emmaus, and the crusading ruins of Kherbat el Jos. (Ibid., Vol.ii, 108.)

7. This is probably Kubebeh, although the site is disputed. (Ibid., Vol. ii, 107.)

8. This was probably in the church of Cleophas which was in the Castle of Emmaus called Kubebeh. (Ibid.)

9. The first is the Chapel of St. Mary of Golgotha, the modern St. Mary of Egypt, owned by the Indians. The Chapel of the Angels was next to it on the east side of the courtyard, owned by the Jacobites. The third is the Armenian Chapel of St. John the Baptist, the modern Church of St. James. The Chapel of St. Mary Magdalene was on the west side of the courtyard. (Ibid., Vol.ii, 124-5.)

10. The Chapel of Calvary was beautifully decorated in the middle ages with marble, a mosaic pavement and a gilded ceiling. (Ibid., Vol.ii, 120.)

Page 41

1. The stone of Unction is still where it was in the fourteenth century and is greatly venerated. (Ibid., Vol.ii, 121.)

2. Fabri describes the Holy Sepulchre as follows. It was a low, twelve sided tower with as many columns supporting the roof, which projected slightly. In circumference it measured twelve times the span of a man's outstretched arms, and its height was one and a half times that of a man.

The momument was supported by a marble ciborium covered in gilded silver by the Crusaders and supported by six double columns. Above this the open roof let in light, rain and snow. The tomb itself on the right of the chapel was covered in polished marble. (Fabri, Evagatorium, ed. Hassler, 1, 327-9.)

3. This chapel belonged to the Latins. There is no truth in the legend that Jesus Christ appeared first to his mother. The source has not been identified. (Polak, Vol.ii, 118.)

4. There were three legends of the Invention of the Cross. Nompar refers to the one found in a letter of St. Paulinus to Severus in the Breviary of Paris. St. Helena had a dead man brought to the spot where she had found three crosses, and he was revived immediately he touched the true cross. (Catholic Encyclopedia, 4, 523.)

5. This is a dark, windowless chapel, still venerated. (Polak, Vol.ii, 118.)

6. The Chapel of the Vestments is in the centre of the outside wall of the Frankish choir. (Ibid., Vol.ii, 119.)

7. The tradition goes back to the end of the fourth century when crowds of pilgrims came to celebrate the dedication of the Martyrium and the Invention of the Cross in the Crypt below it. (Ibid., Vol.ii, 119.)

8. This is a large chapel with bare rock walls, containing a stone alleged to be the one on which St. Helena sat while supervising the excavations. (Ibid.)

Page 42

1. The idea that Mount Calvary was the centre of the world was current in the fourth century. After the seventh century it became localised in the garden separating the monuments built on the Holy Places. In the Crusaders' church the spot was placed under a cupola in the choir of the Holy Sepulchre, marked by an altar with a circular stone with a hole in the middle. (Ibid., Vol.ii, 122.) The idea could have been borrowed from Delphi where there was a stone (the omphalos) marking the centre of the world.

2. After the Church of the Holy Sepulchre began the traditional 'Way of the Cross'. The order of stations is the Church of the Holy Sepulchre, the house of Veronica, the house of Dives (the first one mentioned by Nompar) the meeting with Simon of Cyrene, Christ consoles the women of Jerusalem, Our Lady of the Spasm, the two stones on which Christ and Pilate sat (the Arch of the Ecce Homo), the school of Our Lady,

the house of Pilate, the house of Herod, the house where Christ forgave the sins of Mary Magdalene (also called the house of Simon the Pharisee). This way became established in the thirteenth century and by the fifteenth the number of stations between the Church of the Holy Sepulchre and the East Gate was twenty one. (Ibid., Vol.ii, 135-7.)

3. The house of Pilate was a handsome Arab house where the governor of Jerusalem lived in the fifteenth century. (Ibid., Vol.ii, 138.)

4. The palace of Herod was located in the street running north from the Via Dolorosa opposite the Antonia. (Ibid.)

5. The Church of St. Anne is the birthplace of Mary in Saewulf 1102-3. The Russian, Abbot Daniel, in the twelfth century relates the same tradition describing the cave beneath the altar which contained the birthplace of Mary and the tombs of Joachim and Anne. The present Romanesque church was built over a Carolingian one which replaced one built in the fifth century. (Ibid., Vol.ii, 138-9.)

6. In the thirteenth century there was a small church of Ste. Marie de Pamoyson near the Arch of the Ecce Homo. Later pilgrims saw its ruins some sixty yards east of the arch. (Ibid., Vol.ii, 137.)

7. The Arch of the Ecce Homo in which were enshrined two stones from Pilate's courtyard according to tradition. (Ibid., Vol.ii, 138.)

8. The Temple was built by Abd el Malik at the end of the seventh century. It was Omar's Mosque to the Franks. The pilgrims thought that it was the original temple. (Ibid., Vol.ii, 140.)

9. The Gate of St. Stephen is the Sitti Maryam or Sheep Gate in the East Wall, often confused with the Damascus Gate (the Gate of Effraim). The Golden Gate is in the East Wall of the Temple area. (Ibid., Vol. ii, 155.)

Page 43

1. The cross was buried by Soloman, who had brought the wood from the Lebanon, after the Queen of Sheba had prophesied its fate. The legend was transferred to the Cedron from Bethsaida Pool in the fourteenth century. (Ibid., Vol.ii, 110.)

2. The tomb of the Virgin is in the crypt of a former church. (Ibid., Vol. ii, 111.)

3. The grotto at the foot of the Mount of Olives was venerated as the place of the Betrayal and Arrest of Christ. (Ibid.)

4. In the fifteenth century the Garden of Gethsemane was a field surrounded by a stone wall with a few olive trees. (Ibid., Vol.ii, 112.)

5. John, 18,10.

6. Matthew, 26,40.

7. It is related in the Golden Legend that Thomas was absent when Mary was assumed into Heaven. He refused to believe the other apostles and to convince him Our Lady dropped the girdle into his hands. (La Légende Dorée, tr. T. de Wyzewa, Paris 1935, p.434.)

8. According to the Golden Legend the palm was to be borne before Our Lady's coffin on the way to her burial. (Ibid., p.430.)

9. Galilee was probably on the northern summit of the Mount of Olives. (Polak, Vol.ii, 113.)

10. See page 35, note 1.

Page 44

1. Under Constantine a church was built on the Mount of Olives dedicated to the teaching of Christ - the Eleona. The Oratory was erected by the Crusaders to enshrine the memory of the Pater Noster and may have been a partial restoration. Towards 1335 the Composition of the Creed (the Church of St. Mark to a fifteenth century pilgrim) was transferred to the ruins of the Pater Noster, while the Pater Noster was probably venerated in the ruins of another oratory where 'Christ wept over Jerusalem'. (Ibid., Vol.ii, 114.)

2. The tomb of St. James was in a cave in the Jewish cemetery in the Cedron Valley. An anchorite discovered the bodies of St. Zacharias, St. Simeon and St. James as a result of a dream. A monolith near some cells in the rock was pointed out as the tomb of St. James or of Zacharias. There were the remains of a church round it. (Ibid., Vol.ii, 114-5.)

3. Siloe is now the spring of Gihon. The legend is that the Virgin and Child lived in a cave formed by the spring when they returned from Bethlehem to present Jesus in the Temple. Siloe was famous for curing eye diseases. (Ibid., Vol.ii, 116.)

4. Isaias was sawn asunder with the tree in which he was hiding by King Manasses. In the thirteenth century this became associated with the Byzantine hermitage, now called the tomb of Isaias. (Ibid., Vol.ii, 117.)

5. The Rock Tombs on Djebel Abon Tor are still called the Apostles' Retreat. (Ibid.)

6. Haceldama was a charnel house or cemetery for the pilgrims. (Ibid.)

7. The stealing of the corpse of the Virgin Mary is an apocryphal story related in the Golden Legend. The Jews stopped the apostles as they carried her corpse to be buried. The Chief Priest stretched out his hand to touch the coffin but it was immediately withered. It was healed by St. Peter. (Ibid., Vol.ii, 134.)

8. The Church of St. Saviour (so called from the fourteenth century) was built over the ancient church of St. Peter. The little church is still extant in the Armenian monastery and was restored in 1480. The place where the cock crowed was marked by a stone engraved with a cock in the courtyard. (Ibid., Vol.ii, 127.)

9. The site alone was venerated. (Ibid., Vol.ii, 131.)

10. The presumed house of the Virgin Mary was a bare site where the Franciscans constantly tried to build a chapel but were continually obstructed by the Saracens. (Ibid., Vol.ii, 130.)

Page 45

1. The station of St. James was marked by a white stone in the wall of the Franciscan cemetery. (Ibid.)

2. St. Stephen had been transferred from Caphargamala, where he was found in 415, to Mt. Sion. (Ibid., Vol.ii, 131-2.)

3. The two stones where Christ preached to the Virgin were surrounded by a ruined church. It was the site of the Oratory of David where the Ark of the Covenant was first placed. (Ibid., Vol.ii, 131.)

4. The washing of the feet and the appearance to St. Thomas were in the lower chapels of the south nave of the church on Mt. Sion. The Last Supper and the upper room of Pentecost were in the Upper Chapel. From 1352 onwards Franciscan tradition said that the lower part of the Cenacle contained on the east the Tomb of David and on the west the two small naves where was placed the end of the Last Supper and with this a piece of the Pillar of Scourging. The washing of feet had moved to the Upper Chapel and the appearance to St. Thomas to a special oratory south of the Tomb of David. The Upper Chapel was the same as it had been. (Ibid., Vol.ii, 133.)

5. The Cathedral church of the Armenian monastery, which is still extant,

has a small chapel to the martyrdom of St. James the Greater. (Ibid., Vol.ii, 127.)

6. The legend had moved up here from the courtyard of the Church of the Holy Sepulchre in the thirteenth century. (Ibid., Vol.ii, 126.)

7. This place was marked by a fountain about five kilometres from Jerusalem. (Ibid., Vol.ii, 140.)

8. Five kilometres from Jerusalem is Mar Elyas, a Georgian church and monastery to Elias. (Ibid.)

Page 46

1. The Church of St. Catherine is the Latin Church of the Nativity. (Ibid., Vol.ii, 141.)

2. See page 36, note 3.

3. On coming into the church from the crypt, the altar where the three Kings prepared their gifts is on the left and the Altar of Circumcision is on the right. (Ibid.)

4. By the fifteenth century it was supposed that the star had fallen into a well in the south-west corner of the cave. It is now localised in the north-west corner. (Ibid., Vol.ii, 140-1.)

5. The tomb of St. Jerome was venerated near the cave of the Nativity. (Ibid., Vol.ii, 141.)

6. The memory of the Holy Innocents was associated with a cave in the crypt of the Nativity after the sixth century. Later pilgrims thought that the cave was their burial place. (Ibid., Vol.ii, 142-3.)

7. The tomb of Rachel was very beautiful and greatly honoured by the Saracens. (Ibid., Vol.ii, 141.)

8. See page 37, note 2. The words are from Luke, 1,63.

Page 47

1. See page 38, note 3.

2. See page 39, note 1.

3. See page 39, note 2.

4. The Dead Sea was not normally visited in the fifteenth century.

5. Biblical Zoar, Genesis, 19,22.

Page 49

1. See page 33, note 1.

2. Famagusta was the chief emporium for the Levantine trade. It was a Genoese possession, which had been captured from Peter ii in 1373. Janus de Lusignan had tried and failed to drive the Genoese out. (C.M.H., Vol.iv, 470-1). The church mentioned in the next line is probably the Cathedral of St. Nicholas, now the mosque of St. Sophia.

3. Janus de Lusignan (1398-1432) soon to be captured by the Egyptians in 1426.

4. Nothing certain is known about St. Anne, and although her cult dates from the sixth century, it did not become widely popular until the middle of the fourteenth. (Butler, iii, 189.)

5. St. Euphemia was a martyr in Chalcedon around 303. She is reputed to have survived terrible torture, and her cult became very popular. (Ibid., iii, 567-8.)

6. Cherines was a very strong castle. (C.M.H., Vol.iv, 471.) It was the ancient Cyreneia and is the modern Kyrenia.

7. Achilles was King of Phthiotis in Thessaly.

Page 50

1. By this date the Kings of Cyprus had assumed the empty title of Kings of Armenia after the death in exile of Leo vi of Lusignan in 1393. His wife and children had already died in captivity in Cairo. Cilicia formed part of the Mamluk possessions until the sixteenth century when it passed to the Ottomans. (C.M.H., 1966, Vol.iv, 636-7.)

2. He is confusing this place with Colchis on the east shore of the Black Sea where the adventure of the Golden Fleece took place.

3. Jason was the son of Aeson, King of Iolcus in Thessaly, but he himself never reigned there.

4. This is perhaps the Prince of Caramania. (Lodge, loc.cit., p.505.)

5. The day of St. Lawrence is 10 August. He was one of the early martyrs who died in 258 during the persecution of Valerian at Rome. (Catholic Encyclopedia, Vol.9, 89-90.)

6. The Knights at Rhodes actively encouraged such piracy to enrich themselves as one tenth of all the prisoners brought in were seized by the Order, which also had the right to buy the rest. (Baron de Belabre, Rhodes of the Knights, Oxford 1908, p.16. Henceforth Belabre.)

Page 51

1. This might be a deformation of the title Chelebi (gracious Lord) given to Mahommet i, the reigning Ottoman Sultan. (C.M.H., Vol.iv, 688.)

2. Nompar gives the total number of windmills which were divided between the two moles. On the mole of the Windmill Tower were thirteen mills, of which three are still standing. On the mole of St. Nicholas there were three windmills, making sixteen in all. (Belabre, pp.27, 36.)

3. Philermo is four miles from Rhodes on the site of the acropolis of the old Greek town of Ialysos. It was fortified by the Byzantines in 1306 and subsequently captured by the Knights who built a castle there and a church to enshrine the icon which they found there. (Polak, Vol.ii, 160.)

4. He is confusing Rhodes with Colossae, the city of Phrygia.

5. The Church of St. John of the Fountain still exists. It gets its name from the well which according to legend could cure fever. The legend was that the head of St. John was discovered by the men digging the well. The Church is almost subterranean as it is so near the ramparts. The walls had frescoes of St. John the Baptist. It was small, the dimensions were twenty five feet high, thirty feet long and twenty feet wide. It was near the wall of Provence. (Belabre, pp.80-81.)

Page 52

1. St. Anthony's Oratory was on the shore near the Tower of St. Nicholas. It has disappeared. (Ibid., p.162.)

2. The present Hospital is built on the site of the old one, built by Villaret in 1335. The new one was begun in 1439. (Ibid., p.123.)

3. St. Catherine of Alexandria was a famous martyr, and her cult was very popular in the East. It became even more popular in the West after the Crusades. Her legend is worthless. The Cypriots claimed her as their saint in the Middle Ages. (Butler, iv, 420-1.) The lieutenant governor was Antoine Fluvian (from May 1419).

Page 53

1. Giovanni ii Crispo (1418-1433). The Crispo dynasty found that Venice was interfering more and more during this century. (C.M.H., Vol.iv, 475.)

Page 54

1. The Cape of Malea was very difficult to round in winter. Ships were often blown back into the Ciclades and sometimes had to winter there. (Polak, Vol.ii, 162.)

Page 55

1. This must be a mistake as Modon was always a Venetian stronghold. (C.M.H., Vol.iv, 434.)

2. The identity of this saint is something of a mystery. It might be St. Leo, Bishop of Modon who died at Samos, from where the Venetians took him to Modon. In a storm a voice revealed that the body was that of the saint, but all the ships were lost except the one carrying the body of St. Leo. The cathedral at Modon was very poor. (Polak, Vol.ii, 85.) This account does not agree exactly with that of Nompar, but he was not always very accurate.

Page 59

1. Savast is an anomalous form.

2. Estrema is derived from the Spanish estremar.

Page 61

1. St. Elmo was the patron of sailors and one of the fourteen Holy Helpers. His biographies are all spurious, but he was reputed to be a Syrian bishop, persecuted by Diocletian. Neapolitan sailors believed that St. Elmo's fire indicated the presence of their patron. St. Elmo was also Peter Gonzalez, a Dominican, born 1190 in Astorga and died 1246 in Tuy. He was beatified in 1254 and was regarded by Portuguese sailors as their patron. Sailors believed that the electrical discharge seen during storms at mastheads and yardarms was the souls of the dead. (Butler, ii, 453-4 and Catholic Encyclopedia, II, 768.)

Page 62

1. He addresses his squires directly, although in l.7 he uses leur, which again suggests that he made notes as events happened.

Page 63

1. Possibly the Lago di Pergusa.

Page 64

1. The Chapel of St. Peter is the Palatine Chapel, built by Roger ii between 1129 and 1140. It is exceptionally beautiful and a masterpiece of Norman art and architecture. (For a detailed description see J.J. Norwich, The Kingdom in the Sun, London 1970, pp.73-7. Henceforth Norwich). There are three vaults, as Nompar says, one over the apse and presbytery and two narrower vaults over the transepts. The chapel was covered in mosaics by Roger ii and William i, while the vaults were heavily decorated with painted frescoes. (O. Demus, The Mosaics of Norman Sicily, London 1949, pp.27-57. See Demus for details of all the Norman mosaics. Henceforth Demus.)

2. Nompar has made a mistake as Frederick ii (1197-1250) reigned half a century after the building of the Palatine Chapel.

3. This chapel may be the Chapel of St. Andrew, also built by Roger ii and destroyed in the sixteenth century. (Demus, pp.25, 58-9.)

4. This is the church of Sta. Maria del Ammiraglio founded by George of Antioch, now called the Martorana after Geoffrey de Marturanu who founded a nearby Benedictine convent with which it was amalgamated in the fifteenth century. (Norwich, pp.93-5.) It is much more Byzantine in style than the Palatine. (Demus, p.76.) This may explain Nompar's lack of interest.

5. Palermo Cathedral. The tomb of the Emperor Frederick was in fact the tomb which Roger ii had had prepared for himself. Norwich says that Frederick was buried there alone and makes no mention of his wife. (Norwich, pp.362-3, 389-90.)

Page 65

1. An arbalestre de tour was a large crossbow mounted on a castle wall and worked by a windlass. It had a long range.

Page 67

1. The cathedral at Monreale was founded by William ii in 1176. (For a detailed description see Norwich, pp.315-22). The cloisters are still well preserved with beautiful carved pillars inlaid with mosaic. The church itself is huge with enormous pillars inside. The walls are covered with mosaics which dominate the church. The small chapel is the

original Baptismal Chapel, a small baldachino of ten colonettes of porphyry and granite. It was destroyed in the time of Archbishop De Los Cameros (1656-1668). (Demus, pp.100-106.)

2. The mosaics are probably Byzantine, although they are clearly influenced by the Italians. They cover a vast area of the church and tell many Biblical stories and among the saints appears the first known picture of St. Thomas à Becket. (Norwich, loc.cit.; Demus, pp. 112-22.)

Page 68

1. The remains of William i were transferred to Monreale from the Palatine Chapel by his son, William ii, in 1183. (Norwich, p.321.)

2. William ii wished to be buried in his Cathedral at Monreale but on his death in 1189 the Archbishop of Palermo ordered that his tomb be transferred to the new cathedral in Palermo. Eventually the King was buried at Monreale but the tomb remained at Palermo and has since disappeared. (Ibid.) This may explain the relative poverty of the tomb.

3. St. Louis died in 1270 while crusading in Tunisia, and his heart and other intestines are preserved in an altar in the Cathedral. (Ibid.)

4. This whole story is a concoction as both Williams died almost a century before St. Louis. It is perfectly true that William i lost all Sicilian possessions in North Africa, and no doubt the two stories were confused. He did not acquire his name 'the Bad' until two centuries after his death and probably owes it to the vilification of him in Hugo Falcandus, the principal chronicler of his reign. (Norwich, pp.210-12, 167-8.) William the Good certainly did not deserve his name which he owed to his youth, beauty and piety. (Ibid., p.355.)

5. The doors of the north porch were made by Barisanus of Trani in 1179 while the main doors were made by Bonnanus of Pisa in 1186. They are interesting as they are very early examples of Italian skill in an art that was a monopoly of the Byzantines. (Ibid., p.317.)

Page 69

1. It was about two hundred and forty years since William had built the cathedral at Monreale. (Ibid.)

2. This seems to be a mistake as the abbot of the new foundation at Monreale was automatically to have archiepiscopal rank. (Ibid., p.315.)

Page 70

1. This was a crushing mill formed by a circular millstone arranged to run in a circle round a vertical pivot and worked by a horse or a mule.

2. The Genoese had been harrying Catalan shipping, and in 1420 Alfonso of Aragon and his fleet were in these waters, subduing Sicily and Sardinia, where there had been trouble and preparing to attack Corsica which had been Genoese since 1360. (Chayter, loc.cit., pp.213-4.)

3. The bonetes were strips of canvas laced onto the bottom of a square sail to increase its area.

Page 73

1. The Salve Regina was probably written b Aimar, Bishop of Le Puy.

>   Salve, regina misericordiae,
>   vita, dulcedo et spes nostra, salve!
>   ad te clamamus exsules filii Evae,
>   ad te suspiramus gementes et flentes
>   in hac lacrimarum valle.
>   eia ergo, advocata nostra,
>   illos tuos misericordes oculos ad nos converte
>   et Iesum, benedictum fructum ventris tui,
>   nobis post hoc exsilium ostende,
>   o clemens, o pia,
>   o dulcis Maria.

(F.J. Raby, A History of Christian Latin Poetry, Oxford 1953, pp. 225-7.)

Page 74

1. St. Elias was one of five Egyptians martyred in 309 at Caesarea. Elias was their leader, and the account is given in St. Eusebius, who had been the pupil of St. Pamphilus who was martyred with them. (Butler, i, 350-51.)

Page 78

1. Gaston Phoebus 1331-1391 became count of Foix in 1343 under the regency of his mother. He became governor of Langedoc in 1380 and in 1381 he refused to surrender it to the Duc de Berri. In 1382 he was imprisoned on the grounds that he had poisoned his son, who had died in prison. He died in 1391. (L. Lalanne, Dictionnaire Historique de la France, Paris 1877.)

Page 81

1. Marbodus (Migne, Patrologiae Cursus Completus, Paris 1854, cols. 1737-78) makes no mention of serpentine. He does mention calssidoine (col.1744) which he says is yellow, and he makes no mention of it stopping blood. The Cambridge Version (Studer and Evans, Anglo-Norman Lapidaries, Paris 1924, pp.170-71) does mention red calssidoine. As regards the stone which is good for eye diseases (p.80, l. 28) the First French Version of Marbodus attributes this quality to the pearl. (Studer and Evans, loc.cit., p.64, l.875.)

2. St. Barnabas is one of the apostles, the companion of St. Paul on some of his journeys. He was probably stoned to death at Salamis before A.D.60. Nothing is known about him except what is in the New Testament. (Butler, ii, 522-24.)

Selective Glossary

References are to the first appearance only of the word.

A

a toudiz mais (11,22)	for evermore	apliquer (60,3)	to place
abesonher (50,26)	to attack	apointtemens (16,9)	agreements
abre (15,35)	wood, tree, mast	aqui (30,19)	there
		arrayzim (49,27)	grape
abscence (12,3)	absence	arreer (39,22)	to equip
absolle (10,30)	absolve	arque (58,37)	chest
acommiz (11,4)	committed	arx (27,7)	arch
acort (14,41)	agreement	asceste (19,29)	brutality ?
adober (60,39)	to repair	aspis (33,14)	snake
advis (12,16)	counsel	assayê (65,35)	tried
advocade (11,16)	advocate	aste (67,21)	shaft
affectuosament (11,8)	affectionately	aster (12,15)	to hurry
afferrê (58,35)	tied to	aryre (14,28)	to welcome
ahourê (13,21)	honoured	auder (19,41)	to dare
(ahourê, vendredi (13,21)	Good Friday)	auzelles (81,28)	incense burners shaped like birds?
ahurter (70,38)	to clash, collide	avantatjose (51,27)	advantageous, well sited
ajude (31,13)	help	avenir (16,26)	to happen
s'alegrer (20,5)	to rejoice	aviser (19,29)	to advise
aluigner (71,9)	to withdraw	d'ayssi en avant (12,7)	henceforth
amblê (29,8)	stolen		
ambolle (82,3)	phial	**B**	
amender (20,2)	to improve	baillié (20,8)	sent
aministrer (14,28)	to administer	barat (19,32)	fraud
		bars (29,7)	block, cradle
amoderê (12,18)	moderate	bas (35,29)	not (once)
amprês (21,11)	after	berge (39,20)	shield ?

bestiars	(30,17)	animals	chier	(11,34)	dear
bonetes	(70,41)	strips of canvas	chieuvre	(30,18)	goat
			cinte	(80,16)	strip
bonnement	(14,13)	well	cogiter	(20,1)	to think
boque	(63,40)	mouth	coller	(31,1)	to worship
bouter	(26,26)	to put	colombier	(33,33)	dovecot
brasse	(27,8)	arm-span, fathom	comanderie	(49,15)	commandery
brandon	(56,6)	candle	complir	(10,6)	to achieve
branqu	(26,8)	forked	contfisant	(11,32)	confident
bombarde	(57,4)	cannon	contribuir	(21,16)	to contribute
busche	(73,14)	wood	cordell	(26,8)	rope
			cort	(10,35)	court

C

			costumes	(32,18)	manners
caire	(69,3)	side	cousique	(13,42)	just as
calanger	(15,2)	to ask	coustatge	(70,17)	expense
calogeres	(33,12)	Greek monks	couvertement	(12,21)	secretly
			covercle	(68,4)	cover
camelot	(80,8)	wool cloth	cranallé	(51,18-19)	crenellated
camoix	(81,23)	chamoix	cugner	(70,9)	to strike
campane	(37,33)	bell	culhier	(70,5)	to pick
cassidoine	(80,22)	agate calcedony	custode	(80,20)	box
cene	(35,15)	supper	cuydier	(25,25)	to think
cervis	(27,5)	deer	cy desoubz	(11,24)	here below
chaut	(18,37)	it matters			

D

charrue	(56,14)	cart			
chaytive	(13,15)	wretched	dague	(29,6)	dagger
cheitivece	(21,26)	wretchedness	dalfin	(26,7)	dolphin
			davaller	(24,22)	to descend
cheveniere	(70,3)	hemp	dé	(67,32)	dice, square
cheviron	(67,43)	rafter, roof truss	debonayreté	(17,19)	kindness

decens	(12,19)	suitable	docturer	(31,2)	learned
decheoir	(64,17)	to fall down	domatge	(25,26)	harm
decoller	(34,13)	to behead	domicille	(17,34)	home
deffallimens	(15,22)	fault	dores en avant	(19,5)	from now on
defice	(25,2)	built ?	duites	(17,22)	endured ?
demontant	(24,22)	ascent			
dementies que	(19,39)	while		E	
demeure	(17,34)	dwelling	egeusser	(13,26)	to grant
denuncier	(12,32)	to mention	emprés	(13,31)	after
deputer	(14,20)	to designate	enchaux	(50,33)	pursuit
derrier, derrenier	(15,33)	last	encluge	(37,8)	anvil
			endresser	(22,25-26)	to instruct
desaise	(66,10)	discomfort	enfermerie	(52,12)	infirmary
descaint	(58,9)	extinguished	enfermeté	(16,31)	sickness
descharrier	(71,5)	to descend	enluminer	(46,29)	to give sight to
descendre	(40,15)	to take down			
deschaux	(39,21)	shoeless	enmurré	(23,24)	surrounded by walls
desconsollé	(21,3-4)	afflicted			
desemparer	(59,19)	to abandon	enseignemens	(10,23)	instruction
despasti	(51,28)	demolished	entente	(11,1)	intention
despensse	(21,16)	expense	ensequent	(39,34)	in order
desplee	(36,21)	unfurled	enteriner	(11,5)	to achieve
despleisance	(14,8)	displeasure	entiegrement	(11,36)	entirely
despuller	(26,18)	to pull off, strip	entriquade	(31,5)	intricate
			eques	(27,5)	mares
dessendue	(57,11)	descent	esbaïz	(26,17)	dismayed
desye	(55,19)	already	escanty	(58,9)	extinguished
devezint	(30,6)	separating	escarlate	(53,17)	scarlet
disposer	(41,23)	to assemble	eschamper	(59,35)	to escape, to flow
disenys	(69,22)	falling into ruins, disunited			
			eschessement	(38,1)	scarcity

eschelle	(30, 23)	strait	forment	(11, 14)	strongly
eschine	(63, 17)	spine, ridge	foyal	(11, 9)	vassal
eschirpe	(47, 26)	sash	fraccion	(40, 18)	breaking
eschiver	(22, 5)	to escape, shun	fulgre	(57, 22)	lightning
esleuz	(15, 40)	elect	fuste	(28, 19)	mast, ship, pirate galley
escondre	(37, 9)	to hide			

G

escripture	(11, 21)	writing			
esmovoir	(12, 15)	to excite	gaing	(21, 1)	gain
espandre	(17, 19)	to spread	ganivet	(81, 25)	scimitar, small knife
espargnier	(16, 19)	to spare	giet	(28, 24)	throw (measure of distance)
espaventé	(26, 19)	frightened			
esperance	(12, 8)	hope	glorie	(10, 36)	glory
estancher	(21, 33)	to take in	gracie	(22, 38)	grace
estoy	(67, 43)	coffret	greppe	(36, 36)	crib
estremar	(59, 22)	to leave	greyne	(53, 17)	seed
eure	(17, 28)	hour, luck	grief	(11, 3)	serious, painful
euvres	(11, 19)	works	grin	(81, 25)	chaplet
evangelis	(16, 16)	gospels	guatz	(33, 13)	cats
exident	(73, 19)	chance, mis-chance	guayte	(55, 4)	watch
			gueredon	(12, 7)	reward
expouser	(11, 5)	to expose	gueyne	(36, 3)	sheath
eyde	(22, 14)	help			
expressemant	(19, 26-7)	deliberately			

H

haut en couverte	(71, 6)	on deck	

F

faisable	(14, 37)	possible	haytiez	(11, 18)	gay
farger	(37, 9)	to forge	heretier	(11, 2)	heir
faude	(38, 16)	pouch	hermiten	(31, 18)	hermit
fermail	(81, 24)	lock, bolt	Hetenesiens	(31, 9)	Athenians
fielx	(35, 7)	faithful	houstinité	(12, 20)	perseverance
fluvi	(37, 43)	river	huche	(80, 5)	chest
fortune	(56, 39)	storm	huellz	(19, 41)	eyes

	I		marour	(61,44)	gale? swell?
indie	(80,11)	blue cloth	marturizé	(34,13)	martyred
iniquité	(16,28)	iniquity	marvezie	(71,30)	malmsey
institui	(13,31)	instituted	memento	(12,30)	memory
	J		menchief	(26,16)	harm
			mendre	(33,26)	less
jassoit que	(57,32)	although	merchande	(34,5)	commercial
joye	(80,5)	precious gift, jewel	mercier	(12,5)	to thank
			mereville	(19,37)	amazed
	L		meryne	(64,3)	shore
lairon	(15,35)	robber	mescler	(39,14)	to mix
landier	(27,15)	fire-dog	mescreans	(29,5)	wicked, infidel
lapareux	(25,32)	young rabbits	mesolle	(70,4)	substance, syrup
lazer	(38,10)	beggar			
lengors	(17,22)	sorrows	messongiers	(14,8)	messengers
lessier	(10,8)	to leave	meyns de	(27,9)	unless by
levadisse	(78,21-2)	drawbridge	miencolie	(14,10)	melancholy
leyne	(50,8)	wool	miques	(42,4)	crumbs
lieupart	(36,22)	leopard	moiller	(31,4)	wife
liez	(12,34)	joyful	montance	(28,24)	height
linatge	(22,9)	race	mot	(23,30)	much, very
lombas	(19,1)	wolf cubs	Mouros	(34,21)	Moors
louvant	(58,12)	praising	murrete	(28,26)	wall
luxure	(39,13)	luxury	muser and musier	(46,21) (46,22)	to hide
lyn	(63,9)	flax	musique	(64,9)	mosaic
	M		musquet	(80,14)	musk
magnanimo	(49,35-6)	great-hearted	myres	(52,11)	doctors
machacollé	(23,25)	with machicolation			
maquanit	(31,6)	workman			
marches	(72,25)	land			

N			partus	(41,23)	opening	
navili	(73,10)	ship	pas	(15,38)	threshold	
necligent	(21,22)	neglectful	pater nostres	(80,13)	rosary	
nef	(24,15)	snow	pecheresses	(10,33)	female sinners	
nessen	(28,24)	except	per	(31,3)	equal	
noise	(14,42)	quarrel	perprise	(28,31)	domain, area	
nomp	(10,5)	name	pestres	(11,10)	priests	
notiffiquer	(10,28)	to notify	pignaillez	(81,7)	striped	
notoire	(17,11)	well known	pipe	(70,43)	barrel	
O			poissant	(15,28)	powerful	
obly, en	(13,16)	forgotten	porfedo	(67,24)	porphyry	
oïr	(12,6)	to hear	porge	(79,7)	porch	
omaing	(22,9)	human	port	(24,22)	col, pass	
ondrances	(68,15)	honours	pourteure	(23,27)	dress	
ordenances	(10,8)	orders	poy	(11,21)	little	
orendroit	(15,27)	straightaway	preguiere	(31,27)	prayer	
orguines	(25,8)	organs	prendre place en le mer	(72,11)	stand out to sea	
ortolen	(41,21)	gardner	primevere	(66,35)	spring	
ossire	(46,13)	to kill	priont	(72,13)	far	
ourdenté	(11,25)	arranged	prodomie	(11,32)	worth	
articles ourdentés	(11,25)	indentures	prosine	(19,25)	neighbour	
ouster	(59,36)	to remove	proufiter	(19,20)	to profit	
oustour	(69,41)	falcon	prousomoyer	(57,22)	to presume	
P			pueple	(10,9)	people	
palenc	(79,5)	fence	puis d'enfer	(21,2)	depths of hell	
panell	(61,32)	pennon	puy	(51,25)	hill	
parells	(81,20)	pairs	**Q**			
paroy	(68,44)	wall	quaire	(28,18)	square	
de partide ou	(14,30)	on their side	querre	(14,33)	to seek	
partiment	(16,12)	departure	quite	(61,26)	free from	

	R		semener	(22,4)	to arouse
rachater	(10,33)	to redeem	serpentines	(81,1)	serpentine
redoubté	(10,29)	respected	siere	(19,41)	wax?
regalice	(65,39)	liquorice	sipres	(81,26)	cypress wood
regiment	(14,22)	control	siri	(72,39)	candle
rescansser	(49,11)	to rest	solempniaumat	(25,7)	solemnly
resemus	(34,17-18)	redeemed	solle	(67,41)	ground
resestir	(60,26)	to re-establish	soubde	(12,17)	sudden
resplendens	(20,11-12)	resplendent	souffisans	(14,12)	able, worthy
reteur	(12,23)	rector	soumiers	(39,19)	pack horses
reveller	(66,8)	to waken	souparé	(18,16)	separated
robin	(81,24)	ruby	sourdre	(12,11)	to arise
rodder, radder	(59,25)	to roam	stele	(46,7)	star
rouberie	(38,4)	robbery	suzaire	(23,12)	shroud
rozee	(18,14)	dew		T	
	S		table	(26,13)	plank
saillant	(26,6)	coming out of	taillant	(32,19)	disposition
			taller	(79,3)	to cut
sabatier	(55,36)	cobbler	talu	(78,17)	stone facing of the inner side of the moat
sauvoizines	(27,24)	wild animals			
savance	(56,20)	knowledge			
secourre	(14,29)	to help	tarde	(21,39)	delay
see	(44,13)	saw	targe	(48,4)	shield
seer	(44,12)	to saw	targe de gorge	(81,31)	neck-cloth
seignal	(12,3)	proof	tele	(80,10)	cloth
segont	(19,23)	second	teneur	(11,27)	meaning
sequont	(34,23)	according to	terren	(17,25)	earthly
semblance	(17,14)	resemblance	test	(52,21)	head
sempmence	(12,26)	week	testu	(39,17)	head
senache	(45,20)	cenacle	tigneux	(20,19)	knave
serement	(10,13)	oath	tinel	(79,7)	hall

tiriaque	(47,5)	theriac
toille	(39,18)	cloth
tournejant	(72,19)	tacking
tracion	(21,25)	treason
tracté	(33,19)	plotted
tramettre	(31,11)	to send
translater	(46,11)	to translate
treitz d'arbalestre	(25,30)	crossbow shots
trenquer	(57,9)	to cut
treuvatge	(35,25)	tribute
treves	(70,25)	truce
tribailler	(58,34)	to torment
triet de pierre	(28,17)	stone's throw
trueill	(70,6)	crushing mill
turpe	(20,24)	mole
tymon	(72,34)	helm

V

vaill	(34,41)	valley
vehue	(58,19)	sight
vennre	(35,6)	to come
vespre	(33,17)	evening
vetade	(80,11)	striped
vitailles	(38,2)	food
voulor	(11,20)	desire
vulguelmant	(31,7)	commonly
vuyt	(66,11)	empty

Y

a la yssue	(36,28)	on coming out

Index of Proper Names

A

Abibon, the son of Gamaliel (45,5)
Adam, the first man (17,15)
Adriane, Ariadne, the daughter of Minos (31,13)
Alarebs, Arabs, formed by the addition of the Arabic definite article which had not been understood (39,16)

B

Baffomet, Mahomet (34,22)
Bonelles Gonsalvo de, one of the squires of the seigneur de Caumont (16,11)
Buquere Michel, owner of the ship, on which the seigneur de Caumont returned from Palermo (66,30)

C

Caramanh, the Prince of Caramania (50,18)
Catalains, the Catalans (70,25)
Caumont Arnaut de, uncle of the seigneur de Caumont (14,20)
Caumont seigneur de, Nompar the pilgrim (10,2)
Caumont Nompar de, the elder son and heir of the seigneur de Caumont (13,22)
Caumont femme du seigneur de Caumont, an unidentified lady (11,34)
Caumont pere du seigneur de Caumont, Guillaume Raimond, recently dead (10,29-30)
Causee Guassion de le, one of the squires of the seigneur de Caumont (17,4)
Cayphe, Caiaphas, the high priest of the Jews (44,23)
Chastel Bertran, one of the squires of the seigneur de Caumont (16,11)
Chaux Sancho de, Sancho d'Echauz, a Navarrese knight (32,14)
Chaux Jehan de, the vicomte de Vaiguier, brother of Sancho (32,15)
Cleophas, a disciple of Christ (40,20)
Colossensses, the people of Colossus in Phrygia (51,26)
Costantin, Constantine i, Emperor (324-337) (40,3-4)
Creissi, possibly a title of Mahommet i, the Ottoman Sultan of the time (51,2)

D

David, King David (37,39)
Dedelus, Daedalus, the mythological craftsman (31,6)

E

Egeu, Aegeus, King of Athens (31,11)
Endrogeux, Androgeos, son of Minos (31,10)
Emperiere, the wife of the Emperor, Frederick ii, but there is no evidence as to which wife (Constance of Aragon, Yolanda of Jerusalem and Isabella of England) it was supposed to be (64,24)

F

Febus, Gaston iii, Count of Foix (78,33)
Fedric, Frederick ii (64,7)
Ferre Ramon, co-owner of the pilgrim ship to Jaffa (25,20)
Ferrier Fransois, as above (25,20)
Ferriol Jean, the scribe (80,3-4)
Foiz conte de, Jean de Grailly (14,17-18)

G

Gamaliel, disciple of Christ (45,4)
Gaubert Nandonet, one of the squires of the seigneur de Caumont (17,4)
Genevois, the Genoans (29,8)
Guilhem, William i of Sicily (67,5)
Guilhem, William ii of Sicily (68,12)

H

Hechilles, Achilles (49,36)
Heleyne, Helen, wife of Menelaus (30,9)
Helie, the prophet Elias (Elijah) (45,32)
Herminis, Armenenians (37,14)
Herodes, Herod (37,2)
Hetenesiens, Athenians (31,9)

I

Indiens, the Abyssinian christians (37,25)
Ignocens, the Innocents slaughtered by Herod (37,2)

J

Jacobins, Jacobite christians (monophysite Copts) (37,27)
Jeson, Jason, leader of the Argonauts (50,9)
Josep d'Arimacias, Joseph of Arimathea (13,21-22)
Judas, Judas Iscariot (45,1)
Juifs (judiens), the Jews (37,10)
Juno, the Roman goddess (30,5)
Jupiter, the principal Roman god (30,35)

L

Lauriole Jehan de, one of the squires of the seigneur de Caumont (17,5)
Lazar, the poor man in the parable (42,5)
Lazer (le), Lazarus, brother of Mary and Martha (38,10)
Loth, Lot (47,21)

M

Malcus, Malchus, the servant of Caiaphas (43,14)
Mauvés riche, the rich man of the parable (42,4)
Menelaus, King of Sparta (30,8)

Minotaur, Cretan monster, half man, half bull (31,5)
Minus, King Minos of Crete (31,2)
Morous, Mourous, the Arabs (34,21; 34,22)
Mote Archambaud de le, one of the squires of the seigneur de Caumont (17,5)

N

Nicodemus, Nicodemus, follower of Christ (13,22)

P

Paris, Paris the son of Priam (30,10)
Pilat, Pontius Pilate (13,23)

R

Rachel, Rachel the wife of Jacob (46,15)
Rois, les trois, the Magi, Caspar, Melchior and Balthazar (46,8)

S

Saint Andrief, Saint Andrew (33,37)
Saint Anthoni, Saint Anthony (52,2)
Saint Barnabé, Saint Barnabas (81,16)
Saint Estassi, Saint Eustace (30,7-8)
Saint Estienne, Saint Stephen (42,28)
Saint George, Saint George (11,7)
Saint Hellie, Saint Elias (74,32)
Saint Helm, Saint Elmo (61,32)
Saint Jacques, Saint James (43,16)
Saint Jacque le mineur, Saint James the less (44,3)
Saint Jehan, Saint John (29,9)
Saint Jehan Babtiste, Saint John the Baptist (37,10)
Saint Jeronime, Saint Jerome (46,10)
Saint Jehachin, Saint Joachim (38,39)
Saint Lion, Saint Leo (55,36)
Saint Lorens, Saint Lawrence (50,20)
Saint Loys, Saint Louis (68,18)
Saint Marssal, Saint Martial (34,7)
Saint Mathias, Saint Matthew (45,1)
Saint Nicolas, Saint Nicholas (32,35)
Saint Paul, Saint Paul (33,17)
Saint Pierre, Saint Peter (33,17)
Saint Silvestre, Saint Silvesteri, Pope (40,3)
Saint Thomas, Saint Thomas (43,18)
Sainte Anne, Saint Anne (42,15)
Sainte Cathelline, Saint Catherine (52,31)
Sainte Coullomme Arnout de, Béarnese knight living in Sicily (64,36)
Sainte Collome Arnaut Guillem de, son of the above (69,38-39)
Sainte Helizabet, Saint Elizabeth (37,9)
Sainte Hellene, Saint Helena (40,4)

Sainte Heuffemie, Saint Euphemia   (49,18-19)
Sainte Lussie, Saint Lucy   (29,2)
Sainte Marie Magdalene, Mary Magdalene   (15,34)
Salungnac Clement de, one of the squires of the seigneur de Caumont   (17,6)
Salamon, Solomon (45,13)
Samuel, Samuel the prophet   (40,22)
Saturnus, Saturn, father of Jupiter   (30,35)
Simeon, Simon who took Jesus in his arms   (42,26)
Simeon le Sirenen, Simon the Cyrenean   (42,9)

T

Tabita, Tabitha, the servant of the apostles   (33,35)
Taris Jehan de, one of the squires of the seigneur de Caumont   (17,5-6)
Tezeu, Theseus, King of Athens (31,11)
Tozeux Galhardet de, one of the squires of the seigneur de Caumont   (14,21)
Turcx, the Turks, probably the Ottomans   (32,25)

V

Venessiens, the Venetians   (30,32)
Venus, Venus the Roman goddess   (30,13)

Y

Ysaye, Isaiah the prophet   (44,12)

Z

Zacharie, Zacharias, one of the prophets   (44,6)
Zacharie, Zacharias, the father of John the Baptist   (37,6)

Index of Place Names*

A

Agen: the capital of the Agenais (23,5)
Agenois: Agenais, a region of south-western France (14,24)
Aguoste: Augusta, a town and castle in eastern Sicily (29,19)
Alchedemar: Haceldama, the field reputedly bought with the thirty pieces of silver on Mount Sion (44,16)
Alcudie: Alcudia, a small port on the north coast of Majorca (25,27)
Alexandrie: Alexandria, the chief port of Egypt (50,21)
Antioche, la petite: medieval Antiochetta, ancient Antioch of Cragus in southern Turkey (50,15)
Aquaram, Caram: Karavi, desert island near the coast of Morea (54,13 and 12)
Arabie, Arabe: Arabia, the modern Jordan (39,15)
Arragoce: Ragusa in Sicily (62,34)
Arcepellec: the Aegean sea (30,20)
As: a barren rock near Cythera (30,19)
Asfa: Arfa near the border between Spain and Andorra (76,22)
Attenes: Athens (31,11)
Avinhonet: Avignonet, a small town in Haute-Garonne (23,14)
Ax en Savartes: Ax les Thermes, a small town in Ariège. The castle has long been ruined (24,11)

B

Babiloyne: Cairo (33,25)
Baffa: Paphos, a town on the west coast of Cyprus (33,7)
Bagua: Baga, a small town in Spanish Cerdagne (24,20)
Balceran: Balsereny, a Catalonian village on the Llobregat (24,26)
Barberie: north Africa (25,25)
Barcellone: Barcelona (23,22)
Bastida: la Bastide de Serou in Ariège (77,18)
Bastide: a castle near the Spanish-Andorrean border (76,29)
Bazadês: a region of Guyenne near the Agenais (14,24)
Béarn: a region of France in the western Pyrenees 64,35)
Bendique: a tower on the Sicilian coast between Capo Passaro and Syracuse (28,13-14)
Berbeguieres: a castle in Dordogne (10,27)
Berque: Berga, a Catalonian town (24,24)
Betanie: Bethany, a town in Palestine (38,8)
Betanie le segonde: where Christ was baptised on the Jordan (47,16)
Bellem: Bethlehem (36,32)
Biguorre: Bigorre, a Pyrenean region of France bordering on Aragon (78,11)

---

* Some identifications remain doubtful.

Bouque deffar: Boca de Faro, the Straits of Messina (61,10)
Boutes port de: Porto Botte on the south-west coast of Sardinia (26,38)
Buffavent: Buffavento, a mountain village and castle near Kyrenia (49,33)

C

Cabre: Skhiza, a small island near Sapientza (54,28)
Cacomo: Kekov off the south coast of Turkey (32,31)
Caille: Cagliari, capital of Sardinia (27,12)
Caille Port de lez: probably Porto Kagio near Cape Matapan (30,2)
Calabrie: Calabria (29,22)
Calassivete: Calascibetta, a small town in Sicily (63,1)
Calataboutero: Caltavuturo, the ruined Saracen fortress Kalat Abi Thaur, captured by Roger i (63,34)
Calatagironne: Caltagirone, a town in Sicily (62,38)
Calemes: a castle in Ariège (24,8)
Caloquirane: either Serna or Tria Nisia in the Sporades (53,7)
Calus: Caslus, a castle in Catalonia (76,1)
Cambrils: a castle in Catalonia (76,8)
Candera: Kantara in north-eastern Cyprus (49,31)
Candie: Crete (30,32)
Candie: Heraklion (31,15)
Canelles: castle in Catalonia (76,17)
Canillo: a village in Andorra (76,32)
Capharneum: Caperneum in Palestine (37,7)
Capoupasser: Capo Passaro, the southernmost point of Sicily (28,9)
Cappoguailh: Kavo Gallo (Cape Akritas) in Morea (54,27)
Caram: v. Aquaram
Carbonayre: Capo Carbonara in Sardinia (74,15)
Cardone: Cardona, a fourteenth century town in Catalonia. Nearby is the Montana de Sal, 260 feet high, of pure rock salt (76,3)
Carol: Latour de Carol a castle on the Spanish-French border (24,14)
Carpas: Carpasia a small town on the north coast of Cyprus (49,30)
Carssin: Quercy, a province of France (23,7)
Caseres: Cazeres in the Landes (79,17)
Casserras: Caserras a village in Catalonia (24,25)
Castrojohan: Castro Giovanni, Enna in Sicily. The castle is perhaps La Cittadella, which had been rebuilt by King Manfred (63,14)
Castroy Anuy: a district in Sicily (63,4)
Cataloigne: Catalonia (23,22)
Cathanie, Catanie: Catania in Sicily (58,25)
Caumont: town and castle on the Garonne near Marmande (10,2)
Caumont: village in Ariège (77,25)
Cedron: brook near Jerusalem (43,2)
Cerdagne: v. Sardaigne
Cervellon: a village in Catalonia (75,23)
Cessile: Sicily (27,22)
Chaque: Sciacca on the south coast of Sicily (28,2)

Chasteau Cullier: Castelculier in Lot et Garonne (17,10-11)
Chasteau de Fer et d'Au: a castle on the south coast of Turkey, opposite Rhodes (51,7)
Chasteau Franc: a castle near Famagusta (49,8)
Chasteau Guallin: Castellvell y Vilar, a village in Catalonia (24,29)
Chasteau Geleux: Castel-jaloux in Lot et Garonne (79,22)
Chasteau Hemaux: Kubebeh in Palestine (40,17)
Chasteau dez Lombars: a castle at Enna (63,19)
Chasteau Navarrês: a castle behind Navarino, the modern Pylos, so called because of the Navarrese mercenaries who settled there in 1381 (55,28)
Chasteau Raupa guolf de: Gulf of Lakonia (30,6)
Chasteau Rog: Castelrosso on the south coast of Turkey (32,28)
Chasteau Sarrazin: Castelsarrasin in Tarn et Garonne (23,8)
Chastelbon: Castelbo in Catalonia (76,14)
Chastel Neuf, Chastelnuef: Castelnau in Dordogne (10,2)
Chastel Nuef: Castelnau in Ariège (77,19)
Chastel Nuef Darri: Castelnaudary (23,16)
Chatsse: a town in central Sicily (62,39)
Cheffallenie: Cephalonia (29,23)
Cherement: Chiaramonte in Sicily (62,37)
Cherines: Kyrenia on the north coast of Cyprus (49,34)
Chicle: Scicli, a town on the south coast of Sicily (28,7)
Chipre: Cyprus (33,6)
Coffres: desert islands in the Aegean (53,10)
Coll Beton: Collbeto, a village in Catalonia (25,9)
Coll de Yau: a mountain in Spanish Cerdagne (24,21)
Colquos: an island near Tarsus (50,8)
Comenge: Comminges, a district in the French Pyrenees (77,22)
Corron, Courron: Coron or Kouroni in the Morea (29,31)
Costantinoble: Constantinople or Istanbul (69,31)
Crestiane: Khristiana, islets in the Aegean south of Thera (53,33)
Cret: Crete (30,33)
Cret guolf de: Sea of Crete (30,34)
Crieu: Krio or Iskandil, a headland on the west coast of Turkey (52,39)
Ciutat: Castellciutat in Catalonia (76,25)
Cuille: possibly Cassibile, a small town in eastern Sicily (28,12)

D

Damiate: Damietta, port in Egypt (50,22)
Das: a village in Spanish Cerdagne (24,19)
Deux: a barren rock near Cythera (30,19)
Durffort: Duhort, a village in Landes (79,13)

E

Endorre: Andorra (76,27)
Entioche: Antioch in Syria (50,6)
Enquant: Encamp, a village in Andorra (76,32)

Escampon: Estampon, a river in Landes (79,21)
Escandeleur: Candeloro on the south coast of Turkey, modern Alanya (50,17)
Escandeye: Dia, an island near Heraklion (31,17)
Eschallete: Scaletta on the Straits of Messina, home of the Princes of Scaletta (61,3)
Esclafena: Sclafani, a castle in northern Sicily (63,35)
Escuells de saint Paul: islets off Cape Kara on the coast of Turkey (32,1) Also Cape Kara itself (52,36)
Esquelh Provenssal: Adasi, island off the south coast of Turkey (50,11)
Escure: Lescure in Ariège (77,21)
Esmarencs: Merens in Ariège (77,4)
Espacaforno: Spacaforno, a castle near Modica in Sicily (62,25)
Esparreguieres: Esparraguera in Catalonia (25,10)
Espital Sainte Suzanne: l'Hospitalet, a village on the French-Spanish border (77,1)
Estampaig: Stampace, the western district of Cagliari (27,19)
Estampaleye: Astipalaia in the Aegean (53,12)

F

Falconayre: Falkonera, an island in the Aegean near Morea (54,11)
Famagoste: Famagusta in Cyprus (49,1)
Foiz: town and castle, now ruined, of Foix (23,18)
Fonhane: Favognana, island off the west coast of Sicily (27,26)
Fournelhs: Fornells, castle on the north coast of Minorca (75,13)

G

Galilee: on the northern summit of the Mount of Olives (35,13)
Gave: river in southern France (78,19)
Ger: town in Pyrênées Atlantiques (78,13)
Gergent: Agrigento on the southern coast of Sicily (28,3)
Gericho: v. Jerico
Gomorre: Gomorrah (39,12)
Grece: Greece (32,3)
Grizolles: small town in Tarn et Garonne (23,11)
Guarone: Garonne (77,31)
Guascoigne, Guasconhe: Gascony (14,24)
Guavata: Cape Gata on the south coast of Cyprus (33,11)
Guolizano: probably Collesano, castle and town in northern Sicily (65,26)
Guyeine: Guyenne (34,8)

H

Hastilimurre: castle and town in southern Turkey, modern Anamur (50,14)
Hermine: Armenia (50,3)
Hortês: Orthez. All that survives of the castle is the Tour de Moncade (79,1)

I

Intimil: Antimilos in the Aegean (54,8)

J

Japha: Jaffa (33,16)
Jassenton: Zakinthos (Zante) (29,24)
Jerico (10,14)
Jherusalem: Jerusalem (10,3)
Jourdeyn, Jourdain: the river of Jordan (10,3)
Jonx port de: Navarino, now Pylos (55,8)
Josaphat vaill de: a valley in Jerusalem (34,41)
Judee: Judea (36,31)

L

Lac: Lacq, village near Orthez (78,35)
Lane de Boc: Languedoc (78,6)
Lanemesan: Lannemezan, village in Hautes Pyrénées (78,7)
Languedoc (23,10)
Languo: Kos (52,42)
Lauregués: Lauragais, region near Castelnaudary (23,15)
Lazenello: castle in northern Sicily, probably Isnello (65,28)
Lebarinte, Nabarinte: the Labyrinth in Crete where the Minotaur lived (31,7)
Lescar: town near Pau (78,34)
Leonde: v. Buffalvent (49,32)
Levetique guolf de: part of the Gulf of Lakonia (30,6)
Lidie: Lydda in Palestine (34,11)
Lieuquate: Licata, town on the south coast of Sicily (28,4)
Lion guolf de: Gulf of Lions (26,3)
Liuyan: castle in Catalonia (76,13)
Lobregat: Llobregat, river in Catalonia (25,13)
Lodose: Douze, a river in Landes (79,20)
Loparto: an abbey near Monreale (69,36)
Lordat: castle near Tarascon, now destroyed (77,12)
Lou: Avqo or Ovo, an islet in the Aegean (30,17)
Lymotges: Limoges (34,8)

M

Maleie, Maleye: v. Matapain
Malhorque, Mallorque: Majorca (25,26)
Mal Voysin: Mauvezin, district in Hautes Pyrénées (78,9)
Marcee: perhaps Marzamemi near Capo Passaro in Sicily (28,10)
Marempne, Marepne: Marettimo off the west coast of Sicily (27,23)
Marguon: Amorgos in the Aegean (53,22)
Marquet: possibly Castell Maniace at Syracuse, occupying the southern end of the island (28,26)
Marsaille, Marsalle: Marsala, a town on the west coast of Sicily (27,34)
Marssan: district round Mont de Marsan (79,14)
Masieres: Mazères in Ariège (23,23)

Matapain: Cape Tainaron in Morea (30,1)
Matzare: Mazara, a town on the west coast of Sicily (28,1)
Maynes: Mani in Morea (54,21)
Menorque: Minorca (26,1)
Menreze: Manresa in Catalonia (24,28)
Mer Morte: the Dead Sea (39,13)
Mertorell: Martorell in Catalonia (25,11)
Messine: Messina in Sicily (58,26)
Meyane: the middle group of islands in the Ciclades (30,24)
Meque: Mecca (34,22)
Miramont: a village in Haute Garonne (77,30)
Mirree: Myra, an ancient city in southern Turkey (32,35)
Modique: Modica, a town in south-eastern Sicily (62,32)
Modon: Modon or Methoni in Morea (29,28)
Moissac: a town in Tarn et Garonne (23,7)
Molin de Rech: Molins de Rey, a small town near Barcelona (25,12)
Molle: the castle, now ruined, on the hill of Mola on the Straits of Messina (61,2)
Montserrat: v. Nostre Dame
Mon Gallart: Mongailhard, a village in Ariège (24,6)
Mont de Calvaire: Mount Calvary at Jerusalem (40,33)
Mont d'Ollivet: Mount of Olives at Jerusalem (35,8)
Montession: Mount Sion at Jerusalem (35,15)
Mont Ferrer: a castle in Spanish Cerdagne (76,23)
Mon Joy: Montjoie, a village near Saint Girons in Ariège (77,23)
Monto Pelegrino: an isolated rock west of Palermo (71,34-35)
Mont Real: Monreale, town and abbey near Palermo (67,5)
Mores: probably Mora, a village near Nicosia (49,12)
Moureye, Mouree: Morea (29,29)
My jour: the southern group of islands in the Ciclades (30,25)

N

Namphi: probably Anidhos in the Aegean (53,19)
Napols: Naples (66,28)
Napolle: a district of Cagliari, possibly the modern Marina (27,17)
Narago: Nargo, a castle in Catalonia (76,18)
Nebusayn: a small region in southern France (78,1)
Nicossie: Nicosia, the capital of Cyprus (49,13)
Nitzere: Nisiros in the Dodecanese (53,4)
Nixie: Naxos (53,18)
Nostre Dame d'Allem: part of Castelsarrasin (23,8-9)
Nostre Dame de Finibus terre: Finisterre in Galicia (10,22)
Nostre Dame de Monserrat: the abbey at Montserrat (24,30)
Nuye: a desert island in the Aegean near Morea (54,10)
Nyeu: Ios in the Aegean (53,26)
Nyl: Melos in the Aegean (54,3)

Orguenhe: Organa in Catalonia (76,19)
Ormonyl: a desert island in the Aegean (54,9)
Ospital de Sainte Suzanne: v. Espital
Ostegue: Ustica, an island in the Tyrrhenian Sea (72,1)

P

Palermo: Palermo (64,2)
Palmesolz: San Antioco, an island off the south-west coast of Sardinia (27,3)
Pals, Port de: Porto Palo, a small village at Capo Passaro (28,11)
Pamies: Pamiers (23,29)
Panaye: Kimolos in the Aegean (54,4)
Pantanallee: possibly Pantelleria (27,29)
Pau (78,15)
Perles: Perlas, a village in Catalonia (76,11)
Philermo: a mountain near the town of Rhodes (51,25)
Pierregour: Périgord (14,24)
Pimorent: Puymorens on the French-Spanish frontier (24,15)
Pintodatol: castle in Calabria on the Straits of Messina (61,5)
Pipi: Ofidhousa in the Aegean (53,16)
Piscopeie: Tilos in the Dodecanese (31,30)
Plane: probably Yianisadhes off the coast of Crete (31,21)
Poentis: Pointis, a village in Haute Garonne (77,29)
Poleno: a strong castle in northern Sicily, probably Pollina (65,43)
Poliquandron: Poliaigos in the Ciclades (54,1)
Pollissi: Pollizzi, an important, medieval town in northern Sicily (63,23)
Polymo: an island in the Aegean (54,2)
Port Sainte Marie: a village on the Garonne near Agen (23,3)
Poussaillo: Pozzalo, castle on the south coast of Sicily near Capo Passaro (28,8)
Pratz: Prat, a village in Ariège (27,28)
Predent: probably Proti off the west coast of Morea (56,34)
Puich Sardain: Puigcerda, capital of Spanish Cerdagne (24,18)
Pujol: Pigols, castle in Catalonia (76,18)
Puyou: Pujo-le-plan near Mont de Marsan (79,18)

Q

Quirane: either Serna or Tria Nisia, desert islands in the Sporades (53,7)
Qurc: possibly Corycus on the south coast of Turkey (50,10)

R

Ramès: Rama in Palestine (34,5)
Rejols: Reggio in Calabria (61,6)
Ressequaram: Capo Scaramia on the south coast of Sicily (28,6)
Riumont: Rimont in Ariège (77,20)
Rodes, Rodez: Rhodes (32,4)
Roquaffort: Roquefort, a village in Landes (79,19)
Roquete: a castle in Catalonia (76,17)

S

Sachim: a town in southern Turkey, probably modern Silifke (50,13)
Sadarcet: Cadarcet in Ariège (77,17)
Saint Andrief: Cape Saint Andreas, the easternmost point of Cyprus (49,29)
Saint Andrieu: San Andres de la Barca, a village near Barcelona (25,15)
Saint Angel: Cape Malea in the Morea (30,4)
Saint Gausens: Saint Gaudens (78,2)
Saint George: a small port on the north coast of Sicily (71,33)
Saint Hellie: a church near Cagliari, probably at Capo Sant'Elia (74,32)
Saint Hellarion: Saint Hilarion, a strong castle in the mountains of Cyprus (50,1)
Saint Jacques de Compostelle: Santiago in Galicia (10,21)
Saint Jehachim: a monastery in the desert near the Jordan (38,39)
Saint Jehan: site of the first church (39,5)
Saint Jolyon: Santa Julia de Loria in Andorra (76,29)
Saint Leser: Saint Lizier in Ariège (77,24)
Saint Martin-Lalande: a village in Aude (23,17)
Saint Nicholas de Carqui: Chalki near Rhodes (31,25-26)
Saint Pierre: an island off Cape Gelidonya (33,3)
Saint Pierre: an island off the south-west coast of Sardinia (26,30)
Saint Pierre de Breze: Abrera, a village in Catalonia (75,26)
Saint Pierre d'Our: Sampedor, a village in Catalonia (24,27)
Saint Piphani: Cape Arnauti, the westernmost cape of Cyprus (33,5)
Sainte Marie de Carbonaire: Santa Maria di Buonaria, a famous church between Cagliari and Capo Sant'Elia filled with offerings by sailors (27,21)
Salat: a small river in the Pyrenees (77,26)
Santo Mauro: hamlet in northern Sicily (65,43)
Sapience: Sapientza, an island off the south-west of Morea (29,29)
Sardaigne: Cerdagne, a Pyrenean region divided between France and Spain (24,17)
Sardeigne: Sardinia (27,1)
Saregosse: Syracuse (28,15)
Satallie: Antalya, town and gulf in southern Turkey (51,1)
Saut de Noalhas: Sault de Navailles, village in Pyrénées Atlantiques (79,11)
Scarpento: Karpathos, island near Rhodes (31,23)
Segor: Zoar, town near the Dead Sea, to which Lot fled from Sodom (47,21)
Sequillo: Anticythera (Cerigotto) between Cythera and Crete (30,27)
Semies: Simi between Rhodes and Turkey (31,32)
Semy: v. Servo
Sentis: a village in Spanish Cerdagne (76,21)
Senturion: Thera or Santorini in the Ciclades (53,28)
Serffine: probably Serifos in the Aegean (54,6)
Seridoine: Gelidonya, cape and island in southern Turkey (33,2)
Servo or Semy: possibly Elafanisos in the Gulf of Lakonia (54,19 and 30,7)
Seticaps: probably Cape Kurtoglu in Turkey (32,24)

Setvilh or Setrilh: Cythera, formerly Cerigo (30,11)
Seu d'Urgel: small town in Catalonia (76, 26)
Sicandron: Sikinos in the Aegean (53,34)
Siloe: valley (44,8) and fountain (44,10) near Jerusalem
Sitaree: Cythera (30,12)
Sipres: Cyprus (31,16)
Sodome: Sodom (39,12)
Sollento: Solunto, castle and port near Palermo (64,4)
Solsone: town in Catalonia (76,7)
Surie: town in Catalonia (76,2)

T

Tabermine: Taormina, castle on the Straits of Messina (61,2)
Tamsphanies, Tamphaines: the Strofadhes in the Ionian Sea (29,26)
Tarascon: town in Ariège, whose castle was destroyed in the seventeenth century (24,5)
Tarba: Tarbes (78,10)
Taulat: Capo Teulada in Sardinia (26,37)
Taurinhac: Taurignan in Ariège (77,27)
Termeniaig: castle near Syracuse (28,17)
Termes: Termini, a town on the north coast of Sicily with an exceptionally strong castle, now destroyed (63,28)
Terre Nove: Terra Nuova, town in Sicily in the Noto valley (28,5)
Tersson: Tarsus in southern Turkey (50,5)
Tessaillie: Thessaly (50,9)
Tolouze: Toulouse (23,12)
Tonys: Tunis (68,21)
Toro: large rock off San Antioco (26,33)
Torroelle: Tarruella, village in Catalonia (75,34)
Tornay: Tournay, village near Tarbes (78,8)
Trapena: Trapani, port in western Sicily (27,22)
Tresmontane: the northern group of islands in the Ciclades (30,24)
Tria: a barren rock near Cythera (30,19)
Troye: Troy (30,10)
Turquie: Turkey (32,34)

U

Urgon: village in Landes (79,12)

V

Valentin: Valentine near Saint Gaudens (78,3)
Vaque: Vacca, a rock to the south of San Antioco (74,42)
Vedell: Vitello, a rock to the south of San Antioco (74,43)
Venetiguo: Venetiko, an island off Cape Ackritas (54,23)
Venize: Venice (23,19)
Ville Navete: Villeneuve, a town in Haute Garonne (78,4-5)
Ville Nove: Villanova, a district of Cagliari lying beneath the old town, the Castello (27,18)

Viro: Yiadi near Cape Krio (53,1)
Volquam: probably Vul$_c$ano, but possibly Stromboli (63,37)

Y

Ybos: Ibos near Tarbes (78,12)
Yuisse: Levanzo off the west coast of Sicily (27,25)

The Author, his Family and his Work

The family of Caumont is very ancient, and its ancestry can be traced back to the beginning of the tenth century. In the year 937 the Comte de Rouergue was Raymond ii. His second son was Hugues and lived from approximately 948 to 1015. He established himself at Calmont d'Olt in the Rouergue, on the southern bank of the river Lot near Espalion, and it is from him that the family of Calmont d'Olt and the various families of Caumont are descended.

One of the cadets of Calmont d'Olt established himself in the Agenais where the name was changed slightly, by the vocalisation of the preconsonantal l, into Caumont. He gave his name to the site where he settled near Marmande. The founder of this branch of the family, the Caumont en Agenais, was almost certainly Etienne, the son of Begon i de Calmont d'Olt and his wife Florence, who lived between 1055 and 1140 approximately. He was one of the leading vassals of Guillaume ix d'Aquitaine[1] and was the founder of three other important families besides that of Caumont en Agenais. The original family of Caumont en Agenais died out in the early 1360's with the death of Guillaume-Raimond. The family of Caumont-Lausun was very prominent throughout the medieval period and only died out in 1723. The origin of the family of Caumont de Sainte-Baseille is still rather obscure, but it seems probable that they were descended in the female line from Sans-Aner ii, the great grandson of Etienne de Caumont. This family died out in 1357, when the last heiress, Hélène, married Bérard d'Albret.[2] The most important of the families is that of the seigneurs de Saint Barthélémy who recovered the lands of the extinct seigneurs de Caumont en Agenais and are represented today by the Duc de la Force. All these families are descended from Sans-Aner ii. It is not always certain which of his sons fathered which grandson, but this problem is now probably insoluble.

The seigneur de Caumont en Agenais in the first half of the fourteenth century was Guillaume, the husband of Miramonde de Mauléon, who brought him the vicomté de Rada in Navarre. Guillaume was devoted to the French and in 1334 he was rewarded with the seneschalcy of Languedoc. In 1333, however, he had disinherited his son Guillaume-Raimond for his devotion to the English and made his daughter Indie his sole heiress.[3] As a substitute for her he named the heirs of his sister, Talese de Caumont, who had married twice, first Arnaud de Gironde,[4] and second Pierre de Galard. It seems

---

1. Bibliothèque Nationale, Fonds Périgord, 126, Fol.33 (extraits par Denis Villevieille). (Henceforth Fonds Périgord.)
2. Ibid. 15, fol.129 and 52, fol.37.
3. Ibid. 126, Extraits de Doat, Vol.ii, fol.188.
4. Ibid., p.57.

certain that Guillaume-Raimond had changed sides while his father was
still alive, as the Remissio for the rebellion of Guillaume-Raimond was
issued before 1344,[1] when his father was still living.[2] This seems to have
had no effect upon the will, perhaps because Guillaume-Raimond had also
been disinherited for making war upon his father. By changing sides
Guillaume-Raimond recovered most of his lands,[3] but until her death Indie
was known as the Dame de Caumont. She made her heir her second husband,
Guy de Comminges,[4] as her daughter had predeceased her without issue,
but despite her will Indie's rights to Caumont reverted to the heirs of her
aunt Talese de Caumont.

Indie died in 1357 and Guillaume-Raimond died between 1360 and 1363.
He had no legitimate children and in his will of 1360 he made the King of
England, with whom he was co-seigneur of Gontaud, his heir. The legacy
was accepted, and after the death of Guillaume-Raimond Caumont was given
to Sir John Chandos. On 13 August 1363 or 1364 Jean seigneur de Caumont
et de Chastelnuef did homage to the Black Prince. It is only reasonable to
assume that this is Chandos accepting the gift from his suzerain on or shortly
after the death of Guillaume-Raimond.[5]

On Indie's death in 1357, there was a division of the property between
the heirs of Talese, Jean de Galard, her son by her second marriage, and
the five children of her daughter Géraude who had married Bérard d'Albret.
How much of the property was theirs at the time is doubtful as Guillaume-
Raimond and the King of England were still in possession of it. When
Caumont was given to Sir John Chandos after the death of Guillaume-
Raimond, Jean de Galard was dead, and his heiress was his daughter
Marguerite whose husband Nicholas de Beaufort protested vigorously on
behalf of his wife. Despite the intervention of the French crown, the case
continued until 1372 when a division of the property was effected between
Nicholas de Beaufort and Amanieu d'Albret through the arbitration of the
Pope.[6] The disputes were only finally terminated in 1396, when Jean de
Beaufort, son of Marguerite and Nicholas, sold his rights to Nompar de
Caumont, the grandfather of the pilgrim.[7] This was followed in 1397 by a
treaty of friendship and alliance between the two men.[8]

Nompar de Caumont is one of the most outstanding members of his family.
He was the elder son of Begon de Caumont, seigneur de Saint Barthélémy,

1. Ibid., 177 Reg. 74, fol.20 and 21, item 418.
2. Ibid., Vol.i, p.76.
3. Reg. du Trésor des Chartres du Roy, C.81, V.774.
4. Fonds Périgord, II, fol.150.
5. Ibid., 57, fol.24.
6. Ibid., 15, fol.129.
7. Ibid., 52, fol.38.
8. Ibid., 15, fol.130.

and Esclarmonde de Rovignan, who brought the seigneurie de Castelculier into the family.[1] In 1383 he and his brother installed themselves
in the Agenais at the ruined site of Caumont of which they had taken
possession. As the area was still dominated by the English, and the
English crown still regarded Caumont as a fief, of which it had the right
to dispose, it is not surprising that Nompar supported the English. He
was not yet so important as to matter, however, and was ordered to surrender the fief to Bernardet d'Albret.[2]

The brothers stayed in the Agenais and quickly became a force to be
reckoned with. In 1389 John of Gaunt appointed Nompar the Seneschal
of the Agenais.[3] In 1391 Richard ii granted him the ruined castle of
Caumont, which he had recaptured, and many small towns near by.[4]
Most of these had to be reconquered from the French. Other lands were
given to him in 1395[5] and 1396,[6] in which year he also bought off the
rival claimant to the Caumont lands. In 1398 the d'Albrets made a
surprise attack on Caumont in revenge for some trouble in 1394 when
Nompar had successfully cheated them of Bourg which they had united to
raid. Nompar complained bitterly to the King of France about this
attack by his supporters during a truce,[7] and orders were sent that he
was to be compensated. This is convincing proof of his importance,
that even his enemies had to pacify him.

In 1399 the King of England confirmed his previous grants and added
some property in Bordeaux and its neighbourhood. He also created
Nompar Seneschal of Aquitaine, one of the most important offices which
he had to give. In fifteen years, therefore, Nompar had risen from
little more than a brigand chieftain to an important office-bearer for the
crown. His rise suggests that he must have been a skilful commander
with great force of character and foresight. He must also have been
amply endowed with patience to pursue his plans so steadily despite the
early setbacks. He made his will in 1400[8] and seems to have died
soon after, leaving as his heir his oldest son, Guillaume-Raimond, who
had been married for some years to a member of another leading pro-
English family, Jeanne de Cardaillac.[9]

1. Cahiers de l'abbé Dubois, 20, p.284 and 26, p.131, Archives Départmentales du Lot-et-Garonne. (Henceforth Dubois.)
2. Fonds Périgord, 126, fol.129.
3. Ibid., 15, fol.130 and 52, fol.38.
4. Ibid., 126, Caumont, fol.117.
5. Ibid., 15, fol.130.
6. Ibid.
7. Ibid.
8. Ibid., 126, Caumont, fol.129.
9. Dubois 20, p.251.

At the death of the seneschal the family was at the peak of its power during the medieval period, but their decline was fairly swift. Guillaume-Raimond is a shadowy figure, appearing infrequently in documents but a reference to him in the Chroniques de Saint Denis[1] suggests that he was an important seigneur whose support or overthrow the French were anxious to secure. Despite some temporary reverses he preserved his property intact changing allegiance whenever it was necessary. He seems to have been a skilful if somewhat unscrupulous politician but so little is known about him that it is difficult to draw any conclusions.

He was succeeded by his son Nompar, who undertook the pilgrimage. He was born in the early 1390's as he was about twenty-five when he went on his pilgrimage in 1418. He died in 1428 when caught in an ambush by Nandonnet de Lustrac.[2] He in turn was succeeded by his son Nompar who was a devoted adherent of the English. He showed little of the family skill at opportune switches of loyalty. His brother Brandelis joined the French in 1442,[3] the year when Nompar finally lost Caumont to the French. In 1435 Nompar had married Jeanne de Durfort,[4] a member of another family which was prominent among the supporters of the English. She had inherited considerable property from her mother in Bordeaux[5] so that after 1442 Jeanne and Nompar retired to Bordeaux where Nompar died in 1446.[6] He was succeeded by Brandelis to whom the King of France had already granted the possessions of Nompar.[7]

Nompar the pilgrim is also the author of Lez Dits et Enseignemens[8] a long, rambling poem for the edification of his children. The style and content of the two works have much in common and show clearly their common authorship. The constraints of rhyme and metre accentuate the clumsiness found in the prose narrative, and it would not be unfair to call much of the verse tortured as the poet endeavours to force his thoughts into rhyming couplets. In spirit the two works are closely related as the author expresses his concern for his soul, his distress at the events of this world and his anxiety about the after-life. He is naive and credulous where religion is concerned but shrewd and even cynical on the intrigues and negotiations of court and feudal life.

1. Chroniques de Saint-Denis, Charles vi, Tome 3, pp.355-57.
2. Duc de la Force, Dix Siècles d'Histoire de France, Paris 1960, p.16.
3. Fonds Périgord, 15, fol.131.
4. Ibid.
5. Dubois, 8, p.226.
6. Duc de la Force, op.cit., p.17.
7. Fonds Périgord, 15, fol.131 and 52, fol.39.
8. Dr. J. Galy, Le Livre Caumont où sont contenus les dits et enseignemens du seigneur de Caumont composés pour ses enfans l'an 1416. Paris 1845.

Nompar's character emerges very clearly in the course of the works.
He is devoted to his wife although we never learn her name and indeed
her identity is the one real mystery left in the family at this period. As
Nompar refers to the Comte de Foix as his cousin, the cousinship could
be through his wife.   If so, she is probably a bastard of the Comte de
Foix's father or uncle but this cannot be proved.   Nompar refers to her
in very affectionate terms when he leaves on his pilgrimage, and when
stormbound in Sicily, his thoughts turn to her again, but in between she
seems to disappear from his mind, so complete is his disassociation from
home.   A dutiful son, he fulfils his father's vow by going on the pilgrimage for him and remembers his soul; he seems also to be an affectionate father but for most of the work he makes no mention of his family.
This is understandable as they are not relevant to his account of the
journey but it does not support the claim by the Marquis de la Grange
that he is distinguished by his outstanding devotion to his family. He is
certainly fond of them but when he is away, his concern is with his own
soul.

His piety and his devotion to religion are his outstanding characteristics.   He hates the idea of war between Christians and is shocked by
the thought that Christians could sack churches.   He longs for the time
when men of rank founded them instead.   On the other hand, he has
nothing but dislike and contempt for the Saracens and is eager to attack
them, as in the episode of the Turkish galley.   He detests the Saracens
because of their religion and notices nothing else about them.

In many ways his piety seems rather selfish.   He is concerned with
the salvation of his own soul and prays for others when it will help him.
He asks the people on his lands to pray for him, but he says little about
praying for them although one must assume that he carried out his promise
to pray for them in the Holy Land despite his failure to mention it.   He
is always anxious to collect more 'caranteynes et pardons' and seems a
little smug about his success in spending several nights in the Saint
Sepulcre especially as each entry and exit cost him more money.   He is
particularly devoted to the Virgin and to Saint George although he also
prays to Saint Elmo at sea.   His relationship with the saints is mercen-
ary assuming that they must be bribed and that they are easily offended.
His relationship with them is very real and personal but it is not very
profound, and Nompar shows himself to be pious and devout but not
really aware of the deeper aspects of the Christian faith.

His account of his journey confirms the impressions of his character
already mentioned.   On the journey out, he confines himself to giving
details of distances or occasionally mentions the local castle.   When
he reaches Crete, he shows a little knowledge of classical mythology.
He gives none of the practical details which would be useful for other

pilgrims but on the spiritual side he is much more informative giving
details of all the shrines to be visited. On the journey home he relaxes
a little and gives more information with vivid descriptions of the hazards
of a sea voyage. He talks about the various churches and the miracles
associated with them and, as on the journey out, he talks about the
castles. He is particularly informative about Sicily where he wintered
but even there his interests are limited and very much what is to be expected from a member of his class. Even his references to the classics
and to the Bible suggest only a superficial knowledge, although he does
10   seem to be able to translate the biblical Latin which he quotes.

       He seems to have no interest in the peoples or places which he visited
as he gives almost no information about any of them except the desert
Arabs. He also gives very little information about the people he met
and with whom he travelled. He rarely mentions his squires, although
we know that they were with him because he consulted them in Sicily.
He shows no interest in them. It is the same with Sancho de Chaux
who accompanied him from Rhodes to Jerusalem to knight him as a Knight
of the Holy Sepulcre. Once he has performed his task, he disappears.
In the same way he gives very little information about Arnaut de Sainte
20   Coullome whom he visited in Sicily. Nompar was not interested in
people either individually or en masse.

       Presumably he travelled 'en grand seigneur' and therefore did not
have to concern himself with the details which would be interesting to
us today. No doubt his squires dealt with the inns, the food and the
guides. Such details would, however, have been of interest to other
pilgrims, especially those with less power and status. It was his avowed
intention to make things easier for other pilgrims so that they would have
no excuse for not going on pilgrimages. He caters most adequately for
their spiritual needs, in his eyes the most important, and neglects the
30   material problems which they would have encountered.

       He can give a vivid description, as in his account of the storms
experienced on the voyage home. His account of his travels in Palestine is also brought to life by the calm tone in which he remarks that
they had to travel by night as many travellers died from the heat during
the day. His report of the conversation between himself and those on
the ship who doubted the efficacy of prayers to the Virgin when they
were becalmed off the Barbary coast sounds alive and realistic. Such
moments are rare, however, and there is little life or humour in most of
his account. He emerges as a serious man, obsessed with religion and
40   primarily concerned with the salvation of his own soul. He is very
much a man of his period, perhaps even slightly old-fashioned. To him
the Saracens are always 'fols et mauvais'. He has complete faith in
miracles and in the tales told by the monks, a credulity which would

not have been shared by all his contemporaries. He is true to the
better standards of his class, when he shows his anxiety that everything
should be well administered during his absence, and he was well aware
of his duties as an overlord. He was anxious to fulfil his Christian
duty to his people and this is, no doubt, connected with his absorption
with saving his own soul. His writings give the impression that his
Christianity did not lead to a love of mankind in general, as he was too
self-centred and uninterested in anything which did not affect him.

His account is interesting both for the man it reveals and for its
picture of the pilgrimage with all its dangers. It also shows the faith
which carried him unflinching through these dangers and which never
wavered. He is content to put himself in the hands of God and is sure
that after the observance of the necessary rituals, he will be brought
safely through to his reward. This life is of relatively little importance
to him, and it is the life to come which matters. He quotes from the
Bible to remind the readers of this, which is perhaps the explanation of
his apparent selfishness. Neither he nor his contemporaries would have
regarded it as such, and it seems probable that he was regarded as a very
good man, whose piety was outstanding. By his own lights he was up-
right, devout and affectionate but to us he seems narrow, selfish and
not very likeable. Deeply religious and rather credulous, he was not
very successful in worldly terms, which is not very surprising. The manner of his death, ambushed by a much smaller force, suggests that he
was not a competent commander and was unsuited to the stormy life of
the period.

It seems unlikely that he composed his own list of places to be
visited in the Holy Land, and his list[1] is probably copied or at least
closely based on an earlier account. His account is very similar to the
one in Pèlerinages et stations de la Terre Sainte, as yet unedited in the
Bibliothèque Nationale.[2] The similarities suggest that they had a common source, although there are considerable differences in that each
includes details which are not found in the other. This text is probably
slightly earlier than that of Nompar, but there is a much earlier Latin
text dating from 1346.[3] This Latin text is very close to the unedited
Pèlerinages as the only major difference is that the Latin text includes
Egypt. Nompar is more long-winded in his descriptions than either of
the others and only includes details of the places he himself saw.

---

1. Text, pp. 39-47.
2. I am most grateful to Professor D.J.A. Ross who transcribed
this manuscript for me. Bibliothèque Nationale, Fonds
Français, 25550 S xiv fol.19 verso - 45 verso.
3. R. Pernoud, Un guide du Pèlerin de Terre Sainte au xve siècle,
Cahiers d'Histoire et de Bibliographie, 1940, Cahier 1,
Mantes, p.15.

The unedited French text is dated as early fifteenth century by Roehricht,[1] and the evidence suggests that it is related to the text of Nompar. Its existence shows that there was a guide book, from which Nompar could have copied his itinerary, which was the custom amongst the writers of pilgrim guides. The Latin text is a possible source for the unedited French text but the differences which exist between it and the text of Nompar suggest that the Latin text is not the direct source of his itinerary. There were reworkings of the Latin text,[2] however, and it seems likely that Nompar used a reworking of the Latin text which he in turn adapted for his own purposes.

---

1.   R. Roehricht, Bibliotheca Geographica Palestinae, Berlin 1890, p.99, no.263.
2.   R. Pernoud, op.cit., p.15.

Family Tree of the House of Caumont

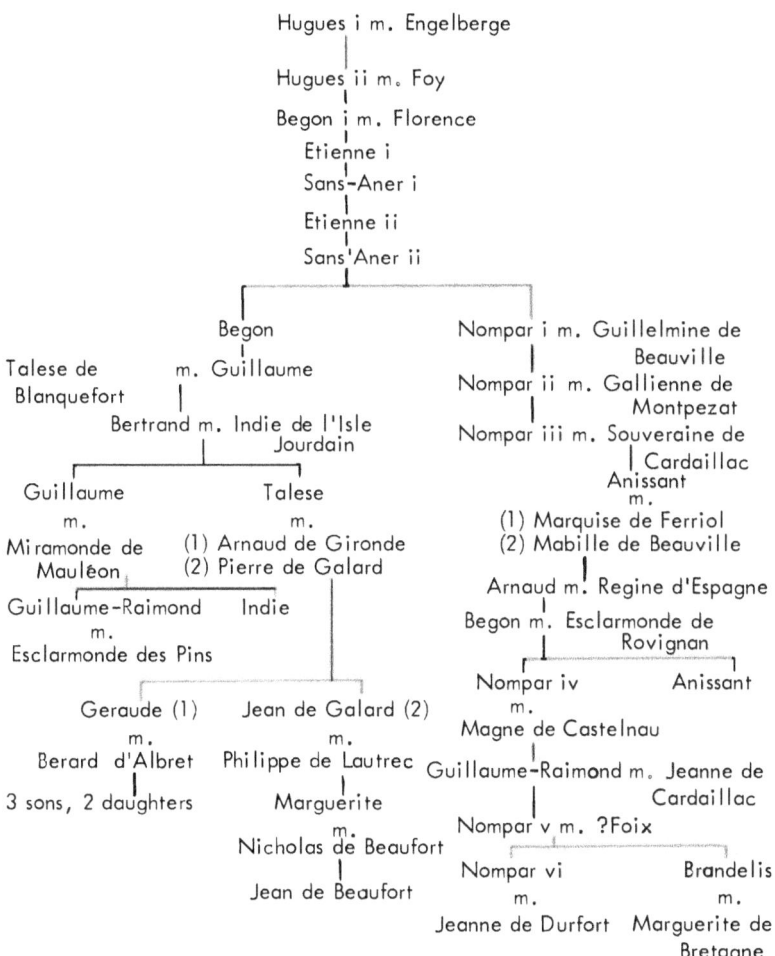

Syntax and Morphology

Syntax and morphology are treated together in the interests of avoiding unnecessary repetition, as the section on morphology would be very short, and much of it would duplicate the section on syntax.

Nouns and the Declension

By the time Nompar de Caumont was writing, the declension had almost completely disappeared from the French language,[1] and in this respect he seems to be in agreement with his period. In the definite article there is no evidence for the survival of the declension, and most nouns, pronouns, adjectives and past participles have also lost their case endings. There are, however, one or two possible examples among the adjectives and the past participles, and one noun does seem to have preserved something of its case system.

With this one exception the examples of the case system surviving in the nouns seem to be either mistakes or so rare as to be unimportant.

Item ung autre romans que je fis d'enseignemens. (10,23)[2]

Romans could be a survival or a mistake. As it is the only example of the word in the text, it is impossible to decide.

... lez eglizes, qui sont temple Nostre Seigneur ... (18,28-29)

This is the correct use of the plural and could be explained as an accepted religious phrase, which has survived thanks to the archaising tendencies of religious language. Another religious noun which poses a problem is vierge. As it is feminine, there should be no question of a declension, but on four occasions (on three of them it is not even in the nominative) it is written with a final -s (11,14; 13,4; 15,28; 22,15). In each of these examples which are all in the first quarter of the book, vierge is qualified by an adjective, but why the presence of an adjective should make a difference is unclear. It seems to be a scribal peculiarity which was discontinued as the book advanced, although the scribe was not changed. Dieu, however, does offer some evidence for the survival of the case system. There are twenty-two examples of dieu in the nominative, and of these twelve are spelt dieu and ten dieux. With one exception all the examples of dieux are in the first quarter of the manuscript, as were the examples of vierges. The almost equal division between the two spellings suggests that this is the last survival of the case system,

1. L. Foulet, Petite Syntaxe de l'Ancien Français, Paris 1930, p.34. (Henceforth Foulet). R. Gardner and M. Greene, A Brief Description of Middle French Syntax, Univ. of N. Carolina, Studies in Rom. Lang. and Lit., no.29, Chapel Hill 1958, p.1. (Henceforth Gardner and Greene).
2. References are to my text by page and line.

owing its existence to the archaising tendencies of religious language which resulted in the older spellings persisting in a few well established forms.[1]

There are nine examples where the past participle has the final -s of the nominative singular (13,44; 19,17; 19,19; 19,20; 19,26; 20,34; 64,22-23; 68,11). Four have religious associations.

Car qui est *amez* du pueple est *amez* de Dieu. (19,19)

These examples could have influenced the others which are mostly grouped very near each other in the text. The examples are so infrequent, however, that it was clearly very unusual for the final -s to be used. The possible examples of the nominative plural (12,9; 13,29) are almost certainly both to be ascribed to scribal error. The evidence suggests that despite the survival of dieux it is very unlikely that the scribe understood what he was doing when he seemed to be using the case system. It is clear that the case system is really dead in this text, and that the apparent survivals owe their presence to the influence of religious language.[2]

Use of the Objective Case

There are three uses of the objective case in Old French which have survived, but they are definitely exceptions. They are (a) the use of the objective case to show the relationship between a determinative complement and the substantive determined; (b) to show the relation of the verb to the circumstantial complement; (c) to show the relation of the verb to the indirect object. In each of these constructions the use of the preposition is not felt to be necessary.[3]

The first construction is the most common with forty-nine examples, almost all associated with religion and twenty-two of them containing the words Nostre Seigneur.

---

1. K. Nyrop, Grammaire Historique de la Langue Française, Copenhagen 1902-32, Vol.ii, 199 says that Dieus or Dieux survives till the sixteenth century in formulaic phrases such as ainsi m'ayde Dieu. (Henceforth Nyrop). F. Brunot, Histoire de la Langue Française des Origines à 1900, Paris 1905, Vol.i, 414. Dieux alone, thanks to formulaic expressions, conserved its nominative to the sixteenth century. (Henceforth Brunot).
2. Brunot, p.414. On peut dire que dès le xve siècle tout sentiment de la flexion casuelle a disparu du français. Nyrop, Vol.ii, 198-99. From the beginning of the fourteenth century the spoken language no longer uses the case system. The written language '... conserve encore longtemps les flexionnel mais on l'ajoute ou on l'omet à tout hasard.'
3. Gardner and Greene, pp.4-5.

> ... le saint Sepulcre Nostre Seigneur ... (11,6).

Even in this construction there are signs of change, as there are four examples where the words are linked by the preposition de (25,19), illustrating the widening use of this preposition. Other words such as the names of saints (42,28) and of places like Jourdain and Jherusalem (47,8) are common in this construction, and de is used more frequently with them than it is with Nostre Seigneur (49,30; 47,9). The survival of this construction can be explained by the existence of set formulae which continued to exist even when the construction had become almost obsolete. This text suggests that the two constructions were coexisting briefly before the construction with de became completely dominant.[1]

The second construction is the use of certain words or phrases without a preposition to relate them to the verb which they are describing. This construction has survived in common phrases where the need for a preposition was not felt as the meaning was instantly recognisable. These phrases are with one exception temporal.

> Et premieremant l'on trouve part dessa ledit fleuve <u>une mylle ung lieu</u> que s'apelle saint Jehan ... (39,4-5)
> ... qui nuyt et jour molent <u>yver et esté</u> ... (51,21)

In so far as it is used with temporal phrases, this construction is far from dead and coexists with the use of prepositions. Otherwise it has almost completely disappeared.

The third construction is very rare, and there is only one example with a noun and three with pronouns.

> ... et vint ung autre qui soffla tiel cop <u>le ditte nef</u> que l'en porta long hors toute celle montaigne de <u>roche</u> ... (59,22-23)

The rarity of this construction makes it clear that it was almost unused.

There are very few examples in which the plural is used as in Old French where modern French would use the singular to express the fact that each person has only one of the things.

> Pour ce nous devrions amender <u>nostres vies</u> ... (20, 2-3)

---

1. Nyrop, v, p.134, says that from the early fifteenth century this is a construction 'en train de mourir'. 'Elle se conserve surtout dans des formules d'ordre religieux.' This agrees with Nompar's practice. Brunot disagrees, p.453. 'Ces expressions se rencontrent encore abondamment au xve siècle.' His examples are not necessarily religious.

By this time Old French constructions were exercising relatively little
influence except where they were supported by the conservatism of religious
language or the well-established usage of temporal phrases. Faint recollec-
tions of the case system and of the use of the objective case survive, but in
his use of nouns Nompar is, on the whole, a man of his period.

The Definite Article

There is no example at all of the case system surviving in the definite
article. The only forms used are le, la and les or lez. Le is frequently
used for la in front of feminine nouns although there is no consistency in this
use, and the same noun can be found with different articles in adjacent
phrases.

    ... et fut getê en le mer dens une caisse ... (56,1)
    ... et la mer le alla porter a terre ... (56,1-2)

This very common usage seems to have its origins in the neighbouring dialects.
It is found in late Anglo-Norman to which it had spread from the northern dialects.[1] Given the close contacts which Nompar must have had with his
English allies and the fact that he had property in Bordeaux, it is easy to see
that his language would be susceptible to Anglo-Norman influence. Le is
also found occasionally as a feminine in Poitevin,[2] and this dialect too might
have had some influence, but the main source is probably Anglo-Norman.

The Old French rule of elision of the article before a vowel[3] is frequently broken. Le, la and du are all found preceding a vowel, although du is
only found in front of the vowel a.

    ... Le Enpire de Grece. (32,3)
    ... la eglize du arcevesque ... (67,6-7)

Examples are found of the definite article contracted with the preceding preposition with all three of the prepositions with which this was common in Old
French, namely en, a and de, but contractions with en are rare, particularly
with the plural article. En contracts to au, ou and es or ez, but it is more
common for en and the definite article not to contract. A contracts to au,
al, oux, as, aulx and aus but only au and aux are really common. There
are also examples of the uncontracted use of a, although these are always in
front of feminine nouns, as is normal where le is used for la.

---

1. M.K. Pope, From Latin to Modern French, Manchester 1952, pp.465
   and 488. (Henceforth Pope).
2. E. Goerlich, Die Südwestlichen Dialecte der Langue d'Oil, Heilbronn
   1882, p.102. (Henceforth Goerlich).
3. Foulet, p.46, but Gardner and Greene, p.8, admit to exceptions.

... a le mort. (18,5)

Contraction of a is therefore closer to the Old French, although there is some variety as to the spelling of the contracted form. De is usually contracted, although de le in front of a feminine noun is quite common, and the forms are in keeping with both Old French and modern usage.[1]

The definite article retains its function of particularising the noun which it precedes.[2] It is absent in the following circumstances; before nouns used in a general sense:

Et ceulx qui veullent guerres, devroient fere comme le loup ...
(18,41-42)

There are no exceptions to this rule.

before abstract nouns:

... a honneur de mon corps et sauvacion de mon arme. (11,19-20)

The definite article is only used with abstract nouns to particularize.[3] Before the names of countries and provinces the practice varied. Both uses are found suggesting that they were coexisting, although the more emphatic was gaining ground.

in lists and series:

... demeurent chevaux, eques, motons, cervis et chiens sauvatges ...
(27,5-6)

The article could be used in front of the first noun only or repeated in front of each noun, but this is by far the least common construction. The definite article was usually absent before a predicate nominative, before nouns in apposition, in adjectival phrases and after expressions of quantity.

Arnaut de Caumont et ... Galhardet de Tozeux ... estre residentement guoverneurs de ... m'amye ... (14,20-23)
... le roy Menelaus, mary de le belle royne ... (30,8-9)
... et cest ouvratge l'on appelle ouvre de musique ... (67,33-34)
Item vi anels de calssidoine vermeilhs ... (81,5)

---
1. Foulet, p.46, gives del, du, dou and des.   Only dou is absent.
2. Foulet, p.49.
3. Brunot, p.463.   Avec les noms abstraits l'article demeure très rare même au xve.

The definite article is sometimes used when a noun in apposition is modified. It is sometimes used with titles but not if the title is in apposition. The definite article is always used in front of quel and, although often written as two words which indicates that it still retains some of its independence, it is clearly losing this as it is also frequently written as one word.

From these examples it seems clear that Nompar de Caumont tends to observe the Old French usages in his treatment of the definite article. It has not yet become an automatic adjunct of the noun and is only used when it has some meaning to add to the phrase, usually that of particularizing a noun. There are exceptions to Old French usage, particularly as regards elision and contraction. His use of the article with proper names is also a break with Old French.[1] He is, however, very close to Old French in his use of the definite article.

The Indefinite Article

There is no example of the case system in the indefinite article, but there are four examples of the plural ungs or unes. All four fit into the categories of geographical features or words connected with buildings[2] and are used correctly.

... en unes roches moult estranges ... (25,2)

The rarity of the construction suggests that it was disappearing, but it was still understood and applied appropriately. The plural of the partitive is expressed in a variety of ways. The most usual is to have no article at all, although if there is an adjective preceding the noun, then the commonest form is de. Des is found very occasionally.

The indefinite article is used to particularize something which has not been mentioned before, and by the beginning of the fifteenth century its use seems to be increasing. Although there are many exceptions, there are five categories in which the article was absent in Middle French.[3]

1) when the noun represented a group or was part of the whole.
2) if 'some' could be substituted for 'a'.
3) after a condition or a negative.
4) before certain adjectives tel, certain, grant, especial, bon.
5) before a predicative nominative.

Only number 4 occurs frequently in this text.

1. Foulet, p.52. Gardner and Greene, p.13 say that the new usage was regular in the fifteenth century but it was not regular in this text.
2. B. Woledge, The Plural of the Indefinite Article in Old French, Modern Language Review, 1956, LI, Vol.i, 17-30, passim.
3. Gardner and Greene, pp.17-19.

The first and second constructions are both very rare (71,11-12; 55,37) and neither is followed consistently as there are exceptions to both. The third construction is more frequent (58,34) but the exceptions are almost as numerous as the examples (17,25). With regard to these three constructions, the author seems to follow no particular rule. There are sufficient examples of the fourth construction to see what rule is followed. There are ten adjectives involved, beau, bon, cruel, estrange, grant, hault, long, parfait, tel and vrai. There are fifty-seven examples of the indefinite article omitted before these adjectives, but there are eighty-eight where the indefinite article is used in front of these same adjectives and petit. The indefinite article is most frequently omitted with grant (21), bon (18) and tel (9) and it is never used with cruel, estrange, long, parfait and vrai, although there are only a few examples. It is rare in front of bon, but there are many examples of it in front of grant. This construction has not stabilised, and clearly the older and the newer constructions coexist with the progress of the newer construction varying according to the adjective. Bon is the most resistant. The newer construction is much the commoner overall, indicating that this tendency is already well established. The fifth construction is also rare but is usually observed. There are very few exceptions to it.

The indefinite article is also absent in expressions like fere oreison (30,13-14), fere veu (44,4), fere feu (73,14), where the expression is regarded as one unit so that there is no need for an article. The article is always absent when two nouns are linked by et even when the nouns are of different genders.

... passay par davant ung chastel et ville ... (65,25)

The use of the indefinite article is in a state of flux, transitional between the uses of Old French and those of the modern period. It approximates to the rules for Middle French,[1] but there are exceptions to all the rules. Clearly there was a state of uncertainty as to the precise functions of the indefinite article, although the Old French uses are losing ground. The use of the indefinite article, unlike that of the definite article, shows that the trend was away from Old French.

Partitive Article

The use of the partitive article is said to be more frequent in the fifteenth century,[2] but there is no evidence of this in this text. As Nompar was very interested in exact quantities, sizes and distances, the opportunities for its use are limited, but even when there is an opportunity to use the partitive, it is not always taken. The partitive article is used twenty-four times

1. Gardner and Greene, pp.16-20.
2. Ibid., p.20.

as against one-hundred-and-six when it is absent and thirty when some other word of quantity is used. Two-thirds of the examples of the partitive are in the second half of the book, where the scribe seems to have abandoned some archaisms. It is used more frequently in the plural than in the singular.

De is always used when an adjective precedes a noun, and the partitive is normal after adverbs of quantity. It is very rare after negatives (two examples both after point (18,9; 21,39)), and there is one example of the partitive after a preposition.

> ... le dit feu escanty et descaint aveques <u>de l'eue</u> et <u>de l'eu</u>lle d'ollive ... (58,9-10)

Stronger words than the partitive are, in fact, used more frequently than the partitive.

> ... sans avoir <u>nulle</u> noise, discencion ne debat ... (14,41-42)

The partitive has only a limited role in the text, and in his use of it Nompar shows a tendency to archaisms and constructions which seemed moribund. In five out of six cases where modern French would use it, the partitive is absent.

Adjectives and Participles

As with the nouns the case system is dead for the adjectives. The adjective normally agrees with the noun which it describes in number and gender. The many examples where an adjective with an apparently masculine form describes a feminine noun are all cases of the survival of third declension adjectives. When an adjective describes two nouns, it almost always agrees with the nearest noun.

> ... <u>aucun grant</u> debat ou querelle ... (15,5)

There are no examples of the adjective in the masculine plural when it describes two or more nouns.

The feminine was formed in the same way as it is today by the addition of -e except where the ending was already a mute -e. Apart from the isolated examples already cited of the survival of third declension adjectives, three such adjectives, grant, tel and quel, have preserved their original feminine. Fort, the adjective usually associated with them in this respect, always uses the newer form forte.[1] There are six examples of tel (24,4)

---

1. Brunot, p.415, considers that it is only in the fifteenth century that forte becomes the usual form. Here Nompar is avoiding an archaism.

and eight of telle (57,40) which is especially associated with maniere (seven examples).[1] Quel in all its various uses shows a preference for the newer form but there are many examples of the older feminine. Grant shows a much more marked preference for the older form (seventy-four to thirty-one). When an adjective with a distinctive feminine precedes grant, this does influence the feminine of grant.

> Aussi l'eglize ... est moult belle, grande et longue. (64,21-22)

Otherwise there is no discernible pattern in the use of grande. Sixteen examples precede the noun, and fifteen follow it.[2] It is clear that the older form is still much more widely used, but that the newer form is encroaching, encouraged by analogy with the more numerous feminines ending in -e.[3] With tel both forms coexist, as they do in quel, but with fort the new feminine has taken over completely. There are no examples of adjectives ending in -el whose feminine is not increased, and only two of adjectives in -al (37,36; 66,2).[4]

Comparatives as in modern French are formed with plus but there are some examples of archaic forms, greigneur, meilleur, majour and pire. The use of greigneur and pire indicates that they were not fully understood and that the more usual construction with plus was gaining ground.

> ... et la plus greigneur partie soubre dourees ... (67,32)
> ... est une de plus pires taches ... (21,24)

Greigneur coexists with a more regular but newer form.[5]

> ... nous avions plus grant navili ... (73,10)

Majour only occurs once (34,12) and suggests a certain degree of Latin influence.[6] The only form successfully resisting the encroachment of plus is meilleur. The other forms are losing their ability to maintain their meaning independently. There are no examples of the Old French construction in which a comparative without a definite article is used as a superlative. The link for connecting a comparative is always que.

---

1. Brunot, p.415, says that tel and quel preserve their early form until the fifteenth century.
2. It is unusual for the position to make no difference. Nyrop, Vol.ii, 265-6, ... grand est variable quand il suit le substantif.
3. Brunot, p.415, says that grand is the usual form at the beginning of the sixteenth century. Nompar, therefore, uses grande relatively often.
4. Brunot, p.416. Increased feminines for -el adjectives only become general in the fifteenth century. Here, too, Nompar avoids archaisms.
5. Nyrop, Vol.ii, 311. It continued to exist until Rabelais.
6. Ibid., 312. Majeur est un mot savant.

The position of the adjective has not stabilised but the commoner adjectives normally precede the noun. Longer adjectives usually follow the noun, but there are exceptions to both practices. Adjectives of colour always follow their noun, and there are no examples of bon or petit following the noun. The tendency is for adjectives to precede the noun unless they are being given a special emphasis. When a noun is described by two or more adjectives, all possible combinations of position could be used. The tendency to put the adjective in front of the noun helps to give the text a slightly colloquial air so that it reads as if it were being dictated, or as if the author wrote as he might have spoken.

Little is fixed about the adjectives. The plural of -al adjectives can be -als or aux, and the feminines of other adjectives are not yet certain. Comparatives and superlatives are becoming uniform at the expense of older forms, and clearly this part of speech is in a state of flux. Old forms and usages continue to exist, although not always understood, while new forms appear and in some cases dominate. It is interesting that in the adjective Nompar gives evidence of conflicting trends. Old forms, such as grand, tel and quel are used, but with forms such as forte he seems to be, if not ahead of his period, very up to date.

Adverbs (formed from adjectives)

The same contradictory trends are evident in adverbs. These are mostly formed in the regular manner, although by analogy he forms some irregular adverbs   (bonnement (14,13), droytemant (58,21), nullemant (16,30)). Despite the fact that he always uses the increased feminine forte, he uses the adverbial form fortmant. On the other hand, he always uses grandemant, and there are no examples of the older gramment.[1] Feminine e, which followed a vowel, was disappearing from adverbs in the fifteenth century, but Nompar still uses vrayement.[2] (71,28) The total number of adverbs is small but no clear pattern emerges. As with adjectives much depends on the whim of the individual writer.

Adjectival -ant Forms[3]

This form is relatively rare as an adjective as in the great majority of examples it is used verbally or as a verbal adjective. It is also used occasionally as a noun. As Latin participles belonged to the third declension, there was no separate feminine, and Nompar observed this rule strictly. Even the presence of other adjectives with separate feminine forms did not influence the -ant forms.

1. Nyrop, Vol.iii, 296, says that gramment was still used in this century.
2. Ibid., 294.
3. For other uses see the section on verbs.

... d'autres pierres belles et moult estranges et <u>roluysans</u> ...
(67,23)

The commonest -ant form used as a noun is mescreans with combatens and partant occurring once each (50,24; 30,31).

... mes puis lez mescreans la tuerent ... (29,6)

The -ant form is used as both a noun and an adjective more widely than it would be in modern French, but the rules of agreement are those of Old French. There are several forms found which seem to be peculiar to this author, as he is the only source cited by Godefroy.[1] (roluysans (67,23))

Past participle

The past participle behaves like an adjective when it is used as an adjective or when the verb with which it is combined is estre. There are a few examples where the case system seems to have survived.

... et la que je fuy <u>retournés</u> en Jherusalem ... (39,28-29)

Most such examples come from the part of the book most strongly influenced by the author's religious outlook which may explain the appearance of this archaic feature. When used as a true adjective the past participle agrees in number and gender with the noun it describes. The past participle dit is used very frequently to reinforce the definite article. It always refers to things already mentioned and usually precedes the noun, although not always. Sometimes it is further strengthened by the addition of sus. This use of the past participle is so frequent that it has little effect and has become little more than a stylistic device, adding to the ponderousness of the sentences. Occasionally the past participle is used as a noun, but this is not a common usage.

... et en y eut nuef de <u>blecés</u> et ung <u>mort</u> ... (57,12)

The past participle follows the rules for adjectives but there is still some uncertainty about its use as the last traces of the case system linger on. The flexibility possible in the function is extended to the form and the rules of agreement.

Personal Pronouns

The subject pronouns closely resemble the forms used today with variations in the spelling.

---

1. F. Godefroy, <u>Dictionnaire de l'Ancien Français</u>, Paris 1881-1902, Vol.x, 532.(Henceforth Godefroy).

	Singular	Plural
1st	je, ge	nous
2nd	tu	vous
3rd	il, yl elle, helle, ella	il, ilz, ilx, ils elles

There is only one example of ge (73,30), and tu is very rare because of the nature of the book. As there is almost no direct speech, tu only occurs in prayers or other communications with God. Il and elle are by far the commonest forms of the third person singular. There are only a few examples of yl (42,9) and helle (71,19) and one of ella (66,29) which might be a scribal slip or might be influenced by the Provençal ela.[1] Nous offers no variants, and there are no examples of vous used with a singular meaning but as with tu, there is little opportunity. Ilz is the commonest form of the masculine third person plural, but all the others occur sufficiently frequently to make it clear that they are not mistakes. There does not seem to be any reason why one form should be chosen rather than another in any particular place. Elles is the only form found for the feminine plural.

There are several examples of the weak and strong forms being used where today the other form would be expected.

... je et mes successeurs vous en soyons tenus d'ayssi an avant. (12,6-7)
... et eulx ne portent nulle armeure ... (39,19-20)

This interchangeability suggests that the roles of the two sorts of pronouns were not yet fixed, and that the subject pronouns retained a certain amount of strength, as they had not yet been reduced to the status of automatic accompaniments to the verb.

Object personal pronouns (weak form)

There is little variation in the form of these pronouns.

me	nous
te	vous
le, la	les, lez
se, ce	se

The indirect object pronouns are identical except in the third person.

lui, li, ly	leur

1. J. Anglade, Grammaire de l'Ancien Provençal, Paris 1921, p.246, gives ela as a Provençal form. (Henceforth Anglade).

Me and te normally precede the verb, and when they are the objects of an infinitive, which is governed by another verb, they precede the auxiliary and not the infinitive.[1]

... que je te puisse rendre grace dez grans biens... (60,31)

There is one example of the replacement of the disjunctive by the weak form after an imperative.

... souviegne te de moy ... (15,36)

In the third person singular the only variant is ce for se.

... pour ce donner le meilleur conssei lh ... (57,31)

There are examples of le used where one would expect an indirect object pronoun.

... et le pourta toute sa faude pleyne de pierres ... (38,16)

The examples are all close together (38,24; 38,27; 38,37) where Nompar is freely rendering the biblical account of the temptation of Christ. This archaic construction - using the direct object pronoun to show the relation of the verb to the indirect object[2] - could therefore be due to the influence of religious language on the author.

Nous and vous show no irregularities while les has the one variant lez. There is one example of lez in an interesting position.

... nostre nef après lez va suyant ... (50,29-30)

Lez is the direct object of suyant which is treated as if it were an infinitive with an auxiliary. Luy is the commonest form of the indirect object in the singular, and leur is the only form of the plural.

Disjunctive pronouns

The forms are close to those used today.

moy	nous
toy	vous
luy	eulx or eux
elle	elles
soy	

---

1. Foulet, p.135. This is normal in Old French.
2. Gardner and Greene, pp.4-5. See also the section on nouns.

The disjunctive is most commonly used after a preposition, and the vast majority of the examples belong to this category. Occasionally it is used as part of a compound subject or object or for emphasis. Sometimes it is used in an absolute construction with participles or to replace indirect and direct object pronouns.

There are several examples of ellipsis which is another of the constructions which help to give a colloquial air to the text.

... a xxx milles de Caille ou nous voullions estre et elle aussi. (74,15-16)

The disjunctive is used for effect.[1]

... que tu as apliqué moy en cest monde pour toy servir ... (60,3-4)

It is also used in the construction in which the pronoun object of an infinitive or participle is treated as the object of the preposition which is governing the infinitive or participle.[2] This is a rare construction, as in many cases the form of the pronoun would not be affected.

... en moy donnant de bon tamps allegremant ... (65,46)

It could also be used in such a way as to look like this construction.

... que nullemant de elle aproschier ne me povoie. (66,14-15)

De elle is actually a prepositional phrase although it looks like the object of the infinitive which is actually me, placed correctly in front of the auxiliary. This shows the fluidity of the word order.[3] The construction which avoided this difficulty is also found.

... Michel Buguere disant li que ... (66,30)

Here the pronoun is placed after the participle.[4]

With regard to the position of the pronoun governed by the infinitive, there is some confusion. Usually the pronoun precedes the auxiliary but

1. Foulet, p.126.
2. Ibid., pp.128-29.
3. Ibid., p.130 says that it is rare for the indirect object of the infinitive to precede the infinitive when, as here, it is a strong pronoun.
4. Ibid., p.132.

there are exceptions where it precedes the infinitive. Nompar wavers between making the preposition governing the infinitive govern the pronoun and ignoring the awkwardness caused by their juxtaposition. He preferred the older construction which obviated this difficulty by putting the pronoun in front of the auxiliary even when this could mean that the pronoun and the infinitive were separated by a considerable distance.

Y and En

Y is always used impersonally, frequently in the phrase il y a or y a. It usually refers to a place but it can refer to abstractions. En can refer to both people and things. The use of these two pronouns corresponds to modern practice although the word order en...y is that of Old French.

... et en y eut nuef de blecês ... (57,12)

Position of personal pronouns

The subject pronoun normally precedes the verbs. There was inversion in questions, and there could be inversion after adverbs but this rule was not followed consistently. Object pronouns normally preceded the verb which governed them. The position of a pronoun governed by an infinitive has already been discussed. When there are two object pronouns, the direct invariably precedes the indirect as was usual in Old French.[1]

... et le te donne entieremant sans fin. (60,38)

Y or en follow another pronoun, but if they are together en precedes y.[2] If the pronoun is the object of two verbs, then it is not usually repeated (18,32), although there are exceptions. In general the pronouns confirm that in his syntax Nompar is content to follow many of the usages of Old French. This is particularly marked in that the word order is usually that of Old French.

Possessive Pronouns and Adjectives

The forms of the possessive adjectives are similar to the modern ones except in the plural.

mon	ma	mes
ton	ta	tes
son, sen	sa	ses
nostre	nostre	nostres, nos
vostre	vostre	vostres, vos
leur	leur	leur, leurs

---
1.   Foulet, p.147.
2.   Gardner and Greene, p.63. This was the regular construction.

Leurs outnumbers leur by eight to one.[1] The separate forms of the plural coexist and are used indifferently. When the possessive is used in front of a feminine singular, all three constructions are found.

... prier qu'elle soit ma advocade ... (11,16)
... ma tresbien amee m'amye et m'amour vraye ... (11,34-35)
... et mon entente estoit d'aller a Venize ... (23,19)

Although all three constructions are possible, the most popular is the use of the masculine form. The elided form is very rare, and the unelided form is more common but both are being replaced by the masculine form.

There are several irregular forms of the possessive adjective. The Anglo-Norman form ces is found on five of the seven occasions on which this adjective is used.[2] It is another indication of possible English influence on the author or the scribe.

... ou il lava lez piêz a cez apostres ... (45,18)

There is one probable borrowing from Provençal.[3]

... par avoir pardonance et remission de mos pechiêz ... (22,10)

There are a few survivals of the early strong forms.[4]

... au saint lieu dez bons esleuz a la sua dextre. (15,40)
... que nous dont le sue grace et amour ... (17,30)
... le quel par se grace je vy ... (61,37)

These forms are so rare that they can be discounted as the regular forms are clearly the ones used normally.

Pronouns

The possessive pronouns are very rare in this text and there are only examples of the following forms:

le tien (4), le nostre (2), le vostre (1), les vostres (1), la leur (1).

There is no trace of the case system surviving, and as in Old French the pronoun could be used without the definite article.[5]

---
1. Brunot, p.424, leurs is the normal fourteenth century form. Leur is, therefore, a survival.
2. Pope, p.466. Other examples: 17,24; 19,1; 45,8; 45,16.
3. Anglade, p.249.
4. Foulet, p.162.   5. Ibid., p.165.

... donne le tien en dementres qu'il est tien ... Car après le mort ne sera pas tien ... (20,38-39)

There are also two examples of the pronominal form used as an adjective, presumably survivals of the strong forms.[1] (59,34; 71,25)

There seem to be no irregularities in the use of the possessive adjective, although the form is another matter. The use of the possessive pronoun is so sparing that any comment becomes difficult.

Demonstrative Pronouns and Adjectives

The forms which are now called pronouns and adjectives seem to be largely interchangeable, as in Old French.[2] The forms can be divided into three groups.

Cel[3] or ceu[4]

cell (rare)	ceulx
celluy or selluy	
celle	celles
cest	
ce	ces
ceste	cestes or ces
cestuy	
ce or se	

In so far as there is a difference in meaning, cel and its forms indicate things that are distant or not immediately present, as in Old French.[5] Cest indicates greater promixity. In the majority of cases, however, there is no clear reason why one demonstrative should be preferred to another, and the different forms cannot easily be separated by their meaning.

Cel and its forms are common as pronouns but there are only three examples of cest as a pronoun (30,35; 63,35; 78,23). It was possible to

1. Foulet, p.166.
2. Ibid., p.167.
3. Brunot, p.425. Cel disappears early, so this would be an archaism.
4. Ibid., p.426, ceu is a vocalised form of cel. Schwan-Behrens, Grammaire de l'Ancien Français, Leipzig 1923, Vol.iii, 85, gives ceu as a form of ce in south-western dialects. This seems a probable explanation.
5. Foulet, p.168.

use cest as a pronoun but it was extremely rare. The usual subject of the
verb estre is ce, and there are no examples of cest used in this way. There
are no examples of -ci used to reinforce cest, although it is used with other
parts of speech.[1] The commonest form of cel, whether as adjective or pronoun is celuy. Cil is never found.[2] Celuy, ceulx and celles are the only
pronominal forms, and they could be used as the antecedent for relative pronouns. There are no examples of the demonstrative pronoun replacing the
personal pronoun as the subject, except when it means those or the ones.

    ... et entrerent ceux de nostre barque ... (74,8-9)

The demonstrative frequently replaced personal pronouns, when they were the
object or after a preposition where a disjunctive could have been used.

    ... je pris celluy pour lez choses sus dittes ... (32,17)

The demonstrative pronoun can also replace the possessive adjective, although
no greater clarity is achieved by this.

    Ce is found as the subject, object or as the object of a preposition. As
the object it could precede the verb. It could also be used to turn certain
prepositions into conjunctions but the only preposition which required this was
pour (11,21). There are examples with après (38,38), jusque (73,36) and
sellon (18,5), but it was not always included with these. Cela (3) and ceci
(1) are both very rare (36,29; 39,27; 66,12; ceci (21,29)). Cela can
be used in an absolute construction with a participle. The prefix i- or y-
is very common with the cel forms, perhaps because they were felt to need
strengthening. It is very rare with the cest forms.

    There is no trace of a case system in either form. Both forms are used
as adjectives but only the celuy form is important as a pronoun. Differences
in meaning are slight, but cest can indicate nearness and presence. The
demonstratives are still flexible parts of speech but it is clear that the separation of the roles was beginning, some forms becoming adjectives and others
pronouns. The Old French freedom is not yet lost, but the modernisation of
the forms and their role has begun.

Relative Pronouns and Adjectives

    Qui and que are found as both the subject and the object of the verb.
Qui is usually the subject but there are a few examples where it appears to

1.   Brunot, p.426. These reinforced pronouns increase rapidly from the
         fourteenth century. Their absence from this text is another archaism.
2.   Gardner and Greene, p.69. It was still current. Brunot, p.424. It
         exists in the seventeenth century.

be the object. This is probably a survival of the strong form cui phonetically identical with qui.[1] Both people and things could be the antecedent of either qui or que. Que is more than twice as common as qui as the subject. This probably reflects popular speech of the period, as it was a feature of popular language even earlier than the fifteenth century.[2] Qui is quite common in the sense of whoever, and both ce qui and ce que are frequent, although ce was very often omitted (12,2). It is rare to find ce qui used to refer to a whole clause (13,41).

Le quel is found as a pronoun, used as the subject, the object or after a preposition. As quel was a third declension adjective, there are examples of the survival of the original feminine (31,20). After the preposition a the contracted form is usual, although the uncontracted form is found. With de and en the uncontracted form is much commoner. After prepositions qui, que (very rare), lequel and quoy are used. Quoy never refers to people but qui and lequel can refer to people and things. Dont is very rare and refers to a clause (72,27). Cuy only survives in standardised expressions, probably owing its survival to the archaising tendency of religious language.

... mon pere, cuy Dieux absolle par sa sainte pitié ... (10, 29-30)

Le quel is also used as a relative adjective, sometimes so close to the antecedent that the repetition seems unnecessary. Que is used as a temporal conjunction and seems to suffice on its own.

... despuis le jour que je parti de Caumont ... (22,29)

The use of the relative is very regular although there is a slight tendency towards archaisms such as cuy, the undifferentiated feminine of lequel and perhaps the use of que as a subject, although this may well reflect the tendency to reproduce contemporary, popular speech.

Interrogative Pronouns and Adjectives

As there is almost no direct speech in this text, there are very few examples of interrogatives, and those that there are are all from indirect questions. There are no examples of interrogative possessives nor are there any of the longer forms of the interrogative. There are no examples of quel as an interrogative pronoun but it is used as an interrogative adjective (22,22; 64,42; 72,19). There are only two other certain interrogatives, qui (74,6) and que (19,19), and all that can be said is that the examples conform to

---

1. Foulet, p.181.
2. Ibid., p.177. Brunot, p.429, says that in Middle French qui and que are found fulfilling each other's functions but that in the fifteenth century qui was extending its range, although que was still very frequent.

accepted medieval usage without any irregularities.

Indefinite Pronouns and Adjectives

Of the many forms of indefinite pronoun and adjective available in this period, some are very rare in this text, and a few of the more complicated compounds do not appear at all. Maint is used only as an adjective and un, on, tant, rien, quanque and autrui appear only as pronouns. Tel, mesme, autre, plusieurs, chacun, aucun and nul are used as both adjectives and pronouns.

There are twenty-eight examples of tel of which only three are of it as a pronoun, indicating its rarity in this use. Maint appears only once as an adjective in a formalised phrase which would explain its survival.

... l'en delaisse aler dehors en <u>maintes</u> pars ... (22,21)

Plusieurs is replacing maint and is common as an adjective with twenty examples as opposed to five as a pronoun and one as an adverb of quantity, which is easy to understand logically although grammatically unjustified.

... mes pluseurs ne le font pas ains acquerent le puis d'enfer en <u>pluseurs</u> de manieres ... (21,1-2)

Mesmes is not very common as either an adjective or a pronoun. It is mostly used as an adjective to give emphasis to the time or the direction. As a pronoun it is always spelt mesmes, presumably a faint recollection of the case system, but as the final -s is used regardless of case, it only proves how decayed the system is.[1]

Un is used frequently as a pronoun, particularly in the phrase l'un l'autre. Autre is used as both an adjective and a pronoun. When used as an adjective it occasionally occurs without any other qualifying word, showing that the Old French construction was just surviving.

... et menerent evesques et pluseurs chapellens et <u>autres</u> gens ... (56,11-12)

It is very common as a pronoun. Autrui is very rare, occuring once only as a pronoun so that there is no trace of the Old French adjectival use surviving (38,4). On is frequently used as the indefinite subject of the verb, but the more common spelling is l'en. Both were usual in Old French. There seems to be no rule as to when l' could be omitted. Chascun and chescun are used as both an adjective and a pronoun. Tant is rare as a pronoun (73,46) and

---

1. Nyrop, Vol.iii, 282. Mesmes is still found in Corneille.

is found twice as an adjective (22,9; 69,32).[1] Quant, quant que and quanque all occur infrequently as indefinite pronouns, and there is one example of quant as an adjective (16,17).[2] Tout and the intensifying trestout are very common as adjectives and pronouns. Quelque occurs thirteen times, always as an adjective. There are no examples of quel ... que, perhaps because it is never used as a pronoun.[3] Rien is rare in a positive sense and is only used in a clause which is negatived in some other way. Nul is used more frequently in this way but always as an adjective. Nul as a pronoun is always negative. Nul could be used positively.

... si tost comme il veusse nulle nef en Palermo ... (66,25)

It is more usual for it to be preceded by a negative or a word such as sans which has a negative sense. Aucun is used in the same way as nul but both as a pronoun and an adjective. It is much commoner as an adjective. It is not used in a negative sense in this text, which is consistent with Old French.[4] Souvant appears once as an adjective and is presumably a synonym for maint and plusieurs. It may be a reflection of current speech.

... me faizoit souvante foix le journee d'elle avoir le souvenir ... (66,5-6)

Quelconques appears twice, once as an adjective (16,21) and once as a pronoun (12,35). Its rarity can be explained by Nompar's interest in giving precise details. Certain is used as an indefinite adjective in contexts where it is clear that the quantity is known or could be found out but that Nompar is not sufficiently interested to do so (52,13).

It is clear that there is a tendency to concentrate on certain words with indefinite meanings at the expense of the others. The more old-fashioned words such as maint, quelconques, autrui and quanque are as a result very rare. Words like plusieurs, aucuns and phrases such as d'autres were replacing them. The indefinites provide clear evidence that, although the language was still in a state of flux, the older uses were dying out.

Verbs

As in his treatment of other parts of speech, Nompar shows a tendency towards archaisms in his treatment of the subject pronoun. Although in the

1. Godefroy, Vol.vii, 639. A regular Old French usage. Nyrop, Vol.ii, 410. It continues to the Renaissance.
2. Ibid.
3. Foulet, p.190. The non-separable form was already in existence in the twelfth century in that the quel and the que were adjacent, but not joined. Nompar is using a well-established form which has not yet acquired its modern meanings.
4. Foulet, pp.247-8.

fifteenth century omission of the subject pronoun is supposed to be followed to only a small degree, Nompar omits it four-hundred-and-seven times.[1] It is certainly present more frequently than it is omitted, but it is usually omitted when there is no room for confusion as to who or what is the subject of the verb. There are examples from every person and almost every tense. Many of the examples of the omission of the first person singular are from verbs like avoir and être where there can be no confusion as to the person involved.[2] The only -er verb in which the first person singular pronoun is regularly omitted is prier, which is used in near formulaic expressions. The pronoun is most commonly omitted with the first person singular of the past historic and also the first person plural. Both of these have distinctive endings.

Where the verb ending makes the person of the verb clear, the author felt under no compulsion to use the pronoun, although he does use it more often than not in the proportion of two to one. The relative frequency of the omission is in keeping with the other archaic tendencies shown. There are frequent examples of the omission of the third person singular pronoun in impersonal constructions, especially in the il y a construction where il y a is far outnumbered by the use of the verb alone.[3]

Number

Nompar is very careful in his use of number, and it is rare even to find a compound subject with a singular verb, although this does happen (59,29-30). There is one example of the Old French construction of uniting the two parts of a compound subject by entre and et (35,40-41). Where the subject is a series of alternatives, the singular is always used.

Mood

Subjunctive. This mood is found in a variety of constructions but Nompar uses it very flexibly, and for almost every rule there are exceptions.

It was used after impersonal expressions of necessity (56,16-17) but the infinitive was preferred after this construction; after verbs expressing will, wish, command, necessity, preference, permission or prohibition. Sometimes after such verbs there is no conjunction (71,17), and although this is not usual,

---

1. Gardner and Greene, p.90.
2. Nyrop, Vol.v, 207 ... on en trouve des exemples dans la littérature du xve et xvie siècle, surtout quand il s'agit de formes verbales qui présentent une terminaison spéciale. This text fits this description.
3. Ibid, 209, says that the omission of il with impersonal verbs persists until the sixteenth century, although il had appeared much earlier. This suggests that its absence is another archaism.

it is too frequent to be considered a slip.[1] It was used after expressions of
disbelief (19,20-21), after verbs of thinking (58,39) and very commonly after
a superlative (20,26). This last construction is almost invariable in this text.
It was used after an indefinite antecedent which is followed by an adjectival
clause (67,7). It was used after que(lest) (60,6-7) and after all the following types of conjunction: result (11,22-23), concession (20,6), temporal
(26,5), but there are very few examples to work from. Often an infinitive
after a preposition is used (16,18-19) where a subjunctive after a conjunction
would have been possible, suggesting that on occasion the author did not
hesitate to avoid the subjunctive. The subjunctive was also used in compound
relative clauses (14,10-11) after comme (since) (11,29) in the subordinate
conditional clause (14,5-7), even although the main verbs were not in the
subjunctive. Presumably this indicated that the subordinate verbs were even
further removed from reality than the verbs in the conditional clause. The
subjunctive was also used in subordinate clauses to express doubt (21,38-39),
futurity (15,11-12) and hypotheses (66,24-25). Its only use in main clauses
was in standardised phrases of wish or exclamation, usually associated with
religion (15,16).

Conditionals

The subjunctive is found in both clauses in an unfulfilled condition.
In a past unfulfilled condition the sequence si...pluperfect subjunctive...
pluperfect subjunctive is the classic formula,[2] but this was already old-
fashioned and from the middle of the fourteenth century was being replaced
by the construction si...pluperfect indicative...conditional perfect.[3]
Nompar de Caumont gives further proof of his linguistic conservatism by using
the older construction. The other tense sequence which he uses is also old-
fashioned by this period.

... ne n'eussent rompu leur costume ... ce ne fust pour l'amor
de moy ... (52,27-28)

In the fifteenth century the imperfect subjunctive was being replaced by the
pluperfect subjunctive almost everywhere. It was surviving only in stylised
phrases such as ce ne fust.[4]

---

1. Foulet, p.333. Parataxis with omission of que after vouloir was common in Old French.
2. R.-L. Wagner, Les Phrases Hypothétiques commençant par Si dans la
   Langue française des origines à la fin du xvie siècle, Paris 1939, p.246.
   (Henceforth Wagner).
3. Ibid., p.247.
4. Ibid., p.193.

In other sorts of conditional sentences the indicative tenses are usually found. Si with the imperfect...present was known in the fourteenth century.[1] Si with the imperfect...imperfect was not a regular sequence and was probably an attempt to express the simultaneity of the verbs (13,10-11).[2] Si...imperfect...future was regular in the fifteenth century,[3] as was si...imperfect... conditional, and si...present...present.

There are also examples of conditionals in which the moods are mixed, a subjunctive in one clause and an indicative in the other. Si with the imperfect subjunctive...imperfect indicative (26,21-24) dates from the fourteenth century, and the use of the imperfect subjunctive was old-fashioned in the fifteenth century.[4] Si with the imperfect indicative or subjunctive... present indicative was quite regular in the fifteenth century (15,5-8).[5] The mixture of moods could occur in the same si clause unless the si were repeated before each verb.

The use of the subjunctive in conditionals relating to the past confirms the tendency towards archaisms. The commonest conditional construction is si...present indicative...present indicative, and some of the other constructions occur in one example only. The impression that Nompar has a liking for archaisms and a rather carefree attitude to syntax is confirmed by the conditionals in which both archaisms and irregular constructions are to be found.

Infinitive

The use of the infinitive as a noun is not common in this text, but there are examples of reveller (66,10), disner (67,4), aler and venir (10,5), perdre (69,23) and enbarchier (72,31). The commonest use of the infinitive is after a modal auxiliary or another verb, sometimes with a linking preposition such as a or de. It is also used after sans, par, pour and en. This last construction was already disappearing in the twelfth century and must, therefore, be considered another archaism.[6]

The prepositional infinitive with an object was not as common as the gerund in Nompar de Caumont, although still very much alive. It is most common to find the infinitive used without a preposition. The commonest

---

1. Wagner, p.471.
2. Wagner gives no examples of this sequence which suggests its irregularity.
3. Ibid., p.474.
4. Ibid., p.458.
5. Ibid., p.476.
6. C. Aspland, A Contribution to the Syntactical Study of -ant Forms in Twelfth Century French Verse, unpublished Ph.D. Thesis, London 1967, pp.325-7. (Henceforth Aspland). Examples: sans (12,15), par (13, 35-36), pour (14,8), en (18,34).

prepositions are a and de, but the examples of a governing the infinitive are only one in nine and those of de one in twenty. The verbs which do take such prepositions are usually found with more than one construction. There was still great confusion about the use of a and de to govern an infinitive, and the normal usage was for the verb to govern its infinitive directly, although the prepositions were extending their range. The infinitive is used quite frequently in this text, although its range seems to have contracted since the twelfth century.[1] It provides clear evidence of the survival of archaic constructions in this text and also illustrates admirably the state of confusion and flux surrounding the uses of some parts of speech.

Imperative

There are few examples of the use of the imperative as the nature of the text limits the opportunities for its use. There are no examples of the third person imperative, and there seems to be no difference between the use of the imperative in this text and in modern French.

Tenses

In the subjunctive the full range of tenses is used, and the regular sequences are observed. There are two survivals of the etymological forms which still existed in the fifteenth and sixteenth centuries, especially in 'locutions toutes faites'.[2] (dont, 13,27; 17,30). The imperfect subjunctive has some unusual forms in the third person singular. Two are north-eastern, for which there is no obvious explanation in this text (aidaist, 42,9; lavaist, 39,8).[3] An alternative third person singular is used quite frequently. This seems to be a very early use as Fouché considers that these forms belong to the late fifteenth century and to the sixteenth. He explains their form by the influence of the first person singular.[4] (fusse, 19,21; eusse, 58,20; semblasse, 15,6; allasse, 74,6). Vouloir has a variant form of the first person singular of the imperfect subjunctive (vouzisse, 65,8; 65,10-11). This is based on the form vousis of the past historic which was quite common in Old French.[5]

The present tense. Present time is expressed by the present indicative, and there are no examples of the compound present continuous. There are several examples of the Old French construction of a present tense in the

1. Aspland, p.245.
2. Nyrop, Vol.ii, 107. Brunot, p.434, considers that these forms were the commoner forms in the fourteenth century, and still very much alive in the fifteenth.
3. P. Fouché, Le Verbe Français, Etude Morphologique, Paris 1967, p. 342. (Henceforth Fouché).
4. Ibid., pp.344-5.
5. Ibid., p.293.

midst of a list of past tenses, where the present is not an historic tense (41, 3-5). This use of the present in prose narrative is closely related to its use in epic.[1] The effect of this use is to denote the aspect of continuance or to focus attention on an action.[2] It is another archaism as the thirteenth century was the turning point in the use of the present. Later prose works look forward to 'modern' tense relationships.[3] Another Old French survival is to be found in the first person singular where a few verbs do not always have final -s (voy, 21,39; croy, 21,14; croiy, 26,21). Voi is an Old French form.[4] The spread of final -s in this position was very slow during the fifteenth century, but these are rather isolated examples in this text.[5]

Past Historic. This is the second most frequent tense and is used to describe a simple, completed action in the past. It is also used occasionally in reported speech, indicating that it was used in direct speech, which was still regular. In the -ir verbs the first person singular frequently lacks the final -s, still regular at this period,[6] although modern forms have begun to appear.[7] In the -er verbs the third person plural is sometimes -arent, condemned in the seventeenth century as a Gasconism[8] and indicating the influence of the south-west on the language. There are no examples of the past historic used with the force of an imperfect, but there are some unusual forms. Mesimes occurs once (72,46) and is an archaism.[9] The other forms are tenuy (66,43), venuy (79,22) and tenu (74,25), all first person singulars. Tenui is an eastern form[10] and tenuy and venuy are orthographical variants. Tenu is presumably based on the past participle.

Imperfect. The imperfect is the third most frequent tense and is used descriptively for continuous action or a continuous state. This aspect of time is also expressed by soloir with the infinitive. The difference between the two seems to be slight, but the soloir construction is rare. The ending -oie is very common, although not the only form for the first person singular. It also occurs, rather infrequently, as the ending of the third person singular.[11]

---

1. M. Blanc, Time and Tense in Old French Narrative, Archivum Linguisticum, Vol.16, 96-124.
2. Ibid., 113-8.
3. Ibid., 122.
4. Fouché, p.153.
5. Brunot, p.435.
6. Nyrop, Vol.ii, 129-30.
7. Brunot, p.436.
8. Brunot et Bruneau, Grammaire Historique de la Langue Française, Paris 1933, p.459. (Henceforth Brunot et Bruneau).
9. Fouché, p.283.
10. Ibid., p.331.
11. Brunot et Bruneau, pp.450-1, -oie is already slightly archaic.

This indicates a slight degree of uncertainty as to the exact forms of this tense. There are no examples of the past progressive.

Perfect. This is a rather rare tense and is used strictly with a perfect meaning. It is noticeable that the rules governing the use of the auxiliaries are not so strictly observed as in modern French and have not yet stabilised.

Pluperfect. The use and formation of the pluperfect do not differ from those of modern French, apart from two examples (45,32; 55,22), where the tense is formed with past historic of the auxiliary, as was the tendency in Old French.[1]

Past Anterior. This tense is used regularly in temporal clauses introduced by quant, après que, sitost que and la que, when the verb in the main clause is in the past historic.

Future Perfect. There is one example of this tense (18,5).

Auxiliaries. The great majority of verbs are conjugated in the compound past tenses with avoir. There are some differences from current practice, and the following verbs are found with both avoir and être: aller, entrer, être, loger and passer. Aller, entrer and être normally take the auxiliary to which we are accustomed, as there are only two examples of aller with avoir (58,18) and one of entrer (39,31). Etre is found twice with être (52,4) and this could be a sign of Provençal influence. Loger is found once with each auxiliary (27,17; 39,1) and passer divides two to one in favour of être (62,7; 56,37). Other verbs conjugated with être are despuillier (57,30), tourner (a synonym for retourner which may explain the usage) (71,26), cesser (72,26) and disner (36,32). Clearly there was still some freedom of choice as to which auxiliary was used.

Future. The future is used to express futurity, frequently after quant and occasionally after comme.

Conditional. This is a rare tense, as the subjunctive is still preferred in conditions. It conveys the idea of 'would' or 'should' (59,11). It could also be used in indirect questions (72,21-22).

Passive. The passive is used frequently by the author, and there are few examples of the use of on or pronominal forms instead of the passive. This results in clumsy, strained syntax, but no effort is made to avoid the passive. This may reflect popular speech, as the more literary forms are avoided.[2]

---

1. A. Ewart, The French Language, reprint 1956, p.254.
2. Brunot, pp.464-5. This century sees an increase in the use of the pronominal forms, but this is not apparent in this text.

There is a slight reluctance to use the passive of dire and appeller, although the passives of both are found. Otherwise the passive is used regardless of the syntactical heaviness caused by an accumulation of passives.

Pronominal verbs

The pronominal verb is used in three ways in this text: to express the true reflexive with the subject of the verb as the agent; to express the passive; with verbs of movement and the adverb en. There are sixty-four examples of the true reflexive, one-hundred-and-eleven of the passive and thirty-four of verbs of movement. All these constructions were well established by the early fifteenth century.[1]

The true reflexive is used with verbs with which it is traditionally associated (se laver, se baigner). There are also examples of the reflexive preceding the auxiliary governing the infinitive to which the reflexive is attached. This construction could be used actively or passively,[2] and there are examples of both in this text (37,11; 38,22-23). The number of examples quoted for the use of the reflexive to express the passive is slightly misleading as the majority come from three verbs (s'appeller 60, se nommer 15 and se trouver 14). The other twenty-two examples are of the pure passive meaning of the reflexive.[3]

The use of the reflexive pronoun and the adverb en with verbs of motion such as aller was well established in Old French and offered the possibility of adding greater precision to the meaning of the verb. There was great freedom in this, and s'en aller could cover a range of meanings from aller to partir to giving a precise idea of the movement.[4] The use of en with aller without altering the meaning of the verb probably explains its spread to other verbs of movement where it could add a 'nuance d'aspect' without affecting the sense.[5] Nompar uses this construction with most verbs of motion.

In the remaining twenty-five examples Nompar seems to anticipate the writers of the late fifteenth century. Towards the end of the century the use of the pronominal form became 'une véritable manie' in certain authors. This spread of the pronominal form from the positions where it was essential to others where it had been possible is the probable explanation of these

---

1. J. Stefanini, La Voix Pronominale en Ancien et en Moyen Français. Publication des Annales de la Faculté des Lettres, Aix en Provence, Nouv. Série, 31, 1962, passim.
2. Ibid., p.615.
3. Ibid., p.609.
4. Ibid., pp.403-8.
5. Ibid., p.408.

examples.[1] In this respect Nompar does not show his usual archaising tendencies. In his use of the pronominal he seems to be very much a man of his period and also to be anticipating the developments which were to take place later in the century.

Verbal -ant forms. When an -ant form is used as a gerund after a preposition or as part of the verb, it is always invariable. All -ant forms are gerunds when their function is verbal.[2] The gerund can take an indirect object and can refer to the subject of a clause.[3] (61,28-29) The gerund can also refer to a noun or a pronoun, not the subject, elsewhere in the sentence.[4] (60,30-31) A common construction in this text is the use of the gerund absolutely. This had been rare earlier,[5] but in this text it is frequent with verbs of motion (26,6). The -ant form is not used to form progressive tenses. The use of the -ant forms in this text remains in many ways very close to the rules which applied in the twelfth century, suggesting again that the syntax is tending towards archaisms. Nompar has introduced a little more freedom into his handling of this part of speech, giving his style a certain colloquialism. The verbal -ant forms, therefore, reinforce the impression of archaism and of carefree syntax.

Past Participles. When the past participle is combined with être it normally agrees with the word which it describes. The exceptions (31,24; 79,10) are probably scribal slips as there are no obvious reasons for the lack of agreement. As already mentioned, the passive is extremely common. It is formed with être and the usual rules of agreement apply.

In compound tenses the past participle is invariable if the auxiliary verb is avoir, unless there is a preceding direct object, but even then it did not always agree.

... honneurs, que m'as donné en cest monde ... (60,31-32)

There are also examples of the participle agreeing in anticipation of the direct object.

... s'il avoye passee le nef ... (57,15)

The verbs conjugated with estre are the same as in modern French with the additions of issir, cheoir and trespasser. As indicated in the section on the auxiliary, the auxiliary used by each verb is not yet completely stabilised,

1. Stefanini, p.646.
2. Aspland, p.335.
3. Ibid., pp.342, 348.
4. Ibid., pp.323-4.
5. Ibid., p.352.

and there are some examples of avoir and estre used with verbs which would be expected to take the other. On the rare occasions when reflexive verbs are used, they take estre. There are four examples where the form of the past participle can only be explained as a survival of the declension system (70,28; 13,44; 16,22; 65,4-5). In all four the cases are correctly used and add a little further evidence to the case for a faint recollection of the case system.

There is great freedom and flexibility about the position of the past participle. It can be separated from the auxiliary verb by an adverb or an adverbial phrase, and it can even precede the auxiliary. Apart from this freedom it shows no signs of either archaisms or particular freedom of use. It is used normally in all the usual constructions.

Negatives

Ne is much more frequent than non in this text, partly because ne is nearly always used in compound negatives and partly because there is almost no direct speech where non would often be more appropriate. Non is found in four constructions, which are, with one exception, very rare. It is used once on its own when the verb is understood (69,15). It is found twice helping to form a compound conjunction to negative the whole clause which follows (20,6; 22,1). It is also found as a substantive (60,36).

There are three examples of non negating a verb or an infinitive (36, 17; 38,20-21; 38,36), but two of these are translations of quotations from the Bible, and the third is also formulaic as it is part of the wording of the oath for the fellowship of knights which Nompar joined. Non is used twice where the verb of the clause has been omitted and is understood from the previous clause (16,20-24; 78,22-23). Non pas is found twice with an infinitive (18,1-2; 20,21) and non is also found following se, so that the word or phrase enclosed between them is made an exception.

... et estre ne puis aquitté se par toy non (60,10)

When se introduces a clause which is to be negatived, however, ne is used, and there is only one exception (16,20-24).

There are no examples of nenil in the text. As nenil does not occur, and non is rather rare, by far the commonest negative is ne, used on its own. There are one-hundred-and-sixty-four examples of ne used by itself, thirty-four of ne...pas and twelve of ne...point. The idea of neither...nor is usually expressed by ne...ne, which was normal in Old French. There are very few examples of the full construction, and more usually it is just the nor which is expressed, and the word used is ne. There are only seven examples of ni and one of ni used together with ne.

... ne arque ni table ne riens que liens fusse ne povoit se
tenir ... (58,37)

There are also two examples of ne used with a positive meaning, introducing an alternative (39,22-23; 51,22). This was normal in Old French.[1]

Auxiliaries of negation. Aucun is very rare used negatively, but nul is common both as an adjective and a pronoun. It is sometimes found supporting ne.

... ne vueillez croire nul d'eulx ... (14,11)

Nulluy is not found at all. The adverbs used as negative auxiliaries are onques (6), jamais (3), ja (2), gueres (5), which is always spelt guieres, and plus (5), which is divided between the meanings no...more and no... longer. Both jamais and onques can precede the negative particle by beginning the clause. Que is one of the commoner auxiliaries.

A large number of nouns are used as negative auxiliaries. Pas was fairly common, and point, rien, mie and nient are found. There is one example of goute, but personne does not appear at all, although it is found as a negative in the previous century.[2] Nul is always used instead, as was normal in Old French, where it had been the most important negative auxiliary in the twelfth and thirteenth centuries.[3] Pas can be used with any verb but it is still rare for it to be used with a direct object. It is very rare for it to precede the verb and the negative particle (66,8). Goute appears only once (19,42) and seems to have retained something of its substantival meaning. There are six examples of mie in which it seems to have retained part of its substantival meaning as there is no other direct object. It is found once with a reflexive verb (73,8) where it has lost its substantival quality. Point has completely lost its substantival sense and is found as often in a sentence with a direct object as not. It never precedes the verb or the negative particle. Rien can be used as either the subject or the object of the verb, or it can be governed by a preposition. Whatever the case it is spelt riens. Nient is very rare (13,12; 20,27; 66,16). In the last two examples it is in the more modern form neant.

The use of the negatives confirms the impression that Nompar inclines towards the archaic in his syntax. The preference for ne alone shows that it has not yet lost its meaning and does not require the support of auxiliaries. The survival of mie and goute, the comparative rarity of pas and point and the complete absence of personne, add to the impression that the syntax is

---

1. Foulet, p.288.
2. O. Bloch and W. von Wartburg, Dictionnaire Etymologique de la Langue Française, Paris 1950, p.472. (Henceforth Bloch and von Wartburg).
3. Foulet, p.246.

slightly old-fashioned for the early fifteenth century. On the other hand
the absence of ne...mais and the rarity of non suggest that the style is not
consciously archaic. The use of the negative is flexible in that the combination of words used can vary widely, and its position is dictated more by the
need for emphasis than the rules of word order. Otherwise there is little
attempt to use it stylistically. Its function is to negate words or clauses, and
there is no attention paid to euphony or the flow of the language.

Invariable Words [1]

The following conjunctions are found in this text: et, mes, ne, ou, si
and car, but with the exception of et, they are all rare. Et is extremely
common, all the more so because Nompar has a style which involves the
accumulation of clauses or phrases, not necessarily closely linked in content,
but joined in the sentence by et. It is also used frequently to link related
clauses, pairs of nouns, verbs and adjectives or to attach the last word in a
list to the preceding ones. Et can also be used to join every element in a
list, although when that happens, the items in the list consist of more than
one word. There are several examples of y used for et, all in the first quarter of the book (25,24; 27,9; 31,5). The only explanation would seem to
be a possible Spanish influence, but if so, it is hard to see why it should be
confined to the first part of the book. Et is frequently found beginning sentences but it seems to have very little extra meaning. It acts as a link between loosely connected groups of words and gives no extra emphasis.

Mes is not a very common word and is always found in this spelling
when used as a conjunction. It is used to contrast two clauses. It is found
beginning sentences to contrast them with the previous sentence. It is also
combined with que (71,20; 20,33; 19,41). Si is even rarer than mes, found
only half as often. It is never found as a substitute for et, as it always has
the meaning of so. Et and si are sometimes combined to mean and thus (39,
21). Si is also found introducing the second clause in a sentence with the
effect of reducing it to a slightly subordinate status (56,3). The use of si
is very limited and it always has an explanatory meaning in addition to its
function as a linking word. It is not a substitute or a synonym for et.

Ne is found meaning or or nor depending on whether the rest of the
sentence is positive or negative (39,22-23; 17,31-32). There are a few
examples of ni meaning or (14,31). There are no examples of ne used to
mean and. It is an alternative to ou, although often the context in which
it is used is negative. Ou is another rare word. Its only meaning is or, and
there are no examples of either...or. Occasionally it is spelt ho or he, but
otherwise it is regular. Car is frequently found beginning a sentence and is

1. In this and the following sections textual references are omitted for
common words and phrases.

also found linking two independent clauses always meaning for. It provides a very strong link between closely related clauses or sentences and has the effect of slightly subordinating the clause which it is introducing. It is used very frequently to introduce sentences which is consistent with Nompar's liking for linking his narrative as much as possible.

Subordinating conjunctions.   Excluding si and quant there are forty-seven conjunctions found in this text, although several are extremely rare, occurring only once or twice.

> A cause que: because. (11,20)
> A celle fin que: in order that. It takes the subjunctive. (11,22)
> Ains que: before. (65,15)
> Ainçoys que: before. (14,14)
> Ains que and ainçoys que are synonyms which have since been replaced by avant que. Ainçoys que is the only one which does not take the subjunctive.
> Ains: rather, but. This is a common conjunction, used to negate a negative clause. It is always oppositive. It is sometimes found as ain. (14,42)
> Ainssi: and so. It is rare as a conjunction on its own. It is also found infrequently with comme, meaning just as. Much more common and with the same meaning is ainssi que. Occasionally it has a temporal meaning (46,30), and there is one example where it means with the result that (55,12). There is also one example where it means in this case that (22,18).
> A par que: apart from. There is one example (15,13).
> Après que: after. It is always followed by the past anterior. The verb in the main clause can be in either the past anterior or the past historic. There is one example (35,36) of the verb in the present, but it is substituting for a past tense and retaining the past meaning. It could be a use of the present to focus attention on the action.[1]
> Attendu que: because. There is one example (13,11).[2]
> Aussi que: as. (11,35)
> Au tamps que: at the time when. (64,7)
> Combien: how or how long. A rare conjunction. (22,28)
> Combien que: although. This is a rare conjunction, surviving from Old French. (73,16)
> Comme: as. It can be used temporally or as a conjunction of manner. It is found in combination with aussi bien to mean just as well as. There is one example of comme meaning as soon as (50,24) and one where it means such as. (30,17). This indicates the flexibility with which it could be used.

---

1. M. Blanc, op.cit., pp.113-4.
2. There is no example in Godefroy, although he used this text as a source.

Comment: how, in or by which, such as and as. Despite its large
number of meanings it is a rare conjunction.
Cousi que: just as. There is one example. (13,42)[1]
Desso que: because of what. There is one example (65,14), possibly
de ço que, with a lengthened initial consonant.
Dont: wherefore.
Encontinent que: as soon as. (67,13)
Encores que: furthermore that. (14,14)
En dementies que: whilst. There are two examples (19,39; 20,38),
the second of which is written en dementres que, the form given
by Godefroy.[2] Both examples come from the part of the book
where he is quoting the Bible, where his language seems to be
influenced by the style of the Bible. This would suggest that the
conjunction is either archaic or very formal and little used in normal speech or writing.
En maniere que: in the way that. (26,15)
Ens se que: as. There is one example (56,18). This compound
conjunction indicates the distaste felt by the French for combining
a preposition and que without any intermediary, here supplied by
the se.
Jassoit que: although. (73,9-10)
Jusques que, jusque ce que, jusque tant que, en jusque tant que:
until. There is one example of jusques que followed by the indicative (44,4), one of jusque ce que with the subjunctive (73,36),
one of jusques tant que with the indicative (70,14), and one with
the subjunctive (59,29), one of en jusque tant que with the subjunctive (65,4), and one with the indicative (51,4). There is a
state of complete confusion as to which mood should follow the
jusque conjunctions.
Lors: then or thereafter. A common copulative conjunction, always
found at the beginning of a clause or sentence. There is only one
example where it is not preceded by et (56,9).
Maugré que: despite that. There is only one example (71,24).
Mayntenant que: once or as soon as. There is one example (55,21).
Mes que and au mais que: but that, unless and at most.
Non obstant que: notwithstanding that. There is one example (20,6).
This is another conjunction which only occurs in a passage closely
associated with the Bible.
Non pourtant que: notwithstanding that. There is one example (22,1).
Par avant que: before. Par acts as an intensifying particle (35,24).
Par le maniere que: in the way that. There is one example (16,14).
Par se car: because. This is a synonym for par ce que with car replacing its synonym que, which is unusual (33,13).

---

1. There is no example in Godefroy.
2. Godefroy, Vol.ii, 498.

Par se que: because. There are two examples of this form (68,35; 71,3) at what seems to be an early date for it to appear.[1] The usual conjunction is pour ce que.

Par tel que: in such a way that. This conjunction takes the subjunctive. (48,7)

Pour ce que: because. This is the common causal conjunction and at this date still greatly outnumbers its rivals.

Pour quoy: wherefore, why. It is always written as two words when it means wherefore, indicating that each word has kept its own meaning and that the interrogative had not yet become the sole function of the word, although it did exist. (60,29; 71,22).

Quant: when. This is an extremely common conjunction, always spelt in the regular Old French form. The tense sequences observed correspond to those of today.

Que: that, except. It is a very common conjunction meaning that, but is rare meaning except (63,43). There is one example of que used as a synonym for car (64,38), which might, however, be an example of the use of que to avoid the repetition of the conjunction.

Sellon que: according as (60,18). There is one example of cellon ce que (18,5) which indicates the reluctance to attach que directly to a preposition.

Si, or se: if. It is extremely common and is combined with non que and ne to mean unless. The tense sequences have been discussed in the section on conditionals.

Si que: so then. This is a common conjunction, especially favoured for the beginning of a sentence. It has the effect of summing up the previous sentence and linking the two sentences.

Sitost come: as soon as. There are four examples of this conjunction (72,41) and one of its synonym sitost que (62,26).

Tant comme: to the extent that, as far as. It can be used of any quantity of time or space or anything measureable.

Tantost que: as soon as. There is one example (41,17).

Tant que: so much or so far that, until. There are many examples, mostly of tant...que. It is followed by the subjunctive in three out of sixteen examples (71,41), but there is no clear reason for the presence of the subjunctive in any of them. The subjunctive seems to express a nuance of doubt and to owe its presence to the context and meaning rather than to the effect of the conjunction.

Tellement que: to such an extent that. (71,6)

---

1. Bloch and von Wartburg, p.455, say that parce que appears in the fifteenth century and cite Commynes, writing much later than Nompar de Caumont. Its very first appearance is in 1272.

The number of conjunctions used in the text is very large and indicates the great liking which the author had for linking his text as closely as possible. He shows a readiness to use the more complex compound conjunctions. There are several synonyms among the conjunctions listed, and many of the conjunctions are rare. Some such as the concessives are rare becuase the text did not offer many opportunities for their use, others are obsolescent, and some are formations of his own devising. The rarity of the concessive conjunctions, which were certainly not rare in general usage, indicates that it would be unwise to draw many conclusions from the rarity of those conjunctions which do occur in the text. Nevertheless the conjunctions do indicate that tendency towards archaisms already noticed and the carefree attitude to syntax, illustrated by his liking for an accumulation of clauses linked often very loosely by conjunctions, some of which are themselves extremely cumbersome.

Adverbs. There are many adverbs and adverbial phrases to be found in this text, but many of these are found in only a few examples, and most of them are relatively infrequent. The only adverbs which are at all common are ainsi, bien, liens, molt, plus and tout. By far the commonest is bien which is used mostly as a synonym for the modern très, which is itself not uncommon.

A bas: down. An adjective used in an adverbial phrase which has the effect of making the sentence an order. There is one example (71,11).
A destre: on the right. An adverbial phrase of place formed by the ellipse of main. There is one example (42,30).
Adonc: at that time. An adverb of time. There is one example (46,25) although it did not go out of use until the seventeenth century.[1]
Affons: to the bottom. An adverb of place formed by combining a and fons with a lengthened consonant. It is used with entrer.
A force: forcibly. An adverb of manner. There is one example (71,24).
Aillors: elsewhere or furthermore. There are two examples of this as an adverb of place (58,36; 68,37) and one where it has the second meaning (66,8).
Ainsi: thus. A common adverb of manner used to sum up a previous action and to link two clauses or sentences.
Alentour: round. An adverb of place used to refer to buildings. (78,17).
Alevant: forward. A not uncommon adverb of place. It is usually written as one word (64,40) but sometimes it is separated into its component parts (58,16) which suggests a faint recollection of its substantival function. It is always used adverbially, however.

1. Godefroy, Vol.i, 107.

Alors: then. An adverb of time. (33,26)

A main cenestre: on the left. An adverbial phrase of place. There is one example (63,2).

A paynes: with difficulty. An adverbial phrase of manner but paynes still retains some of the characteristics of an independent noun and could be qualified by an adjective. This happens in two out of ten examples.[1]

A point: ready, suitably.[2] An adverbial phrase of manner. There is one example (50,25).

A present, ou present: at present. An adverb of time. Three examples out of fifteen have the contracted form (34,14) showing the presence of the definite article, which suggests that the substantival function of present is not completely forgotten.

Après: afterwards. An adverb of time.

Aqui: there. An adverb of place, borrowed from Provençal. It refers to a place just mentioned, but at some distance geographically from the writer.[3] (71,29)

Arriere: backwards. An adverb of place.

Assés: very much. An adverb of manner. It is used as an intensifying adverb, a synonym for moult and tres. It is not very common. It is found once followed by de (70,41).

A toudiz mais: for evermore. An adverbial phrase of time. There is one example (11,22).

Aucune foix: once. An adverb of time, a synonym of une foix. There is one example (45,8).

Au davant: ahead. An adverb of place. There is one example (50,33).

Au derrier: at the last. An adverbial phrase of time. There is one example (18,3).

Aujourduy: today. An adverb of time. Sometimes the parts are separated (50,7), suggesting that they still retain their individuality, although they are always used adverbially.

Auprés: next. An adverb of place found only in the catalogue of holy places. Clearly it was not in common use, and it could be archaic.[4] (44,12)

Au revers: the reverse. An adverbial phrase of manner. Revers is treated as a noun. There is one example (18,32).

---

1. References: 19,30; 21,21-22; 34,31; 49,24; 59,28; 61,20; 61,22; 61,23; 61,43-44.
2. Tobler-Lommatzsch, Vol.vii, col.1313, a point means angemessen (suitably or befittingly).
3. Godefroy Vol.i, 367, gives references to this text only. Tobler-Lommatzsch does not give aqui at all.
4. There is no example of this form given in either Godefroy or Tobler-Lommatzsch, who does give au pres (bei or nahe an used adverbially). Vol.vii, col.1783.

Aussi, oussi: also. An adverb of manner. There are three examples of oussi.

Aussi tost: immediately. An adverb of time. There is one example (70, 36).

Au tamps passé: in the past. An adverbial phrase of time. There is one example (33, 19-20). Each of the components retains its own identity and function.

Autour: round. An adverb of place, usually combined with tout. (28, 22; 63, 26)

Autre foix: again, in the future. An adverb of time. There is one example of each meaning (73, 27; 60, 30).

Autrement: otherwise, on the contrary. An adverb of manner. (71, 21; 67, 43)

Avant: before, in front, forward, further on. An adverb of time or place. This form is commoner than davant with twenty-five examples to ten. In the comparative it is always avant. There is one example where avant is used as a noun (33, 15). It can also be used with de to form an adjectival phrase, but this applies only to cases where it is used to indicate time (36, 29). This is a common adverb and is used very flexibly.

D'ayssi en avant, dessi avant: henceforth. An adverb of time. It is an intensification of avant. (12, 7; 58, 15)

Bas: down. An adjective used as an adverb of place. There is one example (38, 39).

De bas: down. (38, 31)

En bas: downwards. (67, 28)

These combinations have rather more of an idea of movement than the adverb on its own, but they are all rare.

Bien: well, very. An intensifying adverb. It is very common and is found with every part of speech which an adverb can qualify.

Chief en amont: with the top upwards.[1] An adverb of place. Both examples come in his description of the church at Monreale. It could perhaps be a technical word. (68, 46)

Couste et couste: side by side. An adverbial phrase of place. There is one example (68, 45-46).

Cy desoubz: below. An adverbial phrase of place. It is always found with the past participle escript. (11, 24)

Davant: before, ahead. An adverb of time or place.

De davallant: descending. An adverb of place. There is only one example (24, 22). It is formed by the combination of de and the present participle.[2]

Dedens: within. An adverb of place. It can express state or movement.

---

1. Godefroy, Vol. i, 273, gives amont as en haut or par en haut but no examples of this phrase.

2. Godefroy, Vol. i, 506, gives avallant (qui s'abat, qui tombe) as a present participle.

Dehors: outside. An adverb of place. It can express state or
movement.
De la hault: from up there. An adverb of place. It is rare for la to
be linked to another adverb. There is one example (65,35).
De lassus, de lassus hault: from up there, from high up there. An
adverb of place. (34,22)
Demein: tomorrow. An adverb of time. There is one example (18,
7) as lendemain is preferred.
Demontant: rising. An adverb of place. There is one example
(24,22). 1
Dens: within. An adverb of place. There is one example (57,25)
as dedens is preferred.
Depuis, depuis ensa: since. An adverb of time (69,26). There is
one example of the adverbial phrase depuis ensa (68,34).
De retour: back. An adverb of place. There is one example (51,11).
It is an unusual formation and might be taken from popular speech.
Dessus: above. An adverb of place. It is used to refer to something
already mentioned in the text or, more rarely, to something physi-
cally or geographically higher. (46,24)
Desye: already. An adverb of time. There is one example (55,19).
It is, presumably, a distorted form of deja.
De tour: in circumference. An adverbial phrase of place. There is
one example (63,2).
De toutes pars: on every side. An adverbial phrase of place. There
is one example (76,9).
Don: wherefore. An adverb of manner.
Donques: and so. An adverb of manner. There is one example (18,1).
Dores en avant: from now on. An adverbial phrase of time which is
meant to strengthen both parts of the phrase by joining them and
thus emphasising the contrast. There is one example (19,5).
Droit: straight. An adjective used as an adverb of place. It can
be used of state or movement. There is one example of the true
adverbial form, droytemant: immediately (58,21).
D'une part...d'autre part: on both sides. An adverbial phrase of
manner. (67,31)
En: from there. An adverb of place. There is one example (64,13)
where en exists independently. There are many examples of it
attached to verbs, usually verbs of movement.
Encontenant: at once. An adverb of time. A variant of incontinent.
(55,17-18)
Encontre: against. An adverb of place. There is one example (71,
18-19).
Encores: again, still. An adverb of time.

---

1. Neither Godefroy nor Tobler-Lommatzsch gives demontant or de
montant.

En general: in general. An adverb of manner. (14,40)
En gre: favourably. An adverb of manner. There is one example (15,12).[1]
En hors: onwards. An adverb of place. There is one example (35, 14) as dehors was preferred.
En nulle part: anywhere. An adverbial phrase of place used in negative sentences. (57,39)
En reont: round. An adverbial phrase of manner, used with the force of a predicative adjective. (69,18)
Ensemble: together. An adverb of manner.
Ensequent: in sequence or in order. An adverb of manner. There is one example (39,34).
Enssa: ago, then. An adverb of time. (29,8; 68,34)
En...tamps: in or at...time. An adverbial phrase of time. There is always an adjective to define the period of time to which the phrase refers. (51,26)
En tant: meantime. An adverbial phrase of time. Its function is to link the action of one clause to the duration of the related clause. (71,30)
Entiquemant: of old. An adverb of time. (30,33)
Entour: around. An adverb of place. It is a synonym for autour. (79,3)
Environ: about, around. An adverb of degree, used for number or place. (73,41)
Guieres: scarcely. An adverb of quantity.
Hors: out. An adverb of place. There is one example (59,41) as dehors is preferred.
Huy: today. An adverb of time. (18,6)
Illeques: there. An adverb of place. (28,24)
Ja: already. An adverb of time. In compound tenses it comes between the auxiliary and the participle. (73,41)
Jadis: formerly. An adverb of time. (33,8)
Jamais enquore plus: as ever. An adverbial phrase of time and manner. There is one example (73,7)
La: there. An adverb of place. (63,42)
Liens: within. An adverb of place. It can be used of either place or movement. It is a variant of leans.[2] (63,39)
Lonc tamps: for a long time. An adverbial phrase of time. There is one example (63,20). The fact that it is written as two words indicates that each is still seen as fulfilling its own function.
Long: far. An adverb of place. (61,41)
Maintenant: now. An adverb of time. It is always in a stressed position and it never has the Old French meaning of immediately. (29.17)

---

1. There is no example cited in Godefroy.
2. Godefroy, Vol.iv, 699. Liens is the more unusual form.

Majorment: especially. An adverb of degree. There is one example (57,34) but it is found in other texts.[1]
Mal: badly. An adverb of manner. There is one example (57,32)
Mallement: badly. An adverb of manner. (58,22)
Meins: less. An adverb of quantity. (50,24)
Mieulx: better. A comparative adverb of manner. (78,32)
Molt: very or very much. An adverb of quantity.
Ore: now. An adverb of time. It is always at the beginning of the sentence or clause. (39,34)
Orendroit: now. An adverb of time. There is one example (15,27) but it is common in other texts.[2]
Par: very. An adverb of degree. It is very common with other adverbs. It is also found attached to such adjectives as durable, giving the form perdurable, usually written as one word, although in this use it is really an intensifying prefix.
Par avant: first of all, formerly. An adverb of time. (36,4; 50,4)
Par aventure: perchance. An adverb of manner, used only in religious contexts. (21,18)
Par consequent: consequently. An adverb of manner. There is one example (13,43)
Par or part dedens: within. An adverb of place. (79,5)
Par dehors: outside. An adverb of place. There is one example (77,6).
Par or part dessus: above. An adverb of place. (37,37)
Par or part devant: before. An adverb of time or place. (55,9)
Par entier: completely. An adverb of manner. (14,17)
Par especiel: especially. An adverb of manner. There is one example (19,13).
Par jamais: for ever. An adverb of time. There is one example (12,6) which is in a stressed position. It suggests that jamais was already beginning to lose some of its strength, if it needed reinforcing by par.
Par mesmes: in the same way. An adverb of manner.[3] (13,41)
Par tamps: at one time. (30,28) Par lonc tamps: for a long time. (43,4) An adverbial phrase of time, found in several forms, which seem to have very similar meanings. The examples using lonc tamps are from the list of holy places and suggest that this expression was not used regularly by Nompar. There is one example with pour (50,11-12) but as the two words are interchangeable as prepositions, it is not surprising to find pour used here too.
Part dela: overseas. An adverb of place, used with reference to the Holy Land or the next world. (15,41)
Part dessa: on earth, at home. An adverb of place. There is one example of each meaning (18,5; 16,34).

1. Godefroy, Vol.v, 103.
2. Ibid., 627.
3. It is not given in either Godefroy or Tobler-Lommatzsch.

Plain or a plain: fully. An adjective used as an adverb of manner. (74,41)
Plus: more, most. An adverb of quantity. It is common both on its own and in combination with other adverbs.
Plus outre: further on. An adverb of place. It only occurs in the list of holy places, which suggests that it was a word not in normal use. (45,27)
Poy: little. Poy a poy: little by little. An adverb of quantity. It is used once with de. (38,8)
Premier, premieremant: first. An adverb of time or place. The two forms seem to be used in exactly the same way. (45,4; 72,44)
Pres: near. An adverb of time or place. Pres de was an alternative to pres que. (59,29)
Pres que: almost. An adverb of degree. (35,22)
Puis: then. An adverb of time.
Sa et la: here and there. An adverbial phrase of place. All the examples are connected with the sea. (58,30)
Sans doubte: probably. An adverbial phrase of degree. There is one example (17,24).
Souvant: often. An adverb of time.
Sus dit: mentioned above. Sus is an adverb of place within an adjectival phrase.
Tant: so much, so long. An adverb of quantity or degree.
Tantost: straightaway, at one time. An adverb of time. There is only one example of the second meaning (18,10).
Tantsolemant: quite alone. An adverb of degree. There is one example (76,10).
Toujours: always. An adverb of time. It is only once written as one word (12,2).
Tout: completely. An adverb of degree. It observes the modern rules of agreement.
Toutes foix: nevertheless. An adverb of contrast. (30,29)
Toux tamps: always. An adverb of time. It is a synonym for toujours. (32,8)
Tout a cop: suddenly. An adverb of time and manner. This seems to be quite an early use of it as the first examples seem to be in Joinville.[1] Tout can still be used adjectivally. (51,22)
Toux dis: always. An adverb of time which is a synonym of toujours. There is one example (13,39).
Tres: very. An adverb of degree, found only with adjectives and adverbs, reflecting its origin as an intensifying prefix. Sometimes tres is joined to the adjective, which it qualifies, showing that it still retains its role as an intensifying prefix. This only happens with tout. There is one example of tresque (57,3). Tres is not

---

1. Tobler-Lommatzsch, Vol.ii, col. 962.

as common as bien, but it is nearly as common as molt. Its uses
are more restricted, as molt is found with more parts of speech.
Trop: too much. An adverb of quantity. (20,28) In several examples trop is linked with plus, presumably for the sake of extra
emphasis. (61,46)
Ung poy: a little. An adverb of quantity. (33,17)
Voulentiers: willingly. An adverb of manner.
Yci: here. An adverb of place. It is sometimes reduced to ci,
but the commonest form is yssi.
Yssi: thus. An adverb of manner. There is one example (60,28).

It is difficult to form many conclusions about the adverbs, as so many are used infrequently. Many well-established adverbs from Old French are not used at all, but words such as beaucoup, which was coming into use in the fifteenth century, do not appear, while molt and par which were generally in decline by this period still seem to be full of vigour. The use of adverbs indicates clearly the state of flux in which the language found itself. Words typical of Old French have disappeared, and new words are taking their place. On the other hand words, which were about to disappear or had done so in the texts of some of his contemporaries, are found in numerous examples, and the new words which were gaining ground in the fifteenth century do not appear at all. The use of the adverb indicates clearly the transitional state of the language and also shows the archaising tendencies in Nompar de Caumont, in this instance in his choice of vocabulary.

Prepositions. Only three prepositions can be described as common - pour, par and en (not counting de and a which are often linked with other words to form a preposition). By far the commonest is en which has more than twice as many examples as any other preposition. There are some archaic forms, and there is a strong tendency to regard any adverb as a possible preposition with or without the addition of de.

A: with. There is only one example (76,24), which confirms that
this use had almost disappeared.
A: on. A is used as a synonym for sur or sus. (61,6)
A contre: against. There is one example (59,4). It is a variation
of encontre.
Adroit de: opposite. There is one example (63,12). [1]
Al large de: out at. There is one example (72,13). The adjective
is treated as a noun to form a prepositional phrase. It is used with
the sea.
Alentour de: around. Alentour is also found as an adverb. Its use is
flexible and depends on the addition of de. (33,14)
A le veue de: in sight of. There is one example (72,8-9).

---

1. Godefroy, Vol.i, 118, cites examples from Autun, which suggeststhat
it is a recognised but rare usage.

A maniere de: in the style of. There is one example (68,9).
A memoyre de: in memory of. There is one example (68,17).
A meyns de: at less than. There is one example of this prepositional phrase, constructed with an adverb of quantity.[1] (72,23-24)
Aprés: after. It is common as a preposition but almost always used to express time.
Au: in. This form is probably a contraction of en with the definite article.
Au bort de: at the edge of. (64,30)
Au bout de: at the end of. (38,14)
Au chief de: at the top of. (47,1)
Au costé de: beside. (36,23)
Au davant de: in front of. There is one example of this phrase (69, 40-41).
Au dehors de: outside. Another example of an adverb treated as a noun to form a prepositional phrase. (41,19)
Au lonc de: along. There is one example (51,20).
Au milieu de: in the middle of. (40,25)
Au my de: in the middle of. (75,25)
Au pié de: to the foot of.
Auprés de: near. There is one example (61,1).
Autour de: around. It can be used of movement or state. (67,16)
Avant: before. Both examples are of time. (10,9; 21,7)
Avec: with. It is by far the commonest preposition meaning with. It is almost equally divided between the two spellings avec and aveques. It is widely used in accordance with the trends of the period.
Chiere pour chiere de, chere par chiere de: face to face with. A prepositional phrase of place. There is one example of each (51,15; 69,35).
Contre: against. It is used mostly of people opposed to one another and also with words such as droit. In one example (71,18) it seems to mean facing.
Cousté de: beside. There is one example (63,1-2).
Davant: in front of. A common preposition used of places or people. There is one example of time (74,24).
De cousté: beside. There is one example (33,35). It is similar to cousté de in form and meaning. The form of this preposition is not yet stable.
Dedens: inside. It is used to give a certain emphasis.
Dehors: outside. It is often coupled with another indication of position to make it even more precise. (46,10)

---

1. Godefroy, Vol.v, 363, gives three examples, one from the Chroniques de Rains and two from Estienne Boileau.

Dens: in. There is very little differences between dens and dedens, except that dens is used more often of movement.
Derriere: behind. There are no examples of movement. (37,25)
Despuys: since. (10,6)
Dessa: this side of. There is one example (22,28), a survival from Old French.
Dessus: above, upon. (72,10)
Desoubz: beneath. (57,13)
Devant: in front of. There is only one example of movement (33,16), as the others are all of state.
Devert: towards. (28,23)
Droit et droit de: opposite to. There is one example (61,7).
Emprés: after. There is one example (13,31). It is a synonym of aprés.
En: in. This was the all-purpose preposition, used in many ways, as well as expressing every meaning of in.
On. This is not common but it is an easy extension of meaning.[1] (63,12)
With. This use survives in set phrases such as en Dieu, but en was also a synonym for a, which could mean with.[2] This use is a survival from Old French. (69,41)
At. This is a regular Old French usage, which was dying out towards the end of the middle ages.[3] (51,35)

The other examples can mostly be translated by in, but they illustrate the many uses to which en could be put and show that Old French usages were still alive, although by this period en should have been losing ground. This indicates the archaising tendencies of Nompar de Caumont.[4] En is also found occasionally in the contracted forms esquelx (en lesquelx) (12,1) and es (en les) (70,2).

Encontre: against. It can be used with God, people and things.
En my: in the middle. It is used only with voye. (64,34)
Entre: between. It can be used of time, place or movement.
Entour: around. There is one example (19,13), and it is another case of an adverb used as a preposition.
Envers: towards. It is used with people or God.

1. Nyrop, Vol.vi, 118-9. Ainsi la vieille langue attribuait parfois à en le sens de 'sur' ...
2. Ibid., 118 ... dans certains cas en a été remplacé vers la fin du moyen âge par à ...
3. Ibid, 112.
4. Ibid. Vers la fin du moyen âge, le domaine de en commence à se restreindre, et, dans un certain nombre de cas, il est remplacé par à ou par dans ...

Environ: about. It is more common in this text as an adverb. (63, 25)
En voie de: on the way to. It is used only with the expression estre peris en le mer. (71,21)
Excepté: except. This is quite an early use as the first recorded appearance seems to have been in Froissart.[1] (34,11)
Fors que: except. This is much commoner than excepté.
Hault sur: high above. The adjective is used to form a prepositional phrase.
Hors de: outside. There is one example of hors alone (34,41).
Jouste: beside. A preposition surviving from Old French. It is found with people and places. (25,14)
Jus: under. It is used only with seignorie, suggesting that it was restricted in its use, although it had been common.[2] (30,32)
Jusques a: until. This is a common preposition, used occasionally without a in expressions of time. (48,20)
Jusques en: as far as. There is only one example in the formal heading to the list of places of pilgrimage (40,6). It may therefore be a borrowing as jusques a is the form preferred by the author.
Le lonc de: along. It is always strengthened by tout. (64,1)
Loing de: far from. (50,6)
Ou: with. There are only seven examples in this text, indicating clearly its declining popularity compared with avec. (79,9). It is not yet an archaism.[3]
Outre: beyond. There are two examples, in one of which it means on the other side of, its original meaning (47,21), while in the other it means in addition to (48,12).
Par: by. This is a very common preposition, second in frequency only to en. It could express action by people or things,[4] (61,20), but in this text it is interchangeable with pour (20,27), which may be a dialect feature.[5] It governs infinitives (13,35-36), indicates time (55,32) and expresses for the sake of (13,1). It expresses distribution, the place one passes, cause and manner.[6] It is a very versatile preposition with a wide range of uses, some of which seem to be peculiar to this text. It is also used frequently as an intensifying particle, a use which persisted into the sixteenth century.[7]

1. Bloch et von Wartburg, p.242.
2. Godefroy, Vol.iv, 675.
3. Nyrop, Vol.vi, 127.
4. Ibid., 128.
5. Goerlich, p.117.
6. Nyrop, Vol.vi, 128-9. (Examples: 12,36; 18,34; 28,14; 11,34)
7. Ibid., 128.

Par cause de: because of. This is par expressing cause.[1] (23,20-21)
Par dedens: within. Par is an intensifying particle. (78,26)
Par dehors: outside. There is one example (77,11).
Part dela: beyond. It is used with riviere and is an example of an adverb used as a preposition. (77,26)
Part dessa: on this side of. There is one example (39,4). The adverb is used as a preposition.
Par dessus: above. Par is an intensifying particle. (69,14)
Par devant/davant: in front of. It is almost always used of movement and devant is preferred to davant in the ratio of four to one.
Part devers: towards. There is one example (64,37).
Plus bas de: lower than. There is one example (74,30-31).
Pour: for. Pour is found with a variety of meanings, all perfectly regular - in order to, for the sake of, because of and on behalf of. Pour ce often introduces a sentence (19,16). Pour could be used instead of par (35,4), but this is not so common as the reverse process. Pour is the third most frequent preposition after en and par. No doubt through its link with par, pour can be used to mean by, through, from and along, although all these meanings are rather infrequent. (33,32; 39,14; 49,13-14; 64,40)
Pour tamps: at one time. There is one example (50,11-12).
Pour cause de: because of. It is a parallel construction to par cause de. (51,30-31)
Pour davant: in front of. It is synonymous with the more common par davant. (26,1)
Pres de: near. This is a very common preposition. De is occasionally omitted. (32,5)
Sans: without. This is a common preposition used with nouns or infinitives.
Sellon: according to.
Soubre: on top of. This is the Provençal form of super. (62,35)
Soubz: beneath. There is one example (29,2). Desoubz is slightly more frequent.
Sur: on. It is common when used of place. It is also occasionally used of time when it means about. (34,29)
Sus: up, on. It is usually a synonym for sur, but there is one example (50,20) where it is used of time and means towards, a regular meaning.[2]
Sus haut en: high up on. There is one example (69,34).
Ver: towards. This is a common preposition used of movement and place. There is only one example of time (61,18), although this was a regular use.[3]

1. Nyrop, Vol.vi, 129.
2. Ibid., 139.
3. Ibid., 140.

There are several examples where the preposition is redoubled for emphasis. This use is not quoted in the dictionaries, so it may represent popular speech. It is uncommon even in this text where it is found with only four prepositions: droit et droit (61,7), face to face; de chief en amont (67,22), standing on end; couste et couste (68,45-6), side by side; pres et pres (70,29), close together.

Prepositions confirm the impression produced by other parts of speech. Words which belong to the Old French period are still in use - for example, jouste. More modern words such as sur are also found. The large number of forms gives the author considerable scope for variety, and he is fairly free in his use of prepositions, not always conforming to the rules which are supposed to govern which preposition is used for which purpose. The most distinctive feature is the blending of par and pour. Orthographically distinct, they share their functions which seems to be a feature of a neighbouring dialect. The other noticeable feature is the wide range of en, which, despite the existence of its rivals, fulfils all its traditional roles and shows clearly the influence of Old French on the author's syntax. The prepositions do not stand out so much as the adverbs in that at this stage of their development they are already fairly close to modern uses, but they represent accurately the transitional state of the language.

Numbers

The scribe shows a preference for writing his numbers in figures. Nearly all the distances in his lists and many of the quantities in his list of presents are given in Roman numerals. Ordinal numbers are almost never written out in full, but are given in Roman numerals with an -e at the end. In dates mil is always written out in full, although the rest of the number is in Roman numerals. Both cardinals and ordinals are found for dating the day of the month, but the cardinals are all early in the book. There are some archaic features such as his use of the ordinals quart and quint in a list,[1] (36,16-17) and the presence of the Old French final -s in deux cens (50,23-24). Otherwise his use of numbers is unremarkable.

Word Order

The position of individual parts of speech is discussed under the appropriate heading but there has been no discussion of the positions in the clause of the different components of the clause. There are six main groupings of the different parts of a clause: subject, verb and complement.
1. subject - verb - complement.
2. subject - complement - verb.
3. complement - subject - verb.
4. verb - subject - complement.
5. verb - complement - subject.
6. complement - verb - subject.

1. Brunot, pp.418-19.

The first of these constructions is by far the commonest in this text. It occurs more than twice as often as all the others put together. The disappearance of the declension had made its adoption a necessity, and it was felt to be the most natural construction. The second construction is the next most frequent. Out of five-hundred-and-sixty-one examples, all except twenty-six have as the complement a pronoun. The rarity of this construction, except where pronouns form the complement, indicates that it had almost disappeared from general use and was becoming specialised.

The third construction is the third most frequent but it, too, is gradually becoming confined to a specialised usage. Out of two-hundred-and-one examples only forty are not relative pronouns or related words. It was still possible where the form of the verb made confusion between subject and complement impossible. It could also be used to give the complement special emphasis. Its rarity suggests, however, that good reasons were needed to use it. The fourth construction only occurs forty-eight times, and in ten of these the verb is dire or faire introducing direct or indirect speech. Otherwise this word order is adopted to give emphasis to the verb. It is a rare construction but not yet eccentric.

The fifth construction is the rarest of the six. There are only fourteen examples of which eleven are imperatives, and no subject is expressed. The sixth construction is rather commoner with sixty-eight examples of which seven are relatives and three questions. The construction is used when the author wants to draw attention to the link between clauses.

There can be no doubt that the first construction is established as the normal one. The others have specialised uses, but the disappearance of the declension has made them less immediately comprehensible. Word order is replacing the word ending as the device which indicates the syntactic function of each word.

There are variations on constructions one and three in that adverbial phrases are sometimes inserted. The modified constructions are:

1. subject - verb - phrase - complement.
2. complement - phrase - subject - verb.

There are thirty-six examples of the first of these and seventeen of the second. This indicates that a certain flexibility in the word order was possible and that phrases could be placed so as to gain emphasis or to throw the emphasis onto another part of the sentence. This flexibility is indicated by another, much commoner construction, the separation of the subject and the verb by a phrase or even a clause. There are one-hundred-and-forty examples of this and the separation can be caused by anything from an adverb to a relative clause, sometimes occupying several lines of text. There are two reasons for this construction. An adverb is placed in this position to give it stress, while the phrases and clauses which describe the subject are put there so that they will not be tacked on at the end of the main clause. In avoiding this awkwardness another is created, because it does not feel natural for the verb and subject to be separated to the extent which is possible in this text. It makes the style clumsy, suggesting the author's lack of professionalism.

This clumsiness is shown in other constructions for it is possible to separate almost any combination of words. The possessive can be separated from its noun (four examples, 12,30), the infinitive can precede the governing verb (twelve examples, 71,7) which gives great emphasis to the infinitive, the participle is frequently separated from either its verb or its noun (66,8). This flexibility adds variety to the style but sometimes at the expense of clarity, while it makes the style seem jerky and to some extent clumsy.

One rule of Old French which is losing ground is that concerning inversion after an adverb or a conjunction. Although there are one-hundred-and-ninety-six examples of inversion after an adverb or an adverbial phrase (17,35-18,1), there are five-hundred-and-forty-six in which no inversion took place.[1] (20,2) Inversion is in decline together with the constructions in which it played a part. The three word orders in which there was inversion are all rare, and likewise post adverbial inversion is replaced by the word order which was becoming standardised. Inversion is very much less of a rule than in Old French, and the tendency is to replace it.

The position of the object of an infinitive has already been discussed with regard to pronouns. Nouns tend to follow the infinitive but they could be found, like pronouns, preceding the auxiliary verb (42,4-5). It is not a common construction in this text, but it is found.[2] Verbal ellipse in lists of distances or items was very frequent (23,5). Less frequently the verb is omitted to avoid repetition (23,31-24,1). The ellipse of conjunctions is very rare and is probably due to scribal error (71,17). These constructions all add to the impression of clumsiness as do the very long and complex sentences in which he indulges. Although he by no means always writes in long sentences, he can add clause to clause until the end result is far too long and unwieldy (15,25-34).

Modern word order is already emerging as the normal one as far as this text is concerned. There is still considerable freedom and flexibility with regard to the placing of the minor elements of a clause, which are usually put where the stress seems to demand them or else adjacent to the word they qualify, frequently preceding it. This can result in a clumsy separation of

1. Brunot, p.481, says that inversion of this type was obligatory in the fifteenth century. This is not supported by the evidence of this text.
2. Gardner and Greene, p.145. The noun often preceded the infinitive which governed it at this period.

the main components of the clause and even in a loss of clarity. Old French rules are in decline, and the author seems to be using a word order fairly typical of his period, although he is, perhaps, more committed to the order, subject - verb - complement than might have been expected at the beginning of the fifteenth century.

Conclusion

In his syntax Nompar is both individualistic and conservative which may be explained by the fact that he was a provincial, remote from the main northern centres. He reveals that Old French was still exercising a considerable influence on the syntax of the early fifteenth century, although its influence was declining. Old French usages are usually in the minority, sometimes there are only isolated examples, and they are not always fully understood when they are used. This applies to what is left of the declension system in particular.

He is individualistic in that he writes in places as he might have spoken. His use of word order, his fondness for conjunctions and his liking for the passive suggest that he is not a man of great culture, but that he is writing because there is something that he wants to say and that style is a secondary consideration. This sometimes means that he is less than clear.

Although he is not obviously archaic and does not seem to have used archaisms deliberately, his language does reflect the influence of Old French and shows less influence than one might have expected of the trends appearing in the fifteenth century. Perhaps his most modern feature is the failure to invert after adverbs or conjunctions, a feature in which he seems to be almost ahead of his time. Some of the rare verb forms which he uses were current later in the century, and again his liking for them shows that he is not conservative in every aspect of language.

In spite of such features, the overall impression must be that his language and syntax are influenced by Old French and that his uncertainty as to the exact construction reflects the state of flux in which the language was at the beginning of the fifteenth century. A study of the syntax suggests that he wrote as he spoke, with some understanding of the construction which he was using. The undisciplined state of the language as it sought to adjust to the decay of Old French is clearly illustrated.

Orthography

Despite the date of this text, post 1420, the orthography is not as erratic and inconsistent as might be expected.[1] The spelling is very varied, but certain rules appear to be observed, some the result of the influence of Old French and some of Provençal. There are examples of doubled consonants and of superfluous letters but not to excess.[2] There are one or two spellings which suggest that the text was dictated to a scribe with little culture who had to attempt to spell phonetically.

There is a considerable interchange amongst the vowels especially a and e in front of nasals where they had become interchangeable[3] (vant, 73,33) Provençal influence shows in the occasional use of a for final mute -e[4] (tourmenta, 74,37). Old French spelling survives in amer for aimer, an example of the vocalic alternation of Old French as this verb resisted the levelling tendencies of Middle French.[5] The interchange of e and ai in the middle of a word is common in this text as it was in the period (lessay, 10,8), but there are no examples of -e replacing -ai in the final syllable of verbs.[6] E is frequently found for a (trevail, 17,35) but only rarely for the other vowels and never for u (heretier, 11,2; ergull, 20,12). There are many examples of e surviving or being introduced into words where it was not strictly necessary (serements, 10,13;[7] vievront, 16,3). More rarely an existing e was doubled, representing an attempt to spell something that could not be represented by a single e (seel, 47,23). Very rarely e is omitted (juner, 20,35).[8]

There are very few examples of ii, which is so frequent in the northeast of France,[9] but it does exist (paiis, 64,35). The use of y which is

---

1. C. Beaulieux, Histoire de l'Orthographe Française, Paris 1927,p.153. Jamais, au contraire, nous n'avons eu une aussi mauvaise graphie en même temps qu'uneplusaffreuseécriture qu'au XVe siècle. (Henceforth Beaulieux).
2. Ibid., p.181. Au XVe siècle, l'abus est porté à son comble.
3. Pope, p.285.
4. Levy, Provenzalisches Supplement Wörterbuch, Leipzig 1892, Vol.viii, 286. Turmenta is the Provençal form. (Henceforth Levy).
5. Pope, p.351.
6. Beaulieux, p.161.
7. Pope, p.133. Serements is the normal Old French form.
8. Ibid., pp.438, 488. Juner is the normal spelling in late twelfth century Anglo-Norman and is a feature of northern dialects.
9. Beaulieux, p.163.

particularly common in diphthongs where i is the second element confirms the provincial nature of the manuscript.[1] In this text it is the rule that pronouns and verbs end with y. Y is very common in diphthongs in the middle of words (deyvent, 19,12). It is less common when it is not in a diphthong but it is found (ylles, 66,17), and it can also be the final letter of the past historic (il me vy, 67,13-14). Very occasionally i is used where y is normal (soians, 20,10). The use of i for any other vowel is rare, but it is found for e (chivallerie, 36,6-7).[2] I is sometimes omitted, especially in front of e (pluseurs, 12,12)[3] and is frequently inserted in front of g (saigemant, 12, 17).[4] O is never inserted and only rarely replaces other vowels (sojour, 21,19). It is occasionally found for the diphthongs eu and ou especially in front of r or rr (demorer, 21,36; morir, 13,12[5]). U is often found after g, especially initial g, indicating that it is a hard g in front of e and i (guerendon, 15,18).[6]

The reduction of diphthongs during this century is rarely reflected in the spelling[7] which is largely true of this text. The diphthongs in Middle French were often interchangeable because they had been affected by sound change[8] as they had been in Old French when the sounds fell together. Only a few of these interchanges are common in this text, however. Ei for ai is the commonest[9] as most of the examples are concerned with faire and related words (feire, 12,32). Au is frequently replaced by al which reflects the spelling which existed before the vocalisation of l (royalme, 10,36). Both spellings coexist, indicating the state of uncertainty which existed, as well as the author's tendency towards archaisms. There are a handful of examples in which eu is found for e, oeu, ou and u, all of which are Old French spellings (ceu, 58,16; euvres, 11,19; veulu, 25,25; peussent, 14,13). Ie is commonly found for e, especially in infinitive endings, which is still normal [10] (aidier, 14,29). Oi is the regular form for the imperfect and conditional endings. Ou commonly replaces o in front of l, r and s [11] (pourter, 10,18; chouse, 11,21; voulenté, 12,8). Ue and eu had been interchangeable since the twelfth century [12] and this is common in vouloir

1. Beaulieux, p.165.
2. Pope, p.453. A form common in Anglo-Norman.
3. Nyrop, Vol.ii, 313. The normal Old French form.
4. Pope, pp.165, 494, 499. Widespread in Middle French and common in the dialects of the eastern and south-central regions.
5. Ibid., pp.201, 250. Both belong to Old French.
6. Ibid., p.279.
7. Beaulieux, p.167.
8. Pope, p.285.
9. Ibid.
10. Ibid., pp.192, 335. Nyrop, i, 205, says that in the fourteenth century this was becoming e, and the later forms are only a graphy.
11. Pope, p.210. This is a trait belonging to the southern region.
12. Ibid., p.284. Also p.203. This spelling was frequent in the west.

and pouvoir in this text but rare in other words (vueillés, 11,25; pueple, 10,9). Ue and oeu were also interchangeable,[1] but in this text the rule is that it is always ue in the middle of a word (buefs, 56,14).

There is a certain degree of flexibility in the use of the vowels but there are rules, such as the use of oi in the endings of the imperfect and the conditional, the use of ay in the endings of the first person singular of the past historic and future and the use of y as the final letter in most pronouns. The use of ue in vouloir and the use of interconsonantal ue in nouns are also strictly observed. Many of the diphthongs are interchangeable, and this can result in a wide variety of spellings for the same word. To take one example, the verb laisser can be written in five different ways, the modern laisser, the normal Old French laissier, lasser, which is probably a dialectal form, leesser and leisser where the change of diphthong is quite regular.

Old French spellings clearly have considerable influence. They have survived to a remarkable degree, sometimes only in isolated examples, such as ceu, sometimes as the normal spelling, pluseurs. This supports the evidence provided by the syntax. The influence of various dialects can be seen, including Anglo-Norman, which can be explained by the alliance of the author with the English. There is also evidence of the influence of Provençal. The result is a state of considerable confusion in the use of the vowels with many influences at work.

The use of consonants is marked by the interchangeability of certain letters such as c and s and by the insertion of silent or redundant consonants. This text is not an example of the most exaggerated behaviour in the use of consonants and so is not wholly typical of its period.[2]

There are many examples of inserted consonants, often under the influence of Latin or Provençal. B is regularly inserted between ou and d or t (soubde, 12,17).[3] C is inserted on the grounds, sometimes false, that it comes from Latin (auctorité, 11,14; scet, 21,29).[4] D is inserted on the grounds that it is derived from Latin in compounds with ad, and it appears occasionally in parts of verbs influenced by their infinitives or as a survival from the Old French (advenir, 12,20; vindrent, 26,7).[5] There is one example of f inserted where it is a case of the terminal consonant of the masculine adjective introduced into the feminine, which is usual for the period (veufves, 36,18).[6] G is frequent in front of n, which was the regular

1. Pope, p.284.
2. Beaulieux, p.178.
3. Ibid., p.189.
4. Ibid., p.179.
5. Pope, p.377. These forms are early Old French. Nyrop, Vol.ii, 29, 139. They survived until the sixteenth century. Beaulieux, p.186. Avenir is the normal spelling but it is the exception to the rule.
6. Beaulieux, p.190.

combination in Old French to indicate palatalisation (besoignes, 21,27).[1]
H is frequently used as an initial letter, occasionally to mark an hiatus,
which is a regular usage,[2] or combined with n and l. This is a feature of
both Provençal and the north-east. The combination lh for the French ll,
l mouillé, is common at the end of a word, where it is a Provençalism
(hennemix, 20,23; Guasconhe, 22,39; ourgulh, 20,16).[3] L is common
after the diphthongs which represent it vocalised (hault, 24,9). M and n
survive in a few Old French variants (amprés, 21,11; prins, 10,18).[4]
P is inserted because of the influence of Latin or Provençal and is quite common, combined with nasals (nepveu, 38,5; cipté, 23,5; dampnez, 17,16).[5]
S is by far the commonest redundant letter. Words such as nostre, vostre,
chasteau and certain parts of être are regularly spelt with a silent s. Many
other words keep their Old French s (escripture, 11,21; mestier, 14,29).
T is regularly inserted between a vowel and g. This is the normal spelling in
the text and is a Provençalism (voyatge, 10,3). Another sign of Provençal
influence is tz for s (pourrietz, 73,38).[6] X is very rarely inserted, and
when it is, it is to duplicate another sound (rocxs, 30,18).

Certain consonants are frequently doubled. A very common feature
is that, when a monosyllable is closely linked to a word beginning with a
consonant, a lengthened consonant is formed, and the two words are written
as one. This is a survival from Old French.[7] It is also common for the
second consonant to be omitted where it would normally repeat the first.

C is occasionally doubled, usually in front of -ion (fraccion, 40,18).
F is often doubled especially as an initial consonant (affin, 12,20). L is
occasionally doubled as an initial consonant but often as a final consonant.
Aller was often written in the Old French form aler (perill, 18,24, ally,
33,34). M and n are rarely doubled, and although the tendency was to
double nasals,[8] the single m and n of Old French often survive (Damme,
23,9; home, 20,26; unne, 26,4; done, 15,42). R is sometimes doubled
after o, less often after other letters (norri, 14,18). S is frequently doubled,
especially as an initial consonant. Double s can represent c with which it
is, on a very limited scale, interchangeable (ainssi, 13,19; assavoir, 10,28;
forsser, 18,26).[9] T is frequently doubled in parts of dire and faire, but
otherwise its doubling is rare.

1. Pope, p.277.
2. Ibid., p.288.
3. Ibid., p.277. Levy, Vol.v, 519.
4. Nyrop, Vol.ii, 139.
5. Levy, Vol.i, 256.
6. Nyrop, Vol.ii, 43.
7. Pope, p.147.
8. Beaulieux, p.188.
9. Ibid., p.179. -ace and -asse are particularly prone to confusion.

In this text it is rare for the single consonants of Old French not to be doubled, although in this period the existing double consonants, with the exception of rr, were normally reduced.[1] The doubling of consonants can be attributed to Latin influence.[2] Certainly there is such a great degree of inconsistency in the doubling of letters that it cannot be explained by the traditional explanation, that the scribes doubled every letter possible.[3] The uncertainty is due in part to the influence of Old French and in part to the trends of Middle French. The use of doubled consonants shows the importance of the influence of Old French and that the writer was not a professional scribe. It also shows the confusion about the spelling, which, like the syntax, was in a state of change.

The use of final consonants indicates that they were in a state of change. C was already giving way to g in the thirteenth century,[4] but there are still examples in this text (ranc, 51,21). G is common which is in keeping with the trend in the fifteenth century where the scribes kept the silent g. It was added to words ending in n to indicate nasalisation (ung, 10,21).[5] Qu was interchangeable with c in a variety of positions, initial, final and in the middle of the word. It was common in front of e, but less so in front of o which is found in this text (aveques, 16,5; en quore, 69,23).[6] S is sometimes omitted in the first person singular of the past historic, which is not uncommon in the period (parti, 10,26).[7] Final t, which is the older form, although still common at the beginning of the fifteenth century,[8] is frequent in quant but rare in other words (segont, 19,23). Where it does survive it is due to the influence of Old French, and final t is frequently omitted from masculine plural adjectives, due to the same influence (petis, 11,35).[9] It is sometimes omitted from verbs or nouns, the verbs harking back to the thirteenth century when final t started to be restored (fu, 22,18).[10] X usually follows u to mark the plural, even when the vocalised l is restored. It also appears after the diphthongs oi and ai, all of which is normal for the period (lieux, 10,5; ceulx, 26,17; foix, 12,10).[11] Z is the normal final letter after é and after il, which is regular (dez, 10,5; filz, 11,2).[12]

1. Pope, p.147.
2. Ibid., p.281.
3. Beaulieux, p.146. The scribes were paid by length.
4. Ibid., p.193.
5. Ibid., p.194. Pope, p.288.
6. Beaulieux, p.178.
7. Nyrop, Vol.ii, 129-130. This spelling continued to the Renaissance. Beaulieux, p.207. This represents a survival from Old French.
8. Beaulieux, p.193.
9. Ibid., p.200.
10. Ibid., p.372.
11. Ibid., pp.195-6.
12. Ibid., pp.195, 203.

The use of final letters indicates that the spelling is broadly that of the beginning of the fifteenth century with several traits which indicate archaising tendencies. This is in keeping with the syntax.

The use of one consonant for another is quite common amongst final consonants but elsewhere there are relatively few examples for any one letter. Examples tend to be isolated and to reflect the influence of Old French or Provençal. B is found occasionally for p and v (pueble, 12,32;[1] obrir, 60,13[2]). C is found for s and ss. This was a frequent change at this period,[3] but it is rare in this text (cellon, 18,5; abaicerent, 71,12). There are six examples of ch for c, five of them in front of a (enbarchay, 48,23). The nasals are easily confused, and there are examples of m and n used for each other and of mp for n (comfiance, 13,1;[4] enpereur, 51,5; estiomps, 26,21[5]). R is found for n and d, both probably examples of assimilation[6] (derrier, 30,5; vourront, 22,19). The normal spellings of both words are commoner. S is found for c, ch, t, x, and z, while changes between s, ss and c were numerous at this period[7] (plasses, 11,36; serchier, 35,19[8]). S for x and z is rare in this text except in the second person plural of the present indicative. S for t is very rare and is probably a scribal slip. Z is found for d and s. The former may represent an attempt at phonetic spelling, as it formerly represented the sound dz.[9] As z had the same value as intervocalic s, it was found in its place (azouré, 34,7; rozee, 18,14).[10]

A study of the use of one consonant for another confirms the impression that the usages which were current practice are to be found in this text, and in addition there are some rather idiosyncratic ones. The erratic and uncertain nature of the writer's orthography is clear.

Very few letters are regularly omitted. The exception is initial h, but even here there is little consistency as it is frequently inserted where it does not belong (orrible, 20,13; ome, 78,16). The other examples of letters omitted can mostly be ascribed to scribal slips, as can the few examples of transposition (glorie, 10,36;[11] merevillé, 19,37). There are

1. Pope, p.149. Pueble is normal Old French.
2. Levy, Vol.v, 456. Obrir is a regular Provençal form.
3. Beaulieux, p.179.
4. Pope, p.219. M for n in front of labio-dentals is not uncommon, but it is an early feature.
5. Goerlich, p.79. This might be a south-western feature.
6. Pope, p.149. Vourront is found in northern French. P.489.
7. Beaulieux, p.179.
8. Godefroy, Vol.ii, 19. A regular Old French form.
9. Beaulieux, p.180.
10. Ibid.
11. Pope, p.230. A very old form.

also a few Latinisms (redemptor, 10,32; translata, 46,11;[1] flama, 57,21).

The orthography of the period is even more fluid than the syntax, but as far as can be seen, most of the major orthographical trends of the early fifteenth century are reflected in this text, together with many survivals from Old French. These survivals are in a minority but they illustrate the unsettled nature of the orthography. The influence of Provençal is clear, and other French dialects have influenced the writer to a lesser degree. The scribe was not a professional and was probably not very learned as he does not draw on Latin to any great extent. Like the syntax the orthography reflects the confusion of the language at the period, which the author increased by his use of archaisms and his borrowings from the dialects and Provençal. Lack of consistency further complicates the situation. On the whole, however, the influence of standard French is dominant.

---

1. Godefroy, Vol.viii, 18. A learned Old French word.

198

The Influence of Provençal and of Dialects

For the most part the language of the text is standard Francien, but there are traces of the influence of several dialects in the use of individual words or letters. The main influence is that of Provençal which supplies many loan words and influences the orthography in which there are several combinations of letters which are typical of Provençal. The most important dialectal influence comes from the dialects of the south-west, such as Poitou. It is often difficult to decide whether the borrowing comes from Poitou as the Poitevin dialects has many borrowings from Provençal. Where there are the two possible sources, the borrowing probably was direct from Provençal as the Agenais was part of the area of Provençal. The other dialects of some importance are Anglo-Norman and the north-eastern dialects. The influence of Anglo-Norman may be because Nompar de Caumont was the ally of the English who were near the Agenais in Bordeaux where he had property. The influence of the north-eastern dialects is confined to a few forms. There are slight traces of the influence of eastern, western, northern and southern dialects,[1] but their influence is of little importance. The problem occurs again of deciding which dialect is the source of some shared feature. Anglo-Norman and Poitevin both used the forms tiel and quiel which occur in this text. Probably the dialects reinforce each other, and neither is the exclusive source.

Western Dialects. The only feature which this text shares with western dialects is the interchangeability of ue and eu. Spellings such as pueple (10,9), were particularly common in the west. They were also not uncommon in Francien,[2] which may be the more likely source. A more probable borrowing from the west is eue, perhaps a scribal slip for eve, which is a western form.[3]

Northern Dialects. There are two forms vourront (22,19) and vourroient (52,28) which are northern but which could be assimilation of d by r.[4]

South-Central Dialects. The use of ou for o is a southern feature,[5] and there are two borrowings from this area: saigemant (12,17);[6] entencion (11,7).[7]

---

1. These terms are used as defined by Miss Pope.
2. Pope, p.203.
3. Ibid., p.135.
4. Ibid., pp.489, 149.
5. Ibid., p.210.
6. Ibid., p.499.
7. Godefroy, Vol.iii, 253.

Eastern and Burgundian Dialects. This region shares with the last the feature of the insertion of i in front of gn,[1] which is common in this text. There are two words, lassions (20,7)[2] and maul (38,34)[3] which are borrowed from this region. In the syntax the use of que as the subject pronoun may be an eastern feature,[4] but this is doubtful, as it is more probably a reflection of popular speech.

North-Eastern Dialects. In the orthography the use of ii is a north-eastern feature.[5] The use of h with n or l is also a feature of this region,[6] but a more likely source is Provençal. The following verb forms, misrent (29,7),[7] aster (12,15),[8] se lavaist (39,8), aidaist (42,9),[9] are all north-eastern.

Anglo-Norman. There are several forms borrowed from Anglo-Norman, although the standard forms are found as well. The most frequent borrowing is to be found in the words associated with knighthood, perhaps because of his association with the English and their supporters: chivallerie (36,6-7), chivallier (36,8), chivaucher (49,24-25).[10] Other forms associated with Anglo-Norman are juner (20,35),[11] duel (18,18)[12] and tiel (24,4), quiel (64,42).[13] Chiere and chieremant[14] outnumber the standard forms by two to one. The use of le for la, discussed under the definite article, is a feature of late Anglo-Norman,[15] which seems a likely source. Another feature of Anglo-Norman is the use of ces for ses.[16]

Anglo-Norman exercised a slight, but definite, influence on the language of Nompar de Caumont. Anglo-Norman forms and usages are both present, and its influence is clearer than that of any other dialect discussed so far. This is quite understandable in view of his links with the English. The scribe too may have been influenced by Anglo-Norman.

1. Pope, pp.494, 499.
2. Ibid., p.497.
3. Ibid., p.494.
4. Foulet, p.177.
5. Beaulieux, p.164.
6. Pope, p.277.
7. Nyrop, Vol.ii, 139.
8. Schwan-Behrens, III, 120.
9. Fouché, p.342.
10. Pope, p.453.
11. Ibid., pp.438, 488.
12. Ibid., pp.444, 203.
13. Ibid., p.458.
14. Ibid., p.451.
15. Ibid., p.465.
16. Ibid., p.466.

South-Western Dialects. There are several features which suggest the influence of the dialects of Poitou and Saintonge. These dialects showed a tendency to use the masculine form of the definite article for the feminine,[1] which probably reinforced the Anglo-Norman influence. These dialects dropped the final -t of the third person singular of the past historic,[2] which is common in this text. The interchangeability of par and pour, so marked in this text, is found in some documents in these dialects[3] while the use of ceu and seu for ce is another feature of this region.[4] Quiel, discussed under Anglo-Norman, is found in these dialects.[5] So too is the -ey ending of the first person singular of the first conjugation past historic,[6] which is found occasionally in this text.

The influence of these dialects also shows in the vocabulary, where there are twenty-four different words affected by the dialectal forms. Most of these words are rare with only one example but the commoner ones are chescun,[7] dont,[8] longe,[9] pouvre,[10] and reonde.[11] Jherusalem and Jhesus, which are the normal forms in this text, also belong to these dialects.[12]

These dialects from the border of French and Provençal are better represented in this text than those from further north and east, but even their influence is slight. There are three common features - the use of the masculine form of the definite article for the feminine, the omission of final -t in the third person singular of the -ir verbs in the past historic, the interchangeability of par and pour - which are probably in this text because of the influence of these dialects. In addition there are a few common borrowings. All the other examples are isolated or, at most, in a minority, indicating the weakness of the influence of these dialects.

Provençal. The influence of Provençal can be detected in the orthography and in many words which are direct borrowings from Provençal or are influenced by the Provençal form. The use of the suffix -atge, the combination -lh, the use of u after g to indicate hard g,[13] are all clear signs of

1. Goerlich, p.102.
2. Ibid., p.84.
3. Ibid., p.117.
4. Schwan-Behrens, III, 85.
5. Goerlich, p.21.
6. Ibid., p.123.
7. Ibid., p.113.
8. Ibid., p.119.
9. Ibid., p.94.
10. Ibid., p.70.
11. Ibid., p.77.   It is also standard Old French.
12. Ibid., p.94.
13. Grandgent, p.44.

Provençal influence. The grouping -lh is a feature of Limousin where it represents l[1] which is interesting as this would be one of the Provençal dialects near the author. Final -a is another feature of Provençal, although the examples are few in number.[2]

It is unnecessary to give many examples of the common features such as the use of the suffix atge, voyatge, which is the normal ending for nouns which end in -age in French. The combination -lh is also very frequent, ourgulh (20,16), as is the use of u after g, gueredon (15,18). Another feature of Provençal is that the combination nr does not always develop an interconsonantal d, venredi (13,21).[3] The most important borrowing from Provençal is perhaps the list of words which are either direct borrowings or are influenced by the related Provençal word. There are fifty words in this category and ten proper names. Words borrowed directly from Provençal include: advocade (11,16),[4] consols (33,24),[5] lengatge (34,22),[6] pellegrinatge (30,25),[7] pestre (11,10),[8] while words influenced by Provençal include enseignemens (10,23),[9] and ortolen (41,21).[10] Most of these are relatively infrequent but some are commoner: mot (23,30)[11] and nulh (59,18).[12] Examples of Provençal influence on proper names can be seen in Fonhane (27,26), Malhorque (75,15) and Guilhem (67,45). These spellings reflect the local spelling which in southern France would be Provençal. The spelling of the names of the islands may be influenced by the fact that he was in Catalan ships and presumably got his information there, which would mean that the names would be very close to Provençal.

Provençal clearly has more influence than any of the dialects of French. Its influence is quite general throughout the text, both on the vocabulary and the orthography. Even Provençal, however, has relatively little influence on the text. The overall impression is of a text written in standard Francien with only borrowings from the dialects and Provençal,

1. Grandgent, p.56.
2. Ibid., p.90.
3. Anglade, p.188.
4. Levy, Vol.i, 115. This is derived from advocada.
5. Ibid., 338.
6. Levy, Vol.iv, 363.
7. Levy, Vol.vi, 193.
8. Grandgent, p.84.
9. Levy, Vol.iii, 32. Influenced by enseignamens, although the usual form is ensenhamen.
10. Levy, Vol.v, 532. Influenced by ortolan.
11. Anglade, p.78. This word is common in Limousin.
12. Grandgent, p.112.

while the influence of Latin is very slight. Most of the regional dialects leave some trace on the text but the only ones of any importance are Anglo-Norman and the dialects of the south-west. Provençal is more influential than any of the dialects, but its influence is largely confined to certain orthographical traits and the borrowing of certain words.

CAUMONT POSSESSIONS

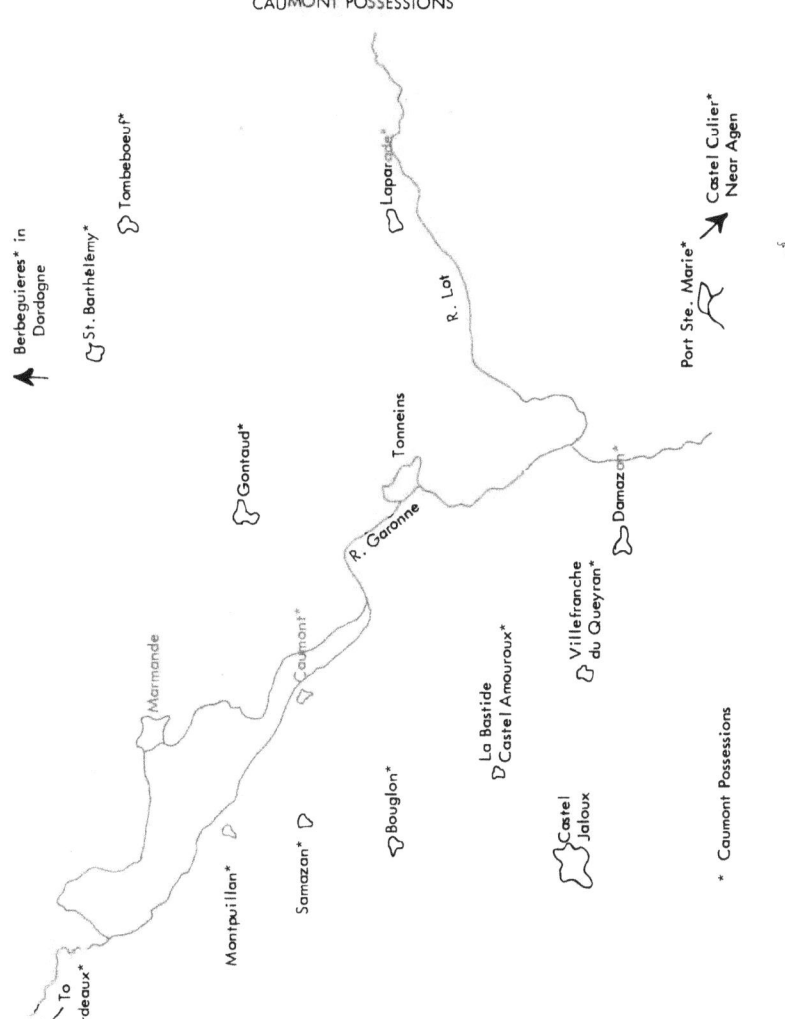

* Caumont Possessions

www.ingramcontent.com/pod-product-compliance
Lightning Source LLC
Chambersburg PA
CBHW021155160426
43194CB00007B/753